A Social Hist
Western Eu
1450–1720

Hutchinson University Library

Hutchinson University Library for Africa

General Editors
Michael Crowder
Paul Richards

Hutchinson University Library for Africa
General Editors: Michael Crowder and Paul Richards

The African City   *A. O'Connor*

African Philosophy: Myth and Reality   *P. J. Hountondji*

The Development of African Drama   *Michael Etherton*

The Development Process: A Spatial Perspective   *Akin Mabogunje*

Forced Migration: The Impact of the Export Slave Trade on African Societies
Edited by J. E. Inikori

A Handbook of Adult Education for West Africa   *Edited by Lalage Brown and S. H. Olu Tomori*

A History of Africa   *J. D. Fage*

Indigenization of African Economies   *Edited by Adebayo Adedeji*

Peasants and Proletarians: The Struggles of Third World Workers   *Edited by Robin Cohen, Peter C. W. Gutkind and Phyllis Brazier*

Rural Development: Theories of Peasant Economy and Agrarian Change   *Edited by John Harriss*

Rural Settlement and Land Use   *Michael Chisholm*

Technology, Tradition and the State in Africa   *Jack Goody*

Twelve African Writers   *Gerald Moore*

West Africa Under Colonial Rule   *Michael Crowder*

West African Resistance: The Military Response to Colonial Occupation   *Edited by Michael Crowder*

in association with the International African Institute

Islam in Tropical Africa   *Edited by I. M. Lewis*

The Drums of Affliction: A Study of Religious Processes among the Ndembu of Zambia   *V. W. Turner*

in association with Zed Press

African Women: Their Struggle for Economic Independence   *Christine Obbo*

A SOCIAL HISTORY OF WESTERN EUROPE 1450–1720

Tensions and solidarities among rural people

Sheldon J. Watts

Hutchinson University Library
Hutchinson University Library for Africa
London Melbourne Sydney Auckland Johannesburg

HUTCHINSON UNIVERSITY LIBRARY FOR AFRICA

Hutchinson & Co. (Publishers) Ltd

An imprint of the Hutchinson Publishing Group

17–21 Conway Street, London W1P 6JD
and 51 Washington Street, Dover, New Hampshire 03820, USA

Hutchinson Publishing Group (Australia) Pty Ltd
PO Box 496, 16–22 Church Street, Hawthorne,
Melbourne, Victoria 3122

Hutchinson Group (NZ) Ltd
32–34 View Road, PO Box 40–086, Glenfield, Auckland 10

Hutchinson Group (SA) (Pty) Ltd
PO Box 337, Bergvlei 2012, South Africa

First published 1984

Set in 10/12pt Garamond by Activity Ltd, Salisbury, Wilts

Printed and bound in Great Britain by
Anchor Brendon Ltd,
Tiptree, Essex

British Library Cataloguing in Publication Data
Watts, Sheldon J.
  A social history of Western Europe, 1450–1720.
  1. Europe—Social conditions—History
  I. Title
  940.2′2   HN375

Library of Congress Cataloging in Publication Data
Watts, S. J. (Sheldon J.)
  A social history of Western Europe, 1450–1720.

  (Hutchinson University Library for Africa)
  Bibliography: p.
  Includes index.
  1. Europe—Rural conditions.   2. Social history—Modern,
  1500–   . I. Title. II. Series.
  HN373.W37   1984   306′.094   84–159439

ISBN 0 09 156091 0 paper

Contents

Tables, maps and illustrations

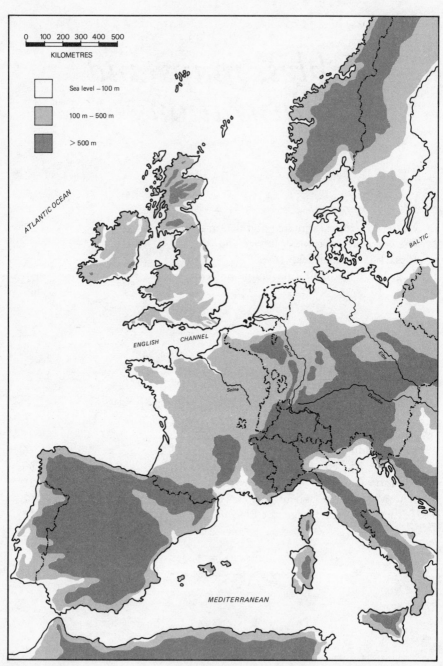

Map 1 Relief map

Map 2 Europe: major towns and regions

Introduction

What is social history? Though no single answer can be given which will satisfy every social historian, most of them would agree that social history is concerned with people's relationships with each other in families, kinship groupings, status groupings, villages, urban neighbourhoods, regions and polities. In some groupings the nature of social relationships remained unchanged for long periods; the social historian wants to know why this was so. In others important changes took place in a relatively short period of time, say over the course of a century or so; unlike political historians, social historians can seldom give precise dates for the things which concern them most. Some of the causal elements for the changes which did take place were fully within the capacity of humankind to control and involved conscious human choice. Others were not, or at least so it seemed to contemporaries living at the time. These changing perceptions are also of concern to social historians.

Most social historians agree that social history is no longer limited to the sports and amusements, clothing styles, patterns of religious observance and marriage patterns of the élite at the summit of society. Instead the social historian's task is to study the social relationships of all sorts and conditions of men, women and children, and especially those who formed the bulk of the population and left few or no written records of their own. It was these people, the inarticulate, whose rituals and belief systems, diversions and myths formed the stuff of popular culture.

In western Europe during the early part of the early modern period, say around 1450–80, the ruling élites freely shared in the rituals and culture of the populace and probably helped to shape them in more ways than historians who would like to study history only from the grass roots upwards would care to admit. Then in the sixteenth century, as a consequence of the élite-inspired reformation of manners first identified by Norbert Elias in the 1930s and more recently (in 1978) described by Peter Burke and Robert Muchembled, a split took place between popular culture and the culture of the élites, particularly those whose point of reference was the culture of the great cities of western Europe. Far more than in the recent past, the sixteenth-century élites saw themselves as separate from the populace and its culture and rejected it in favour of the Great Tradition. This tradition consisted of the written corpus of histories, precepts, religious and quasi-scientific works etc. which in provenance stretched back through the Middle Ages to the time of the fathers of the early Christian Church and to the beginnings of western culture in ancient Greece. The clash between the upholders of the Great Tradition and those who lived within the framework of popular culture forms one of the principal themes of this book. Whether my particular interpretation can serve as a model for similar studies in today's Third World and non-European world remains to be seen. At any rate I hope that other scholars living in the Third World more qualified than I will take it upon themselves to study the relationships between the culture of their own western orientated, or at least non-indigenous orientated, élites and local popular culture in times past.

As one of the newer fields of history, social history has had difficulty in shaking itself clear of its immediate generators, most notably economic history. Since the end of the Second World War economic history has become increasingly concerned with grand theory and statistics which are almost beyond the comprehension of ordinary non-specialist readers. In consequence many social historians have considered it essential to divorce themselves from economic history with its materialistic emphasis, and instead to stress the human-centredness of their profession. In this, whether they openly admit it or not, they are in part working in the tradition of the nineteenth-century German historicists stretching from Johan von Goethe and Johan von Herder to Wilhelm Dilthey. Historicists were primarily concerned to study each unique past society for itself and not to judge it by the standards of their own contemporary western Europe. Using the evidence of artefacts from a past era – pottery, painting, sculpture, architecture – as well as surviving written evidence, historicists attempted to put themselves in a state of mind where they could empathize with the past and so establish a valid interchange between 'I' (the historian) and 'thou' (the people of the past). This attempt to empathize with people living in a selected segment of the past had much to commend it at a time when most history was still being written from the vantage point of the present and when any part of the past which was not seen as relevant to human progress and progressive change – the lost causes and the immobile peasantry – was consigned to the dustbin. However, as Gordon Leff has so ably pointed out, the great flaw in historicism was that it ignored one of the great insights which sets historians apart from the writers of historical fiction or from hack writers in the employ of a government which is seeking historical justification for its current ideology. Historians worthy of the name are aware of the consequences of human action and that these consequences very often have little to do with the intentions of the actors involved in past events; in shaping human history, accident and contingency often play leading roles. So it is that social historians writing in the last decades of the twentieth century like to think that they can combine the best of the historicist tradition with the essential insights of a Western-trained historian (knowledge of consequences and the role of accident and chance).

In their struggle to shake themselves free of the limitations of conventional history social historians who concern themselves with the inarticulate as well as with the élites have been accused of neglecting the role of political history; in this book I myself have made only passing reference to political events or to political personages. In justification, it can be pointed out that in most of the societies of early modern mainland Europe (though to a lesser extent in England) peasants who enjoyed high status in their own village communities were allowed no role in shaping policies at the level of the territory, principality or state. Yet they were the least likely to benefit from the policies of kings and great nobles whose main concern was to preserve or enlarge their patrimony through diplomacy or war. The wars which probably as much as any other human-caused factor shaped the lives of early modern Europeans took place despite the real needs of ordinary people. In this vital area of human concern the inarticulate were indeed only acted upon. Yet in many others, as it is the burden of this book to show, they themselves were the principal actors.

In writing this book I have placed myself in debt to the numerous scholars and specialists whose learned articles and monographs I have drawn upon before coming to my own conclusions. It is only the economics of publishing which have prevented me from giving full footnote references for each scholarly work on which I have based my arguments. In default of footnotes, I have drawn up a reasonably full bibliography of the studies I have used. To all of these scholars I express my thanks.

I am also deeply indebted to my colleagues at the University of Ilorin, Nigeria, and to the many students, graduates and undergraduates alike, with whom I have exchanged ideas during the past six years. Without their insights about their own society, a society quite different from my own, many of the questions about early modern Europe to which I have attempted to address myself would not have occurred to me. A quiet period in London at the Institute of Historical Research in 1982–3 in order to sort things out and to undertake the final writing up was generously provided by the Vice-Chancellor and administration of the University of Ilorin.

In the task of assimilating ideas new and old, a vital role has been played by my wife, Susan Watts. Through her own studies of mobility patterns around Ilorin, she has started many intellectual hares which in one way or another have found their way into my own perceptions. She also took time out from her own scholarly concerns to type the many drafts necessary for the final production of this book and to provide me with constant encouragement. To her I am eternally grateful. I am also grateful for the generous support provided by Michael Crowder, Mark Cohen, Sarah Conibear and the staff at Hutchinson.

Sheldon J. Watts
Ilorin, London, Rose Lake
St Bartholomew's Day 1983

1 *An overview*

Western European sailors, traders and missionaries as well as callous adventurers in search of personal fortunes and fame they could never hope to win at home first came into direct sustained contact with the non-European world in the mid 1400s. By 1520, seeking to tap West Africa's wealth in gold and human slaves, they had established permanent bases along the west African coasts. By that date as well, Europeans, many of them either Spaniards or Portuguese, were establishing enclaves in the Caribbean Islands, in central America and in Asia.

These well-known historical facts prompt the non-European reader to ask a number of questions. Who were these strangers from western Europe who came in during the Age of Exploration? Second, in what ways were the social relationships which existed among the various European social groupings different from those which then existed among Africans, Amerindians and Asians? Finally, how did the actual life-world known to early modern Europeans differ from the mythical, thoroughly sanitized European experience which non-European Christian converts and school children learned about from European teachers and missionaries?

Answers to the second question, the comparison between European and non-European cultures during the Age of Exploration, can best be left to each reader drawing on his or her own perceptions and knowledge of his or her own society and its history. In this book I shall only attempt to provide some answers to questions one and three. Yet even here, the answers can only be tentative. This is because there was no single standard European society which was typical of all the rest. As French social historians put it, *'l'Europe est multiple'*. Even at the level of the peasant village, in the early modern period in western Europe there were thousands of quite different sorts of social systems. For example, a historicist who placed equal emphasis on artefacts and written evidence would notice the difference in types of houses found in late seventeenth-century Lower Saxony in the German Empire. In

'The Four Riders of the Apocalypse' by Albrecht Dürer, c. 1500

the village of Calenberg, as Lutz Berkner has pointed out, full-holding cultivators lived in large 'long-houses' of the Old Saxon type with barns, sheds and living quarters located around a central court. Here all the buildings were covered by a single great roof. But only a few miles to the south at Göttingen, sheds and barns were separated from the family's living quarters following the 'middle German' pattern of vernacular housing. The social historian might expect that in these two villages people's attitudes towards the family and the larger unit of society, the village, would differ. In fact, at Göttingen partible inheritance was the usual practice while at Calenberg impartible inheritance patterns were usually followed. This meant that at Calenberg, where all the sons of the family except one were excluded from a share in the patrimony, there were far more landless young men who had somehow to be fitted into the village agrarian régime as wage-labourers or be sent away to the towns than there were at Göttingen.

Everywhere in Europe each localized social system had its own way of responding to the changing circumstances in which it found itself. In response to these pressures, some local systems changed very considerably between 1450 and 1720; others, for all intents and purposes, remained unchanged.

The special task which social historians have set themselves is the reconstruction of a number of the social systems of western Europe in times past. Though a great deal of progress in this direction has been made since the late 1940s and early 1950s when social history came to find its new sense of direction, a great deal still remains to be done. This is particularly true in the case of Spain and Portugal where social history is still very much the infant brother of economic and political history. To only a marginally lesser degree the same is also true of the social history of the early modern Germanies and the Scandinavian countries. This then means that most of what we now know about the social history of western Europe between 1450 and 1720 is based on evidence derived from France, England, the Low Countries and northern Italy; southern Italy is less well served.

One lesson which social historians (as opposed to say students of international law or diplomacy) have already learned is that more or less complete social systems can only be meaningfully compared with other whole systems; like can only be compared to like. Moreover, in order to be understood, each social system must be placed firmly in its own historical context, which is to say rooted in a definite space and in a definite segment of time. It is important to realize at the onset that there is virtually no explanatory value in abstracting bits of information about one social system and then comparing these with fragments from another. Wrenched out of context, the similarities which seem to exist between the two fragments are often more apparent than real. Thus to compare *only* the inheritance customs of the people of Val des Dunes in Normandy between 1530 and 1540 with those of a group of villagers in early nineteenth-century Igboland in Nigeria – as recorded by oral tradition – is unrewarding except for the antiquarian. It is for this reason that the reader who seeks to compare some of the social systems found in western Europe during the Age of Discovery with those found in Africa, Asia or America must be prepared to think of both as totalities, as holistic systems firmly fixed within their own particular historical contexts. If I seem to be belabouring this fundamental point it is only because it is so often overlooked, even by professional historians.

European ideas old and new

Before we go further, one or two very general observations about the European intellectual context should be made. First, it is important to realize that in the three hundred years which followed the first arrival of Europeans into the harbours of Ghana in West Africa, the position of Europe relative to the rest of the world changed dramatically. With the fall of Constantinople to the Ottoman Turks in 1453 and the closure of the old overland trading routes to Asia brought about by the spread of Islam, Europe's only direct access to the outside world was by sea. This might have led Europeans who cared about such things to become inward looking isolationists, but as we all know, they did not. By 1453 Europe already possessed the ships and the navigational skills needed to meet the new challenge.

For that matter so too did the Chinese. But what set the Europeans apart from the Chinese was the former's insatiable sense of curiosity and uprootedness. Both at the governing and at the middling levels, Europeans were dissatisfied with the everyday world they saw about them. They wanted to discover new cultures and new lands where things were done better than they were at home. Unlike the Chinese who visited the coasts of east Africa in the early fifteenth century to collect tribute from people who were expected to acknowledge that the Chinese Celestial Kingdom was far superior to all others, the Europeans were open to new influences, new ideas and new ways of doing things.

Some of the new lands to which western Europeans initially looked for guidance were actual geographical realities; India under the Moghuls, China, Africa, South America and the home of the 'noble savage', North America. Others existed only in the mind. In the sixteenth century numerous books and essays about *Utopia* (no-where-land) were written and printed on Europe's growing store of printing presses. Yet strange as it may seem to most of us in the late twentieth century, it was not the new lands discovered by the explorers which provided educated Europeans at or near the governing levels of society with most of their inspiration about how to improve existing society; instead this inspiration was provided by the classics of ancient Greece and Rome. Beginning in the fourteenth century in Italy and slightly later in northern Europe, the scholars known as humanists rediscovered this classical pagan past and with it the meaning of historical context and historical perspective. Older-style custodians of the traditions of the people, the men who compiled chronicles and the like, had assumed that they and their contemporaries were the legitimate but debased descendants of an earlier race of intellectual giants – the Ancients. To them history had meant continuity, a continuity associated with the gradual deterioration of humankind since the Fall from Grace in the Garden of Eden and the winding down of the world in preparation for the final cataclysm, the Last Judgement. In contrast, the humanists recognized that an unbridgeable gulf of time – the Middle Ages – separated them from the ancient classical worlds of Greece and Rome. In a word, the humanists were aware of the *discontinuities* of history in a way which was foreign to any society which relied solely on oral history for its ideas of the past.

As the humanists saw it, their task was to recover the most useful of the principles which had guided the much admired but dead men of the ancient classical world and then to refurbish these ideas and apply them to their own contemporary Renaissance society. In their willingness to recover pieces of the classical past, the humanists were eclectic and too willing to dissociate themselves from their own recent and still living Gothic past. Yet at the same time they recognized that whole areas of human concern had been neglected by the great writers of Greece and Rome. For example, no classical author had ever seen fit to devise a strategy to ensure the continuity and prosperity of a family or lineage from one generation to the next. The idea of establishing strategies for family survival was apparently first undertaken in the 1430s by the Renaissance humanist and architect, Leonis Baptiste Alberti, author of *I Libri Della Famiglia*, a pace-setting book on the family.

In their willingness to absorb new ideas from the past as well as the material artefacts they found in use in Africa, America and Asia, early modern European thinkers laid down the foundations of the concept of 'progress'. In its mature form (which it did not achieve until the early eighteenth century), this was the idea that man as a species had the potential ability to control his physical and social environment if, instead of magic, he used his reason to discover the rules governing natural phenomena and then went on to develop the scientific techniques needed to harness nature for the benefit of humankind. Although one of the greatest of the scientists of the late seventeenth century, Isaac Newton, did not fully accept the dichotomy between science and magic, the idea was certainly gaining headway by his time. Already in the 1620s intellectuals of the calibre of Sir Francis Bacon,

Lord Chancellor of England, had arrived at the startling conclusion – anticipated by Aristotle in the fourth century BC – that the material world could not be altered by invoking demons, using magical rituals or commanding changes to be made in physical objects through intensive concentration of the faith moveth mountains variety. Instead, Bacon and men like him perceived that man's mastery over Nature could be achieved by establishing causal connections between relevant pieces of matter and using these materials in accordance with the universal laws of Nature which learned men such as Copernicus and Galileo had already begun to discover.

Yet the new world that science had the potential to create was not intended to be an élitist world. For his part, Bacon concluded that by bringing together the theories supplied by learned scholars with the practical empirical knowledge supplied by artisans and craftsmen like those who had cobbled together the compass, the first printing press and gunpowder, humankind could gain mastery over their material environment and for the first time in human history abolish hunger, poverty and ignorance. In the light of the experience of the Third World in the late twentieth century, it would be well to stress the co-operative nature of the enterprise of human renewal envisioned by Bacon. For him, famine, war, disease, poverty and other human ills could only be banished if there was a unity of purpose between the skilled workers, the hands of society, and the intellectual élite, the mind. In the Lord Chancellor's scheme, the Great Instauration, there was no room for the exploitation of one party by the other.

The social structure of Europe: a simplified view

Nearly all people in early modern Europe lived in polities which were socially stratified and utterly undemocratic. These facts seem to be beyond dispute. However, some historians still hold that the early modern social structure can be meaningfully explained in terms of a 'society of orders'. Devised in the northern Gothic heartland of Europe in the early Middle Ages and unquestionably still relevant in the eleventh century in the high-tide of feudalism and decentralized authority, the scheme assigned to each of the three orders special functions and special privileges. First, in respect of the honour they bore came the priesthood, the members of the First Estate whose function it was to pray for God's people, living and dead. They were followed by the Second Estate which consisted of the warriors – in other words the nobility greater, middling and lesser – whose function it was to defend God's people. The Third Order or Estate was held to consist of the peasant cultivators and artisans whose farm products and crafts maintained the rest. Yet by the late fifteenth/early sixteenth century, in almost all areas of Europe to the west of the River Elbe, this high medieval ordering of society bore little relationship to the realities of most people's lives. This was largely because the urban-based merchants and bankers, people who had been few in number in the earlier period, had now come to play a vital and extremely visible role in society; one thinks of Jakob Fugger of Augsburg, Jacques Coeur of Paris and the Loire valley and of Cosimo de Medici of Florence. In the late thirteenth and fourteenth centuries, the growing importance of the commercial and banking interests was recognized by several western European territorial princes when they called into existence the regional or territorial consultative bodies known as the Estates. In most of these bodies the urban élite gained full recognition as the legitimate representatives of everyone who was not a priest or a warrior knight or noble. In practical terms this meant that the concept of a society of orders was limited to the political nation and no longer took account of the 90 per cent or more of the population who were peasant cultivators, artisans or craftsmen. Among the principal states the only exception to this rule was Sweden under its Vasa kings. In this rude frontier society, which hardly anyone had heard of before Gustavus Adolphus brought his country into the Thirty Years' War on the Protestant side in 1630, the *Riksdag* contained a fourth house consisting of the representatives of the peasants.

So much then for the society of orders. Even less useful in understanding the full complexity of early modern European societies are the modern ideas of class. These can be said to be based on the competing perceptions and interests of a proletariat and their polar opposites, the capitalists who own the means of production. But as Karl Marx, one of the principal creators of modern ideas of class, made clear in his writings in the 1840s, full consciousness of belonging to a specific class which was in permanent opposition to another class had to await the development of a fully industrialized society where, as in late eighteenth- and nineteenth-century Britain, the standard unit of production was the factory. In this sort of context workers who had no control over the means of production and had nothing to offer on the market-place except for their brute labour came to realize that their interests lay with workers living in other parishes and cities. Here then by the nineteenth century the loyalties of some working people at least had become *horizontal* and were based on a sense of community which transcended local boundaries.

As Marx fully recognized, no such sense of class was found anywhere in early modern Europe. In towns and cities the standard unit of production was still the small shop owned by the master and staffed by the master, his journeymen and apprentices and using manual labour. Although workers' organizations were not unknown in urban craft industries most workers lived in the same house as their employers and were counted as part of the family. Much as younger workers might dislike their master, they lived in hope that one day they might become masters. This intimacy and sense of expectation made the development of urban class consciousness in the modern sense nearly impossible. The same was true in rural areas, though for different reasons. Here poor people who were trying to make a living by manual labour were well aware that they were deprived of the special privileges (known to contemporaries as 'liberties') and quantitatively different life-style which the possession of wealth bestowed upon their landlord and the local great magnate. Nevertheless, they continued to regard themselves as part of a localized society which was divinely ordained to be headed by the great men of the neighbourhood. In time of personal hardship or need they expected that they would be the recipients of some token of the great man's paternalism. For their part, great landholders who upheld the traditional ethic still regarded themselves as bound by the obligations of paternalism to demonstrate humanitarian concern for all the local people of the meaner sort who showed proper deference. Exercised either in person or by deputy, the visible and frequent demonstration of paternalistic concern gave firm support to the status ascription which a landlord bore.

Of course, the strength of these ideals of obligation and deference varied tremendously between regions and from one period to the next. For example, there appears to have been little sense of lordly paternalism in the lands and territories of western Germany on the eve of the Peasants' War in 1524. A similar absence of paternalism was found both in seventeenth-century Castile and in Spanish Naples where most of the better off nobles were non-resident city-dwellers, and in Brittany and Poland where resident nobles who were not much better off financially than peasants were particularly thick on the ground. Yet in the Germanies by the late sixteenth century, after the lessons taught by the holocaust of the Peasants' War had had time to become a permanent part of the mentalities of both landholders and peasant cultivators, something resembling paternalism in return for deference had again become part of the German scene. Apart from on the rare occasions when they were in open revolt, and often even then, local non-élite people were bound by *vertical* ties of loyalty to their locally resident social superiors. They had no super-territorial or super-regional political organizations and had no consciousness of forming anything resembling a class which was in permanent opposition to the great landed magnates or the territorial prince.

More appropriate than either the concept of class or the concept of a society of orders in understanding the social organization of early modern Europe is the Neoplatonic concept of the Chain of Being. This concept was much in fashion in ruling circles in the sixteenth century. A century later, after it had been largely discarded by the élite, it continued its hold over the popular imagination. As far as its human members were concerned, at its lower end this Chain of Being began with the most destitute vagrant child and extended upwards through the various gradations of peasantry to the lesser and greater nobility and ended with the king or, in the Holy Roman Empire, with the emperor. Extending upwards beyond humankind were the links in the Chain of Being formed by the angels, archangels, principalities, powers, virtues, dominions, thrones, cherubim and seraphim and finally by God himself. Below humankind were the mammals who had sensitive souls (as opposed to men's intellectual souls), then plants with their vegetative souls and then earth and stones which had no souls at all. Thus, throughout the length of the Chain of Being each grouping shared some of the attributes of the group immediately below it as well as of the group immediately above.

Yet as far as humankind were concerned these groupings were not the same everywhere. In France and Italy and in most other parts of the Continent, nearly all contemporaries agreed that near the top of the links of the Chain of Being occupied by humankind there was a dramatic break. Below this break were the links occupied by all the people – roughly 95 per cent of the population – who worked with their hands, either as peasants, day-labourers or as artisans and craftsmen in villages and cities. Above the break were privileged people who were able to live without recourse to manual labour. Such people included the princes of the Church (archbishops and bishops), the greater, middling and lesser nobility, magistrates and judges, the great merchants and the intellectuals. These were the people who formed the ruling strata of society, the élite to whom we shall so often be referring in the pages which follow.

The situation was slightly different on the largest of Europe's off-shore islands. In England, as anybody who walked up a village street or looked about him in London could clearly see, society was also highly stratified. But in contrast to most parts of the Continent, in England the people known as yeomen, who worked their farms with their own hands and knew how to handle a stubborn plough-animal, were regarded as forming a part of the governing strata of society, though in a capacity which was more humble than that expected of a full 'gentleman', a person who did *not* work with his hands. Around 1600 all yeomen and indeed other countrymen who had a clear annual income from their lands in excess of 40 shillings were entitled to vote in an election for a Member of Parliament from their county. Yeomen served as constables and bailiffs and, after 1599–1601, as Poor Law officials. Together with the better sort of husbandmen, men whose holdings in land and annual income were far less than that of a yeoman, yeomen also served as grand and petty jurors in cases of life and death. No *laboureur*, the northern French equivalent of the English yeoman, was trusted with responsibilities of this sort. Yet even in England by the late seventeenth century, the gap between the few who were rich and the multitude who were poor was perceptibly widening. Using one sly trick or another, the élites had, by 1720, effectively disenfranchised all but a small minority of the population.

In continental western Europe, where most of the population lived in villages, society was also highly stratified. Somewhere close to the village was the great house in which the local landowner lived. In his absence this house might be occupied by the landowner's estate agent. This agent, who might either be a literate professional from outside the village or one of the rich local peasants, made certain that the land held for the direct use of the lord, the *demesne*, was properly worked and the customary tenants and others who held and worked the remainder of the village lands respected the proprieties of rank, degree and order. At the beginning of the early modern period this respect was best shown by the tenants' willingness to serve as foot soldiers under the banner of the landlord and to attend his court on ceremonial occasions. Only later when local territorial rulers, or in France, Spain and England the State, came to have a near monopoly over military force did landlords begin to regard their tenantry less as an essential part of a little commonwealth headed by themselves and more as depersonalized profit-generating units of production.

Within the peasant population of each village, local people awarded highest status to the peasants who had the most land and who generally speaking had the most wealth. In many parts of the German Empire, in the eye of the law, these rich peasants might be serfs whose conduct was more tightly controlled by the lord than was that of free, but poorer, tenants. For example, in the heavily governed territory of Lippe in Westphalia there were many serfs like Mesch Jobst. According to a report from 1620:

Mesch Jobst...is the ruler's serf. Pays castle duty of 9 groschen, one chicken. Serves the ruler like a hop-picker, namely to carry letters, work in the flax and help in the court yard with the harvest.[1]*

In northern France, where, apart from Burgundy, serfs were few, the leading free tenants were the *laboureurs*. These men, at least according to later theory, had enough land to maintain their families on the proceeds of the family farm and to give casual employment and loans of money to village people less fortunate than themselves. In the esteem of villagers, below the *laboureurs* or in England the yeomen, came the *manouvriers*, the English husbandmen. These people's landholdings were generally too small to support their families. This meant that they had to supplement their income by working part-time for more prosperous farmers. Below the *manouvriers* or husbandmen were the cottagers who held only a house and a small yard in which to grow foodstuffs, and the day-labourers or, as they were known in Castile, the *joraleros*. Such men had to work for other people in order to make a living and counted themselves lucky if they could find a paying job two or three days a week: in pre-industrial Europe

*Superior figures refer to the references which can be found at the end of each chapter.

underemployment was a chronic problem. Further down the scale of village social esteem were the people who had given up looking for work and who lived as vagrants or beggars.

Within a peasant village everyone who held a modicum of land by a recognized form was protected in his rights (or in the case of a widowed head of household, her rights) by village custom. Recognized by the villagers as well as by traditional-minded landlords, custom involved both rules and the control of resources; as such it must be regarded as one of the fundamental structures of early modern Europe. Especially if it were still only in oral form, with each application of the rules of custom, the custom itself was renewed even though in the process it might be subtly changed. Disputes about what constituted the custom of a village community, no less than those which concerned the customs of a province or State, lay behind many of the social tensions which will come within our purview in the course of this book.

Within most peasant villages were a number of full-time traders and skilled craftsmen, such as blacksmiths, leather workers, carpenters and millers. Such people were found in greatest profusion in the most westerly and most prosperous parts of Europe. Generally, the further east one travelled especially after passing over the Elbe, the river which passes through Dresden and Hamburg, the fewer the number of specialist craftsmen to be found in each village. Yet whatever their numbers, local skilled craftsmen and particularly traders served as important intermediaries between the village and the world outside.

For many peasants and certainly for most wage-labourers who could not find employment in the countryside and had to cast about for other alternatives, an important part of that world outside was the nearby or distant great city. Some of the peasants who came to a city were able to continue farming. For example, in Montpellier in Languedoc, in some neighbourhoods in the mid sixteenth century, nearly a quarter of the adult males were either *laboureurs* or day-labourers who made their living from agrarian activities which took place either within the city itself or within a short walk from its walls.

In the fifteenth and sixteenth centuries it was in the cities of northern Italy, southern Germany, the Low Countries and the Spanish Kingdoms that employment-generating craft industries such as cloth-making were largely found. As the centres of industrial and merchant capitalism it was to be expected that the social structures of these cities would be altogether more complex than those found in rural areas. Among the most prominent citizens of Seville or Antwerp, Cologne or Genoa, cities which in the sixteenth century served as centres of long-distance trade with the non-European as well as the European world, were the great merchants. Wherever they were found these great commercial capitalists formed the nucleus of the local bourgeoisie, the people who held a special charter of privilege from the Crown or local territorial prince. This charter usually gave the city the right to elect its own corporation and mayor, to hold courts, collect taxes and hold markets.

Before the late 1940s, when J. H. Hexter put his debunking pen to paper, most historians of north-west Europe – i.e. not Italy – held that merchant capitalists formed the core of what they called the 'middle class' and that such people were more or less in permanent opposition to the great landed aristocracy and its backward-looking ideals of paternalism and local autonomy. Admittedly, when writing about social stratification in the north Italian cities around 1500 it was quite proper for historians to use the term 'the middle class' since it was commonly used in more or less its modern sense by sixteenth-century northern Italian social theorists. Brought up short by Hexter's reappraisal of the evidence, most historians other than die-hard Marxists now recognize that in most northern cities other than Amsterdam and its sister cities in the Dutch Republic, where bourgeois values continued to prevail generation after generation, the condition of being a great merchant was simply one phase of development in the history of a successful family. Most northern merchants emerged from the obscurity of the countryside and rose to greatness not so much because they practised worldly asceticism and the Protestant work ethic but because of good judgement and good luck. Once established as great merchants they or their sons and grandsons set their sights on cutting their links with trade – perhaps through holding a government office which they purchased, as in France – and setting themselves up as proprietors of great landed estates in the countryside.

Although in the short term there were often tensions between the bourgeoisie of the Continental cities and the older aristocracy, over the course of three or four generations at most, members of successful bourgeois families merged with the landed aristocracy. Both adhered to a common ideology, the ideology of landed wealth and territorial influence. Moving from the family to the larger scene, the same sort of merger of interests becomes apparent if one compares the fifteenth and sixteenth centuries with the late seventeenth and early eighteenth centuries. During the earlier period when territorial rulers were in the process of building up their state bureaucracies they tended to recruit most of their officers from the middling sort of literate urban people to the near exclusion of the older aristocracy. Hence, with some justification one can speak of a western European-wide crisis of the aristocracy. However, by the late seventeenth century, after the crisis of the Fronde in France and the Thirty Years' War in the German Empire, most aristocrats in the states and larger principalities of western Europe had come to realize that because of the central government's near monopoly of armed force they could never again be semi-autonomous rulers of the regions where the core of their landed estates lay. Instead their future lay in joining forces with the central government by acquiring the rudiments of an education in the classics (the Great Tradition) and by serving as a great officer of state under the Crown or as the Crown's chief representative in a locality. By the early eighteenth century, almost everywhere in western Europe including England, it was the great landed magnates wielding power on behalf of central authority who once again dominated society. Recruited into their ranks, although not always on equal terms – for example, in France there was latent conflict between the nobles of the sword and the nobility of the robe – were the urban based élites who had acquired their wealth through their parents' bourgeois pursuit of trade, commerce or banking. In the north Italian cities, precocious as usual, this merging took place even earlier. Peter Burke suggests that by the 1540s most of the great north Italian cities were dominated by a patriciate which had given up the life-style of the simple bourgeoisie common in the 1450s and instead lived as if they were nobles.

In Venice in the 1550s and 1560s, many families bought up estates on the Terra Firma and commissioned architects like Andrea Palladio to build them houses befitting their noble or near-noble status. Much the same sort of thing happened in the Papal States. Thus, in the half century after 1580 several bankers from Genoa and Florence (true capitalists if ever such existed) came to Rome to help the Pope manage his finances. Seeking rewards for their good services – it was after 1580 that papal largess brought into existence the miracle which is Baroque Rome – the immigrant capitalists arranged with the Pope and the local aristocratic power structure to get themselves set up on the Roman Campagna as great landed proprietors. With respect to their new tenantry they acted in as feudal a manner as did the older Roman aristocracy with whom they intermarried.

Great cities were of course the natural centres of princely and ecclesiastical power. By 1550, after most of the Italian city states had been reduced to a position of dependency on either France or Spain, the idea had caught on that the king of a proper nation state (i.e. France, Spain or England) should spend most of his time in or near a fixed capital rather than touring around his far-flung domains with his courtiers, advisers and baggage trains. The settling down of princely courts and their ecclesiastical hangers-on (even the Archbishop of Canterbury, the Primate of All England, saw fit to spend most of his time in Lambeth Palace across the Thames from Whitehall Palace rather than in his Kentish cathedral city) further facilitated the growth of government bureaucracy. With the growth of this clerical and literate lay element a capital city such as Madrid, Vienna, Munich or Rome – to mention only a few of the booming capital cities in the Catholic world – proved an increasingly attractive place for non-civil servant professional people whose livelihood depended upon having influential patrons; lawyers, medical doctors, artists, architects, musicians and intellectuals.

It was the professional urban people – the respectable lay element – no less than the clerics of the Church who in the years after 1550 were in the vanguard of the phenomenon known as the reformation of manners. For the first time citizens were expected to behave in all things with fitting decorum; not to defecate in public, to wash their hands and face before meals and to uphold the principles of a society in which rank, degree and order were fully respected. Aside from modes of dress, speech and posture, the most visible way in which reformed urbanites could show their adherence to the new, more rigorously ordered society was to support the new forms of religion adopted by their state between 1517 and 1648 (see Chapter 5).

Not only did *men* at the governing levels of society (women were among the victims of the movement) expect courteous, decent and godly behaviour from each other, they came to expect it as well from ordinary people in the countryside. A theme which runs through all the history of early modern western European society is the attempt of learned urban laymen and clerics, who saw themselves as the upholders of the Great Tradition, to impose the reformation of manners upon rural people. Yet the popular cultures which were under continuous assault from high culture from the 1550s onwards proved highly resilient to change. At the deeper levels of lived experience popular culture retained much of its distinctive rural-based identity until well beyond the end of the early modern period. Even then in the context of an increasingly urbanized social setting, the new forms of popular culture remained separate and distinct from the high culture adopted by the ruling elements of society.

Demographic trends

A brief glance at the figures listed in Table 1 might suggest that western Europe had achieved some sort of optimal population level in the four hundred years before the coming of industrialization, the phenomenon which first occurred in Britain between 1750 and 1820. In 1340 Europe's population had probably stood at between 80 and 85 million – in the absence of censuses and similar records historical demographers must resort to educated guesses. In 1680, on the eve of the demographic revolution, Europe's population stood at approximately 71 million; it increased to 116 million by 1820.

Closer scrutiny of Table 1, however, will show that some very strange things happened to Europe's population in the years *between* 1340 and 1680. The population in 1680, to say nothing of the population in 1550, was less than it had been in 1340. In its simplest form, the explanation for this is that after the bubonic plague (popularly known as the Black Death) first

Table 1 *Western Europe: estimated population totals*

Country	1340 millions	1550 millions	1680 millions	Percentage change between 1550 and 1680
France	*c.* 24	17	21.9	+29
England	6	3	4.9	+64
Netherlands	4	1.2	1.9	+58
Spain	14	9	8.5	− 6
Italy	15	11	12	+ 9
Germany	17	12	12	0
Western Europe	80	61	71.9	+18

Sources: A. E. Wrigley, 'The growth of population in eighteenth-century England: a conundrum resolved', *Past and Present*, no. 98 (1983), p. 122. For the earlier period see John Hatcher, *Plague, Population and the English Economy 1348–1530* (London: Macmillan 1977).

established itself in Europe in 1346 as an import from Asia, and then settled down to become endemic until the late seventeenth century, Europe's birth rate was not able to compensate for the high death rate.

In normal years the European birth rate generally stood at between thirty and thirty-eight per thousand. This is low when compared to a birth rate in excess of forty-five per thousand which is not uncommon in many parts of the modern tropical Africa. In normal times, the European death rate was between twenty-eight and thirty-five per thousand. All other things being equal this meant that Europe's population should have gradually increased and perhaps doubled every century. That it did not was because normal years, when these rates held, were more than offset by the abnormal years. These were years when the village or region under consideration was being ravaged by plague or other endemic diseases, or in the throes of war. On the average (a misleading concept which eliminates local variations but is useful to get an overall impression), villages, cities and whole regions were visited by plague, famine or war, either separately or in combination, once every twenty or thirty years. During these visitations the death rate might rise to three or four times its normal level. In some cases a third or a half of the population might be swept away by the angel of death.

Basing his observations on what he knew of Europe's population history (some important facts were unknown to him), Thomas Malthus concluded in 1798 that the standard of living of a growing population which no longer had enough landed resources to support itself would necessarily fall. Under these circumstances a population which did not take preventive steps, by which Malthus meant lowering the birth rate, would be overtaken by a shortage of food. In time, scarcity or dearth would give way to famine and finally to mass starvation, the ultimate in what Malthus called *positive* population checks. Malthusians assumed that killer diseases marched hand in hand with dearth and starvation. Now it is true that this grim equation linking food resources and land, population size and death probably can be applied to a small-scale society of simple cultivators who live in isolation from the larger society. The question is, did it apply to early modern Europe?

The answer must be that it applies only to a very limited degree in particularly ill-favoured regions and not at all in most others. As we have already seen, early modern Europe was very much dependent on the land and required that 85 per cent or more of the workforce spend its time growing crops or tending cattle. Almost all of the food which people ate was derived from the land, either in the form of cereals, root crops such as turnips, from fruit, or from livestock and poultry. Because of their taste preferences most people refused to regard fish as more than occasional food to be eaten on Catholic fast days. In addition to food, the land also provided nearly all the materials needed for non-agricultural work: flax for linen cloth-makers, hides for leatherworkers, wood and timber for barrel- and stave-makers and carpenters, iron, tin, copper and silver for metalworkers.

It is obvious that a bad cereal harvest, or worse a run of two or three successive bad harvests, could have serious repercussions for a localized economy. In late seventeenth-century France, for example, where labourers commonly spent a third or a half of the family's earnings on bread, their staple food, a doubling or trebling of the price of bread at the village bakery (it was not worth the time and effort involved to bake bread at home), could have a devastating effect on the family. The fall in the value of the tithes owing the Church, and of rents and taxes which could be collected on behalf of the élite, meant that bad harvests could also affect people at the governing levels of society.

Historians have now generally accepted the evidence of climatologists who tell us that between 1560 and 1850 Europe was in the midst of a 'little ice-age'. During the worst years of this long period, the late 1590s, the early 1620s, the late 1640s, the early 1660s and the mid 1690s, and in Castile 1698–9, the annual average temperature may have fallen 0.9°C below the norms of a good year in the post 1850 period. This meant that during particularly adverse years the winters were unusually cold and the summers unusually wet. A small drop in the average summer temperature could reduce the time available for cereal crops to ripen by two or three weeks. This meant that areas which were reasonable wheat producers in years with sunny summers were transformed in the cold, wet years into marginal lands which were not suitable for this staple crop.

Less important than the drop in average annual temperatures were the social and cultural responses of the people most directly affected by bad harvest conditions; the peasant cultivators and their landlords. Farmers who were left to their own devices could usually alter their farming patterns and dietary habits to meet variable climatic conditions. Weather conditions did not affect all crops in the same way. A season which promised to be unfavourable to wheat would provide an excellent harvest in coarser grains such as rye or barley, and hay for animal fodder. Thus, wherever farmers were free to grow such crops, no one need starve to death. Fresh meat and rye bread were as good a diet (or better) than one based largely on wheaten bread.

Yet, as we know, crises of subsistence when people starved to death *did* occur during the years when weather conditions were adverse for good wheat harvests, or for some other staple crop. The main reason for this was that landlords were inflexible in their demand that peasants grow wheat. Wheat almost always fetched a good market price because of the European cultural preference for white wheaten bread, a preference which was intensified by the reformation of manners after 1550. Suffering under landlords of this sort, peasants in the parish of San Facundo in Medina del Campo, an area of Spain given over to wheat, suffered a heavy loss of life through starvation in the early 1620s. Similarly, nearly a quarter of the population in the parishes around Beauvais which were given over almost entirely to wheat died in the years 1693–4. Yet, during the same period, in the neighbouring parish of Auneuil, where more diversified farming was practised, the mortality rate was less than half that of the wheat-growing parishes. In addition to wheat, Auneuil peasants grew large quantities of peas and beans which were perfectly suitable for a nourishing soup.

By the 1720s, when western Europe happened to be blessed by a long series of sunny summers suitable for good wheat harvests, the age of subsistence crises had come to an end. In part, this change was reflected in the renewed growth of Europe's population. The change itself was partly the result of better marketing systems, better roads and forms of transport. It was also the result of the introduction of new crops from the Americas; maize (American corn), potatoes and a range of clovers which restored to the soil the nitrates needed to produce better crops even in mildly adverse weather conditions.

What sort of people died during a famine? What did they die from? What effect did their deaths have upon the population structure of the village? Answers to these questions are not easy to obtain. However, in the last thirty or forty years historical demographers and social historians have begun to tap local records for information. The single most important local records for this purpose are the parish registers. Beginning before the 1530s in parts of Italy, Spain and France, and in 1538 in England, parish priests were required by law to keep registers of baptisms, marriages and burials. Though the cause of death was seldom noted, the day or at least the week were. Historical demographers who use this information in conjunction with what they know about the seasonal patterns of killer disease, reports about the outbreak of diseases and the state of local harvests, are thus able to learn approximately how many people died from these diseases.

There is still considerable controversy among historians about the possible connection between dietary deficiencies which might be attributed to local scarcity and death through disease. It might be supposed that people who were debilitated and weak from hunger would be the most likely to succumb to disease. However, the latest opinion is that only outbreaks of typhus and various kinds of fevers were directly associated with periods of famine. Statistically these killers did not occur with sufficient frequency to have a meaningful impact on Europe's long-term demographic patterns. Most other diseases struck and killed regardless of the state of the harvests. One obvious example comes from the years 1556–8 when most of England was enjoying bountiful harvests and low grain prices. Nevertheless, in many regions a fifth of the population died in those two years as a result of the ravages of influenza. Much the same sort of thing happened in the late fifteenth century in wide areas of western Europe. At a time when the population was still low following the plague, and in France the Hundred Years' War, as far as we can determine most people were eating better than their ancestors had a hundred years earlier. Yet mortality constantly kept pace with fertility. In the two hundred or more villages in the peaceful diocese of Geneva the population remained at less than half its pre 1348–9 level throughout the period 1470 to 1518 because of disease. As these examples illustrate, Malthus, in claiming it was mass starvation, was clearly wrong about the nature of the agency which held early modern populations in check.

When death by starvation did occur, it was age and status selective; rich people seldom starved to death. In the rest of the population it was the old people and children who could not contribute their labour to the family economy or who had been deserted by their kinsfolk who were the first to be left to die. People who were in the prime of life – between 20 and 45 years of age – were also the most mobile. When their food resources ran short they thronged to nearby market towns or cities where they thought food was available. Some were disappointed and died along the road, in a barn belonging to a gentleman, or outside the gates of an inhospitable city. The number of people who died in this way depended entirely upon the local social and cultural context.

During a period of disruption brought about by a local shortage or other catastrophe, people postponed their marriages. Because married people were not of a mind to have children or because of miscarriages purposely brought about by the mother or resulting from weakness and malnutrition, fertility rates dropped. But a year or two after the end of the crisis, the young and the able-bodied were back in their villages, producing – among other things – children. For example, local studies have shown that 15 per cent of the adults in the Paris Basin died during the famine of 1693–4. But by the 1705–6 the population had recovered to the level of 1690. Of the larger polities between 1550 and 1680, it was only Spain which failed to at least maintain its population level and ended the period with fewer people than it had had at the beginning.

War was the second of the three cataclysmic ills from which good Christians prayed that their God would deliver them. And for good reason. When the dogs of war were let loose, mortality rates – at least before the mid eighteenth century – were always appallingly high. In Normandy in the course of the Hundred Years' War between the rulers of France and England, 30 per cent of the population of the province died. Similarly high were the levels of mortality among ordinary people in the districts where military operations were carried out during the French Wars of Religion (1562–98), the revolutionary civil war known as the Fronde (1648–52) and during Louis XIV's wars of aggrandizement (1690–1713). Mortality rates were also high in those parts of Spain bordering onto Portugal during the long years after 1590 when Portugal was struggling to regain its independence and, with it, control of Brazil. In the Spanish frontier town of Ceclavin, a population which had numbered 1000 households in 1640 had dropped to only 430 households in 1666. During the Thirty Years' War which shattered much of central Europe between 1618 and 1648, the Baltic provinces in what is now East Germany lost half of their population.

In all of these wars a few of the fatalities could be credited to good marksmanship, skill with the sword, lance, or cannon, and the wilful murder of peasants by sadistic mercenary soldiers. Until the development of the concept of limited warfare using disciplined soldiers came into general use in the mid eighteenth century – perhaps the experience of the Thirty Years' War *had* taught Europe's statesmen to abhor senseless violence – men under arms were a scourge to local populations. Aside from the officers, who were generally of high or middling social status, the soldiers were drawn from the dregs of their societies and were usually misfits who could not get along with other people in their own village. In the long lulls between pitched battles, ill-paid or unpaid mercenary soldiers and their hangers-on sometimes held whole villages to ransom or worse. The fate of the town of Cognoncles in the Cambrésis was typical of many. The province was seized by France from the

Habsburg Emperor in 1477 and became the scene of continuous warfare. Unfriendly soldiers pillaged the plough animals, livestock and standing crops of the people of Cognoncles in 1553. Between 1554 and 1557 they ravaged the town three more times. In human terms the first of these assaults was the most costly. Troops in the employ of His Most Catholic Majesty, the King of France, set fire to the church in which most of the people of Cognoncles had taken refuge; only a few charred bones remained.

Barbarous though such actions were, the main threat posed by soldiers and marauders was the diseases which they carried with them. Cut off from the social controls exercised by their distant homes – few settled villagers would defecate into a stream from which they would later drink – soldiers neglected the most elementary rules of sanitation. When the soldiers of King Charles I were in quarters in the university town of Oxford during the early stages of the first English Civil War (1642–6), it was reported that 'being pact together in close houses, when they had filled all things with filthiness and unwholesome nastiness and stinking odours...they fell sick by troops'.[2]

In France, it has been suggested that the small troop of 8000 ragged soldiers which Cardinal Richelieu sent from La Rochelle to Languedoc in 1628 to crush a few thousand dissident French Huguenots (Protestants), carried death through disease to nearly a million people. Even more disastrous in human terms was the effect of the German invasion of Italy in 1694. Unknown until it was too late, the hireling soldiers carried with them the infected fleas which transmitted bubonic plague. Within a few months of the German invasion in the autumn of 1694, the population of northern Italy had been reduced from 4 million to 2.9 million. Losses of this magnitude require further explanation.

From the terrors of the pestilence, good Lord deliver us!

Bubonic plague had first appeared in the port cities of Italy in 1346 as an unintended consequence of the trade with the Levant. From there it spread throughout the whole of western Europe and into eastern Europe. Between the years 1346 and 1350 it advanced on a wide front. In Italy and north of the Alps it decimated whole villages, others it left virtually unscathed. Overall, in its first attack the plague probably swept away one person out of every three or four. Tragic though these losses were in human terms, they could have been replaced in a generation or two given western Europe's normal birth rate had not the plague become endemic. Thus, in the countryside around Nantes in France, and in the city itself, plague broke out in fifty-three of the years between 1465 and 1566. There were particularly severe losses, a third or a half of the population, in 1500–1, in 1528–33 and in 1544–6. In Castile, the city of Ciudad Real lost half of its population because of pestilence in 1684–5.

In the long term, the endemic nature of the pestilence had a cumulative effect. Expressed simply, the population in the child-rearing stages of life never had a chance to recover its numbers. The young people who were struck down were not around fifteen or twenty years later to replenish the population. In Europe generally it was the endemic nature of the plague and other diseases which prevented a recovery of the population to its 1340 levels. In Spain, even between 1550 and 1680, the cumulative impact of the pestilence and other diseases led to an overall reduction in population. In that collection of kingdoms ruled by the Spanish king from the Escorial near Madrid, population recovery did not begin until the pestilence finally disappeared late in 1685.

The principal form of plague is carried by a bacterium, *pasteurella pestis*, which needs three hosts to complete its work of devastation: rats, fleas and humans. The bacterium is an internal parasite in rats and many other rodents which feeds on the animals' blood. A flea picks up the infection when it bites a rat and soon it finds itself unable to digest its food. The insect then becomes voraciously hungry and after the death by plague of the host rat, transfers its attention to humans. Among people afflicted with the principal form of plague the mortality rate was between 70 and 90 per cent. Death generally occurred within four days. Because of the nature of the life cycle of the bacterium, the principal form of plague was not infectious; it could not be transferred directly from one human being to another. If a doctor or, in Portugal or Spain, a black slave serving in a pest-hospital could only avoid coming into contact with the rat fleas which lived in humans' clothes and hair, he could survive long contact with victims of the plague. However, a second form of plague called *pneumonic plague* was highly infectious. In its pneumonic form the plague was present in the spittle or mucus of an infected person and was spread when he or she coughed, sneezed or spat. This form of plague was 90 to 99 per cent fatal. It seems likely that pneumonic plague worked in alliance with non-infectious plague during the terrible years 1346–50. Whether it did later on remains unknown.

In Europe the plague was more feared than any other catastrophe. This fear is reflected in the late medieval nursery rhyme which English and American children still sing:

> Ring a ring o' roses
> A pocket full of posies
> A tishoo, a tishoo
> We all fall down [– dead]

When it first made its murderous way across Europe in 1346–50 the plague continued summer and autumn, winter and spring. But in later years it tended to become passive during the cold winter months. Then during the spring planting season it would again shoot out its clammy killing fingers, striking unpredictably in one direction in one year and in another the next. It was this unpredictability no less than the lethal nature of the plague when it did strike which made it so feared.

Before 1540 colonies of plague bearing black rats were commonly found in the wood, mud-walled and thatched dwellings in which most Europeans lived. When living in such close proximity to humans, it was easy enough for the fleas to transfer from one host to another. In retrospect we now know that a sudden surfacing of large numbers of rats in the final throes of the disease, like the fleas ravenously hungry because their digestive processes had been disrupted, should have been a signal for all humans to immediately abandon their dwellings and towns and soak themselves and their clothes in powerful disinfectant. Strangely enough no person of influence in early modern Europe recognized the connection between rats and the bubonic plague. Yet occasionally contemporaries did comment on a sudden surge of rats. In the north Italian town of Busto Arsizio in 1630 it was noted that there was 'such a great quantity of rats that people could hardly protect themselves either at daytime or at night from the molesting rage of these animals...one could count them by the hundreds in every house...they were so hungry that they gnawed at doors and windows'.[3] The Busto Arsizio plague of 1630 was the same plague which reduced the population of the great port city of Venice by a third. In 1631, after the plague had finally subsided, the Doge and Council of Venice gave orders that a church be built as a thank offering to God. The result was one of the architectural marvels of the west, the Church of Santa Maria della Salute.

The human response to the plague

The European intellectual and social response to the plague was twofold. One response was to see the pestilence and all other diseases as scourges sent by God to punish His erring people. As late as the 1630s, most of the experts at the University of Oxford, other than the Chancellor of the university, Archbishop William Laud, held to this theory. In an attempt to placate the angry deity, shrines were built dedicated to the saints who were reputed to have special powers over the pestilence, particularly St Roch and St Sebastian. The visible arrows from which Sebastian had died (he was a fourth century Roman centurion who had been martyred for his faith) were analagous to the invisible arrows of the killing plague. Other people, a statistically negligible percentage of the population as a whole, joined penitential orders and went on long pilgrimages beating each other with whips as they went. The effectiveness of such measures is reflected in Table 1 (p. 20). But at the very

least these efforts did reflect the widespread feeling among Europeans that it
was possible for them to do something to counteract the plague. Rather than
simply waiting passively to be struck dead, sinful men and women were
asking God to reconsider His earlier judgement upon them.

The second intellectual response to disease was no less characteristic of
western Europeans who in the years after 1450 created the modern
capitalistic world system. This response led to the organization and
definition of a medical profession and to the establishment of a system of
public health.

The growth of the medical profession

It was in the cultural heartland of the Renaissance, northern Italy, that the
organization of the medical profession first took place. Blending ideas of
individualism and competitiveness with notions of the public good, it was
generally accepted by 1400 that gentlemen of good birth would not lose
status if they came into physical contact with filthy scab-ridden patients. To
become a physician it was necessary to take a degree at a university such as
those at Padua or Bologna. By 1500, degrees in medicine were also being
granted by the Spanish universities of Salamanca and Valladolid. But, as part
of the general weakening of Italian cultural hegemony and the precipitous
decline in the quality of Spanish intellectual life, by 1600 most of the new
innovations in medicine were being made at northern universities such as
those at Leiden in the Netherlands. Once out of university, a student
underwent further on the job training until he was admitted to a physicians'
guild. In London and several other northern cities, barber-surgeons (the
people who had the messy task of amputating arms and legs without benefit
of antiseptics or anaesthetics) were organized into a separate guild as were
the apothecaries, the people who traded in medically proven drugs and
cures (few of their drugs would be acceptable to today's medical profession).

In the Renaissance and Baroque city states of northern Italy the effective
area of a medical guild's jurisdiction covered the whole of the state, rural as
well as urban areas. In early seventeenth-century Tuscany, which comprised
Florence and its extensive hinterland, there were two physicians and two
surgeons for every 10,000 people. This would be a respectable ratio even for
an advanced industrial society today. North of the Alps, however, it was
probably true to say that medical services by university graduates or
competent barber-surgeons were available only to people of substance who
lived in Paris, where medical services were organized on an effective
city-wide basis during the reign of Henry IV (1589–1610), or in London,
Madrid or in the few provincial centres where doctors who wished to escape
the deadening hand of centralized controls chose to live.

The medical profession grew in size and in social prestige because people who were in a position to pay for its services (or who, as in northern Italy, enjoyed the benefits of nationalized state medicine), had confidence in the doctor's ability to effect cures. Perhaps this confidence was misplaced. Before the 1860s doctors had no way of curing any disease other than malaria and syphilis. Whenever any other disease was found, all the physician was able to do was to give his patients psychological relief. Yet today, modern doctors recognize that the provision of this imponderable by a doctor, or in the Third World by a traditional healer, may effect a remission from the disease.

Returning to the sixteenth and seventeenth centuries, it can be seen that by creating medical guilds, entry into which only came through a system of rigorous examinations, a channel was created through which the latest medical discoveries and theories *could be* quickly transmitted to all members of the profession (however, this does not mean that they always were). Yet in the long run it was the existence of these channels rather than the theories which were of most vital importance. Without having some theory to hang on to, however wrong-headed, these channels would have dried up.

In northern Europe two paradigms vied with each other for supremacy, neither of which would meet the approval of the medical profession today, but both of which serve to give us some insight into early modern mentalities. The first was based on the authority of the writings of the pagan Greek philosopher Galen who had lived in the second century of the Christian era. The Galenic school held that bodily health was controlled by the four humours: Melancholy, Phlegm, Blood and Choler. An imbalance in these humours could be put right by severe dietary constraints, blood-letting and purges of the bowels. Treated by Galenic physicians, who were particularly strongly entrenched in the London College of Physicians until the 1650s, it seems likely that as many people died of the treatment as of the disease.

The second system held more hope for the future, although it, too, was based on ideas garnered from the past. Proponents of this school, which in the battle between the Ancients and the Moderns (followers of Sir Francis Bacon must be termed Moderns), held that the secrets of Nature could be revealed by clinical observation and empirical experimentation. Support for this theory was provided by what was known of the work of Hippocrates (died *c.* 377 BC), as well as the work of Andreas Vesalius, Professor of Anatomy at the University of Padua (under whom William Harvey studied before he made his discoveries about the circulation of blood). Support was also provided by the mystical writings of the early sixteenth-century Swiss-German metaphysician Theophrastus Paracelsus (d. 1541).

The Moderns, the empiricists, had plenty of things with which to experiment. Some of the new drugs brought back from the Spanish New World, such as ipecacuanha, were found to give relief from malaria and other fevers. Following the travels of John Tradescant to America in the early seventeenth century, botanical gardens were established to provide the range of herbs which some scholars held might eventually provide cures for all diseases. Other Moderns placed their faith in minerals and in the pseudo-science of alchemy which eventually became chemistry in the nineteenth century. During the early modern period the most important of the cures derived from chemicals was the use of a mercury solution to cure syphilis, the new disease brought to Europe by Italian and Spanish sailors coming from America and Asia.

Yet in the cure of most other diseases the empiricists made little progress. In the absence of anaesthesia, for example, medical practitioners were not able to make much use of the discoveries William Harvey had made in the 1620s, or the discoveries about human anatomy revealed by the dissection of human cadavers. Knowledge of anatomy remained of more importance to artists – for example, Michelangelo, Leonardo da Vinci and Rubens – than to medical doctors.

The basic problem was that, for all their interest in empiricism, the Moderns lacked an empirically tested interpretative structure (a paradigm) which would have enabled them to think in terms of the germs and micro-agents which we now know cause many diseases. Yet, some of the statements made by Paracelsus might have begun to put them on the right track. Unfortunately, Paracelsus had come out in support of the peasants during the German Peasants' War of 1524–5. Because he was seen as a social revolutionary, few medical doctors other than those in revolutionary England in the 1650s were willing to give serious consideration to what he said.

Paracelsus and his followers among the Calvinist precisionists (Puritans) of revolutionary England held that the spiritual regeneration of humankind, the first priority for them, was dependent upon the *revival* of knowledge which would once again enable humankind to prevent and cure disease. In their view this knowledge had been partially lost at the time of the Fall from Grace in the Garden of Eden and totally lost in the late Roman period when physicians became more conscious of their élite status and ceased coming into physical contact with live patients or with cadavers.

Paracelsus based his theories on a strange combination of biblical, gnostic (gnostics were Hebrew and Greek intellectual élitists), and hermetic sources (hermetic ideas were thought to have originated in ancient Egypt but were in reality the thoughts of Hermes Trismegistus who lived in the second or third century of the Christian era). Paracelsus rejected the Galenic ideas that disease was caused by an imbalance of the four humours. This itself was a positive achievement. He replaced this theory with the notion that sickness was caused by the *astrum* of the disease agent which afflicted the body like a parasite, settling in one particular location. But after this hopeful start,

Paracelsus went off on a metaphysical tangent. He held that in its purest form each disease *astrum*, like each human being's *astrum* (that of Martin Luther, for example), was to be found in the great world spirit which hovered about in the realm of the stars, the sun and the planets. In its debased terrestrial form, the human *astrum* or the disease *astrum* gave each individual man or disease its characteristic shape and nature, and its vital spirit. The Paracelsians held that individual human *astrum* which had been attacked by a particular disease *astrum* during the time when the appropriate constellation was dominant in the night sky could be put right if the proper antidote against the alien *astrum* were found. Following this logic, syphilis was linked to disorders which came upon a sufferer between 24 October and 21 November when Scorpio (hence the name syphilis) was the dominant sign of the Zodiac.

Faulty though their reasoning was, the Moderns were eternal optimists. They were convinced that an antidote for every disease which afflicted humankind existed somewhere in Nature, if only Nature could be made to unlock its secrets. This sense of optimism was the greatest contribution made to true progress by the Moderns. If one is convinced that something can never be done, one will never start off on a new venture of experimentation and discovery. Another feature characteristic of the Moderns was their conviction that the regeneration of the bodily health of humankind meant the whole of humankind, the Commonwealth of all men and women. It was this spirit, combined with the lingering humanist concept of society as an organic Commonwealth and the sense of *noblesse oblige* inherited from the feudal age which lay behind many of the public health measures which were put into effect during this period.

The prevention of disease

In practical terms it was again the northern Italians, followed at some remove by the French, the Spaniards, the Scots and the English, who led the way in the creation of state or regional health authorities. Whenever a medical crisis threatened, northern Italian doctors and surgeons paid by the state were required by the board of health to treat all patients. Those who were too poor to pay the doctors' fees were treated free of charge. Serious cases were confined to the state pest-house.

In northern Italy, and later in the great cities north of the Alps, public health officials also made some effort to deal with public sanitation. Health regulations required butchers, leather tanners and other polluters to locate their establishments well down stream from the place where drinking water was drawn. This was done, not because the health authorities knew that these waste products carried infection (nobody yet was thinking in terms of a paradigm based on the germ theory), but because the wastes emitted a horrid smell. It was the smell itself which was thought to be the cause of disease. This false notion remains with us yet in the name given to the disease malaria (Latin, bad air). Malaria afflicted thousands of people who did not bear sickle-cells in their blood and who lived in smelly swampy regions of lowland Italy, Spain and France, as well as in the lowland parts of Essex and Cambridgeshire in England.

In order to cope with the foul smells which were erroneously thought to cause disease, in time of medical crisis public health officials gave orders that foul smells issuing from items which could not be burnt be covered over with what they took to be hygienic smells. Thus, in Spain letters coming from a city where the plague was known to exist had to be rubbed with vinegar. Other items were treated with lye or bleach. To treat their own persons, people of substance covered themselves with expensive perfumes imported from the East; in contrast, ordinary peasants stank.

The concern which early modern health authorities had for the provision of water that did not carry with it foul smells was at least a step in the right direction. However, the fact that water does not smell is no guarantee that it does not harbour waterborne diseases such as cholera, typhoid and dysentery. In some of the poorer parts of rural France where no precautions about water supplies were taken, most people suffered from waterborne debilitating diseases which gave them the appearance of being old people at the age of 25. In such regions the death rate was consistently high. In 1707, in some of the parishes in Anjou where these conditions held, more than a fifth of the population died from dysentery within a few weeks.

One reason why the introduction of tea, coffee and cocoa, products of Asia and Africa, was so important for the demographic history of Europe was that the preparation of these beverages required boiling water. Even if water is boiled for only a few minutes most of the disease organisms it carries are killed, although complete sterilization only occurs if the water is boiled for a full twenty minutes. This of course would require more fuel than a poor person might care to use. Clearly, disease and poverty were often closely linked.

As part of the reformation of manners we mentioned earlier, people were encouraged to pay increasing attention to personal hygiene. In his *Primer*, Erasmus of Rotterdam, the great humanist scholar and popularizer, advised schoolboys to wash their hands, face and teeth in clean water when they got up in the morning and before coming to the table to eat. As any dentist knows, however, it would have been more useful had they brushed their teeth *after* eating. Advice similar to that of Erasmus was given by Andrew Boorde, the first British physician to go into print, in 1547. In the much regulated city of Nuremberg in the German Empire all wage-earners were given half a day off once a week to enable them to go to the public baths to scour themselves clean on the principle that 'cleanliness is next to godliness'. Here, half naked family processions on the way to the baths were a common sight. But in early sixteenth-century Italy and southern France public steam baths were better known as places where roving men made assignations with prostitutes, male and female. A full half century after Andrew Boorde published his helpful hints on hygiene, the Scottish King, James VI, later James I of England, was still unwilling to do more than apply a slightly dampened cloth to his face and hands once a fortnight. Like many other aristocrats James thought it quite enough to cover his bodily odours with perfume.

The conquest of the plague

Two things contributed to bringing an end to the plague in western Europe by the end of the seventeenth century. One of these had nothing whatever to do with human agency or action but instead involved obscure changes which took place in the ecosystem of the disease micro-organism itself. By around 1540, or perhaps earlier, the concentrated pockets of disease known to have existed near Caen and Beauvais in France, and elsewhere in the fifteenth century, were no longer self-supporting. Instead, they had to be replenished by fresh batches of disease organism brought in by rats from the Orient. Even today, in the 1980s, rat burrows containing concentrations of bubonic plague micro-organisms capable of destroying whole populations are found in remote parts of Mongolia in the People's Republic of China.

Nearly two hundred years after the ecosystem of the plague micro-organism changed, which is to say in the 1730s, the composition of the dominant rat population of western Europe also changed. It seems likely that this alteration began with the great surge of brown rats over the River Volga which was noted in 1727. The consequence of this revolution in rat-dom was that the black rats of the sort which had suddenly surfaced at Busto Arsizio in 1630 – 'one could count them by hundreds in every house' – had come to be replaced by brown rats. Brown rats preferred to live in burrows underground rather than in houses as black rats had done. However, these changes in the composition of western Europe's rat population occurred *after* the bubonic plague had ceased to be a permanent scourge and thus can no longer be counted as a cause of its disappearance. Similarly discounted by recent scholarship are the changes in the standards of housing built by people of middling and superior wealth. In London, for example, a year after the plague had visited the city for the last time in 1665, the Great Fire destroyed most of the core of the city. In the wake of this catastrophe, an order was given that all houses be built of brick rather than of wood and wattle and daub. Yet in Scotland, the poorer types of housing continued to be built out of flimsy materials and to have rubbish heaps just outside the door long after the last

occurrence of the plague in 1649 (both places which would prove suitable
habitations for rats). Similarly discounted is the older idea that it was changes
in the dietary patterns of the middling population and above which brought
an end to the plague since the diet of the poor was still not conducive to good
health.

As far as human action was concerned the *sufficient* condition needed to
bring an end to the plague in western Europe was the rigorous application of
quarantine regulations; the *necessary* precondition for the end of plague was
the changes in the ecosystem of the plague micro-organisms. As early as 1563,
Doctor de Boekel of Hamburg had concluded that the causal agent of the
plague which afflicted the city in that year was a ship which had come into the
port from the Orient. This observation led existing boards of health in the
cities and kingdoms of western Europe to redouble their efforts to enforce
quarantine regulations. Ships which were known to have come from ports in
the Ottoman Empire or the Orient where the plague was raging were required
to remain far out at sea for at least forty days. In the case of the ship le Grand
Saint-Antoine, which came into Marseilles from a non-European port in
1720, it was the lapse of quarantine regulations which brought the plague to
Marseilles and its immediate hinterland; this was the last outbreak of plague
anywhere in western Europe.

Quarantine regulations were also enforced in western European cities and
towns where, in the years before 1690, the plague was at work. Such a city was
surrounded at a safe distance by regiments of soldiers who forcibly
prevented anyone from leaving it. Around cities which were not yet affected
cordons sanitaires were also created; soldiers prevented anyone from entering
the city. Such drastic action, of course, completely disrupted normal trading
activities and created serious hardships for urban poor who depended upon
food supplies brought into the city from the surrounding countryside. Yet, in
the case of Madrid the quarantine system worked. Although this sprawling
settlement of destitute people was regarded by foreigners as the most filthy
city in western Europe, during the last twenty years when the plague was
found in Spain (before it made its silent exit in 1685), Madrid remained free
from contagion.

Within a city or town where the plague had broken out, quarantine
regulations were also put into force. In England until the 1630s and the
publication of the *Book of Orders* by the government of Charles I, the usual
practice had been to forbid all members of a plague-afflicted household, the
healthy as well as the sick, from leaving the house. In effect this policy
condemned all the members of the household to being bitten by plague-bear-
ing fleas and eventually dying. The more enlightened policy recommended by
the Book of Orders was to transfer the person who was afflicted from the

household to a special pest-hospital. All of their clothing and bedding was to be burnt and the house thoroughly washed down with powerful disinfectants or liquids which at least smelled hygienic.

The use of pest-houses as isolation centres for contagion in an otherwise healthy city was another of western Europe's legacies from the past and owed nothing to non-European influences. In the Ottoman Empire, Europe's nearest neighbour, neither pest-houses nor quarantine measures were found before 1720; here an outbreak of the plague continued to be thought of as a scourge sent by Allah. But in western Europe, beginning in the twelfth and thirteenth centuries, people who were suffering from leprosy had been confined in leprosaria. This policy of confinement worked. By 1550 most of the 19,000 leprosaria which had been in operation in 1350 stood empty awaiting new uses. After 1550 they came to serve as isolation centres for victims of the plague.

By the 1690s, the bubonic plague had for all intents and purposes disappeared from Europe. This happened because boards of health, heads of state and the great mass of the population, who willingly accepted the inconveniences of quarantine and a policy of isolating the sick in pest-houses, had come to recognize that man himself could prevent further outbreaks of the scourge which had held back sustained population growth since 1346. In western Europe man the thinker, man the idealist, and man the actor found that he could control his own environment and that he no longer needed to be at the beck and call of natural forces. With these reflections we are now in a position to turn our attention to the smallest unit of human culture, the family.

Notes and references

1 G. Benecke, 'Labour relations and peasant society in northwest Germany', *History*, **58** no. 194 (1973), p. 356.
2 L. Clarkson, *Death, Disease and Famine in Pre-Industrial England* (London 1975), p. 46.
3 C. Cipolla, *Cristofano and the plague: a study in the history of public health in the age of Galileo* (London 1973), pp. 17–18.

2 The family, the passions and social controls

The family was the smallest of the social units which gave people a sense of identity and purpose. In recognition of the undoubted importance of this grouping, a small band of historians have set themselves the laborious task of unravelling the secrets of the various family types found in early modern western Europe. Begun as recently as the 1960s, and using computers and other sophisticated techniques, this task is still far from complete. Either because of the shortage of qualified historians who are willing to spend years tucked away in scattered provincial archives sorting through parish registers, notarial and court records and wills and inventories, or because of a shortage of the relevant written records, for large parts of Europe the history of the family has yet to be written.

Although a great deal *is* known about marriage patterns and family types in northern Italy, England, France and urban Switzerland for the years before *c.* 1700, much less is known about these in the Germanies, the Low Countries and Scandinavia. And, as of the moment I am writing, almost nothing is known of the history of the family in early modern Spain and Portugal, except for a handful of cities. This is because the historians of these two countries have devoted themselves almost entirely to sorting out the facts of political and religious history – the interaction of larger social units – and to studying the rise and stagnation of the early modern Spanish economy (why Spain and its Empire was not a thriving centre of capitalist endeavour), to the near exclusion of the history of the family. This means that we still do not know with any certainty whether the dominant family type in rural Spain (most Spaniards were peasants) consisted of the small nuclear family or of larger units.

Detail from 'The Wedding Dance' by Peter Bruegel the Elder

Even in those regions for which the solid foundations of local family history have already been laid, much of the superstructure has yet to be built. We still know very little about the degree of importance which ordinary early modern Europeans placed on their immediate families as opposed to wider kinship groupings, to neighbours of a like age and sex and the village community. Though churchmen and literate publicists, such as Leonis Baptiste Alberti of Florence (d. 1472), wrote a great deal about how families *should* conduct their affairs to the greater glory of God and the well-being of the existing hierarchical social order, there was almost always a considerable gap between these élitist ideals and the social reality known to ordinary people; quite different again was the social reality known to the destitute and homeless. We still know very little about the feeding patterns of ordinary people, whether they gathered around a common table at supper where they chattered about the day's events, or whether they ate on the run when they felt hungry, and, except in passing, seldom met. Similarly, we still have little direct evidence about the degree of romantic attachment which bound a husband and wife together, and about child-rearing practices. In the absence of evidence, some historians have resorted to theory.

Until recently, following the insights of Philippe Ariès (1960), it was commonly supposed that significant changes in the emotive area of family life took place in the early modern period or in the century immediately following. According to Ariès and his followers, relatively hard-nosed impersonal relationships between spouses and between parents and their children gave way to more tender, caring, affective bonds as the family became more inward looking and concerned about its privacy at the expense of its emotive relationships with the wider community of kin groups and neighbours. Without disparaging the importance of Ariès's contribution as a hypothesis to be tested, studies made in the 1970s and 1980s of southern and central England suggest that in these localities – which may not be typical of those elsewhere – the family types and emotive impulses found among ordinary people in 1450 were not much different in kind from those found in 1720; both were recognizably modern. In other words, for England at least, Ariès's hypothesis is not valid.

Monogamy in Europe

With the exception of the Germanic and Netherlandish Anabaptists in Münster in 1534, and some of the radical fringe groups in England in the 1650s, and possibly in Spain among the descendants of the Islamic Moors who had been converted to a superficial Christianity (the Moriscos expelled in 1609), one thing which nearly all ordinary and élite western Europeans had in common was their adherence to the concept of monogamy. Monogamy meant one wife for each husband during the wife's lifetime with the option of remarriage after her death. In most European societies even bigamy (two wives), to say nothing of polygamy (multiple wives), was a capital offence punishable by death. Especially in the wake of the Anabaptist seizure of Münster and the forcible imposition of polygamy on that German city's female population in 1534, Europe's rule-making élite equated polygamy with anarchy and the overturning of all accepted social values.

Hostile as they were to polygamy – with its Islamic and anarchical associations – European men of substance were not averse to keeping a concubine or a mistress (a woman who was not a wife). Before they were overtaken by the reformation in manners which set new standards of respectable behaviour after about 1550, nobles everywhere between Sicily in the far south and Scandinavia and Scotland in the far north openly kept mistresses and found ways of making their illegitimate progeny legitimate.

In seventeenth-century France, where nobles and the idle rich were particularly thick on the ground (all the sons of a French noble were nobles), respectable people's enthusiasm for Tridentine religion led to a great drop in the number of kept women. However, in the following century a reaction against religious enthusiasm set in and with it a great increase in the number of mistresses among the sophisticated rich.

As far as the people who worked with their hands were concerned at no time in the early modern period could they afford to keep both a wife and family, and a mistress. This is not to say that they did not permit themselves the occasional adulterous liaison. But after the 1550s, with the reformation in manners, even this pleasure was frowned upon by those in authority. In late sixteenth-century Basel, for example, a man found guilty of four offences of adultery was liable to be banished; if found guilty of five offences he might be drowned.

Family types defined

In the few brief moments when a government census-taker or a lord's bailiff was asking a householder about the number of people in the household, this particular co-residential group might be one of several types. The simplest was that formed by a solitary householder. Thus, according to the great *catasto* (census) made of Florence and its hinterland in 1427, a sixth of all households consisted of only one person.

The simplest form of family which could engage in the process of human reproduction was the nuclear family. This consisted of the man and his wife (the conjugal couple) and their *co-resident* unmarried children. Among ordinary people – but excluding the aristocracy, the greater gentry and the destitute poor – nuclear families were, by 1500 (if not before), the predominant family type in southern and central England, in northern France and the Low Countries and in parts of western Germany. In all of these regions, before the children could marry and establish nuclear families of their own they had to make provision to set up their own independent household. In northern France where family farms were too small to support more than three pairs of hands – the farmer's, the wife's and the heir's – this might mean that the heir had to wait until his father died before he could finally marry. But in England in the sixteenth century, where family farms were often much larger than those in France and where wage-labour was used to work them, young men who were of a mind to marry could work for a time on a non-related man's farm to earn the wherewithal to marry. Such men did not need to remain at home awaiting their father's death. Here, when all hands were on deck, including the resident living-in servant, the size of the average household ranged from 3.5 to 4.5 people.

It was the absence of opportunities to perform wage-labour on a non-related person's farm, no less than local cultural preferences, which led people in central and southern France and in many other parts of the Mediterranean world as well as in Austria and parts of Germany to establish the second basic family type, the *stem family*. This consisted of two co-residential married couples. Here, at least one member of the elder couple was the parent of one of the younger couple. With the arrival of grandchildren this stem family might become a three generational family.

The third basic family type found in early modern Europe was the *joint family*. This consisted of two or more married siblings (brothers and sisters), their spouses and possibly the siblings' retired parent or parents. In Tuscany in 1427 10 per cent of the people lived in joint families numbering between eleven and twenty-five people. As was the case with the stem family, the economic rationale for calling a joint family into being was to provide enough family labour to run the farm without the necessity of paying for wage-labour. Heavy eaters though the brothers, brothers-in-law and their families might be, in a time when wages were high they were still cheaper to have around than outsiders brought in to work for money. In the Nivernais, in central France, in the late sixteenth and seventeenth centuries, landlords who had created large-scale farms by dispossessing small family farmers often preferred to rent them out to share-croppers who had joint families. Here they could always expect to find at least six or eight pairs of hands – counting those of the women – to work the farm.

Historians who have access only to a single census report, a camera snap-shot as it were, in the developmental cycle of the family, cannot tell whether the members of this particular family would have preferred to live in a nuclear family or in a stem or joint family rather than in the sort of family in which the census-taker found them. In such things cultural preferences varied very much from one village or neighbourhood to the next.

Before historians of the family began their work in the 1960s, it was commonly supposed that simple nuclear family forms had everywhere evolved from more complex joint or stem families and that this evolutionary process was part of the move towards modernization. Enshrined in the writings of Marc Bloch, Karl Marx, Max Weber and other founding fathers of the social sciences, this hypothesis was derived from Charles Darwin's more general theory of evolution (Darwin's *Origin of Species* was published in 1859). However, the facts about changes in family patterns recently discovered by historians of the family show that this evolutionary hypothesis is no longer tenable. Several instances have been found of localities in which the dominant family pattern changed from simple to complex rather than the other way round, because the local people involved preferred things to be so arranged. For instance, in Héricourt, a small town in Franche-Comté, in 1688 95 per cent of the households were of the nuclear type. Sixteen years later, after the Héricourt region had been ravaged by soldiers during one of Louis XIV's wars, the number of nuclear households had dropped to only 67 per cent, and the number of stem or joint families had increased to nearly 23 per cent. Similarly, in the parts of Tuscany which were opened to resettlement in the early seventeenth century, following a period of pestilence and demographic collapse, the young immigrants first formed nuclear families. Yet by 1650, under pressure of population growth and land shortage, cultural norms reasserted themselves and joint families had again become the dominant family form. But in southern and central England changes in population density between the fourteenth century and the eighteenth did not lead to any change in the dominant family type. Nuclear it began and nuclear it remained, simply because English people preferred this sort of household arrangement.

The 'extended family'

Married people who were not of a mind to make the co-resident family their sole emotive centre or were not content to seek emotional fulfilment with unrelated neighbours in their village, might find satisfaction for this need among members of their extended family. Just as is still the case in many parts of the Third World today (and in defiance of professional demographers' use of the term) an extended family consisted of people who did not live together under the same roof. It was made up of distantly-related people for whom an individual who had done well in the world felt a sense of obligation and responsibility. Such a person might be called upon to provide wedding portions (dowries) for poor girls in his extended family and school fees and jobs for the poor young men. Alternatively, among ordinary people who kept close control over their earnings – a characteristic of many of the members of the French peasantry – the members of an extended family might not expect much from each other in the way of money or influence. Yet on festive occasions they would gather at the house of the oldest or most venerated of their number for a family reunion.

Lineage

For men who belonged to one of Europe's élite social systems and who had the leisure needed to cultivate personal relationships, the concept of *lineage* might have been important. Lineage connections might also have been valued among ordinary people in upland regions such as the Spanish Pyrenees or the highlands of Scotland where the practice of pastoralism permitted them a great deal of spare time. However, in a more settled lowland environment, where time-consuming arable husbandry was prac- tised, lineage connections might have been almost totally ignored. Thus, among the peasants of Altopascio in Tuscany in the seventeenth century there was little interest in cousins or other more distant relations; here people's knowledge of their family tree hardly extended beyond the time of their grandparents.

The people who were conscious of belonging to a lineage (the urban and rural élite and underemployed pastoralists) claimed descent in the male line from a common male ancestor, real or fictitious. In western Europe female ancestors counted for very little. Among the élite, symbolic of their sense of lineage was their family coat of arms, their family battle cry (archaic by the seventeenth century), and the family chapel in which the family dead were buried; one well-known example of such a chapel is the Medici chapel in Florence designed by Michelangelo.

The lineage or the sub-lineage (in Italian *casa* or house) also had a highly developed sense of shared honour and shared shame. These might require that the lineage or the broader less coherent unit, the clan, enter into a vendetta or feud with a rival group which had maimed or killed one of their men or raped one of their womenfolk. As every reader of Shakespeare's *Romeo and Juliet* knows, family feuds dominated the politics of many Renaissance Italian city states. They were also important in the politics of France at the time of the Fronde revolutionary civil war between 1648–52 (see Chapter 6), and in many parts of the Holy Roman Empire of the German nation until the settlement at Westphalia in 1648 which ended the Thirty Years' War. Yet even in these feud-prone regions, clan or lineage unity was on the decline by the mid sixteenth century. Responsibility for avenging a wrong came increasingly to rest with the members of the immediate family and of state-provided courts of law.

Among the record-generating élite important decisions about matters which affected the lineage or *casa* were often taken at a meeting of the family council. Though such groupings no longer had control of property as they had in the twelfth century, they were at least an occasion when an ambitious young capitalist of the sort so common in the cities of Renaissance Italy might cement a business alliance with one of his kinsmen. Among Florentine families such as the Capponi or the Rucellai, the family council was presided over by the ablest and most worldly successful of the *casa* members rather than by the eldest male. Unlike councils of village elders in late nineteenth-century Igboland in Nigeria, for example, in the rapidly changing world of fifteenth-century Europe gerontocracy (rule by the eldest) was seen as incompatible with family survival.

Family councils might be called upon to decide who a daughter of the *casa* should marry or what should be done about an orphaned child whose father had died and whose mother had packed her bags and returned to her father's house leaving her child behind. In Renaissance Florence, where élite women tended to marry men ten to fifteen years their senior and had little sense of belonging to their spouses' lineage, such a situation was not uncommon. From the late sixteenth century onwards in families such as the Rucellai or Ginori of Florence or the Richelieus of France, in cases of this sort the family council usually decided that the child should be cared for by its father's married brother or sister. At this level, as in the case of the feud, by the late sixteenth century the importance of lineage was giving way to the more concrete reality of the small family and the immediate kith and kin.

Godparents

One of the institutions which helped to accelerate this movement towards greater co-residential family cohesion was the Catholic Church. In the years before the Catholic Reformation and the Council of Trent (ending in 1563), it had been the practice to have six, eight or more people serving as godparents at the baptism of an infant. Some of these godparents might be children of lineage-group members and themselves little older than the infant whom they were sponsoring. In the eyes of participants and onlookers – a baptism was a public affair – these practices created a tightly knit age-group whose unity was expected to extend to the world beyond the grave. According to the interpretation placed on this phenomenon by laymen, at the last days the entire age-group would intercede before the throne of God on behalf of those of their members who had committed offences deserving of punishment in hell.

It was to this idea that the Catholic hierarchy took exception. In contrast to popular lay concepts, the Church held that people entered into heaven not as part of a corporate group but as individuals. At the time of the Council of Trent the Church limited the number of permitted godparents to one of each sex and decreed that godparents must be old enough to have been confirmed as full members of the Church. These Tridentine injunctions gradually came to be enforced. In the French Vixin, for example, in the years after about 1690, no child seems to have had more than two godparents. Usually one was an adult male from the father's lineage and the other an adult woman from the mother's side of the family. But in the German village of Neckarhausen in Württemberg (after the Reformation a Lutheran region where Tridentine decrees did not apply) it was only after about 1650 that low status peasants regularly began to ask kinsfolk to serve as godparents. Before that time the more usual practice had been to create a client–patron relationship with high-status people in the region by having them serve as godparents.

The Tridentine Church further required that all baptisms be held in the local parish church only a few days after the birth of the infant. In the past baptisms had often been long delayed to allow large numbers of relatives and friends to gather. Very often these festive occasions degenerated into drunken brawls which threatened the public peace. In Brussels in the southern Netherlands and in many of the French and Italian cities civil authorities had frequently banned large gatherings of this sort but to little avail until the Tridentine Church – that sure ally of the reformation in manners – had removed the justification for such riotous gatherings. Whatever the Church's original intentions in diminishing the public nature of baptisms, the consequence was the weakening of lineage and inter-lineage solidarities.

Naming practices

Among ordinary people another development which served to give the co-resident family a greater sense of group identity was the introduction of surnames (last names). The earlier practice, which in remote areas such as Scandinavia continued well into the nineteenth century, was to give an individual only one name, John, Henri, etc. For purposes of further identification this John or Henri might be linked in a word or two to his village – John of Howden – or to his trade – John the Smith (iron-worker). Alternatively, the person might be linked to his or her parents. In Norway, Kirsten the daughter of Lavrans became Kirsten Lavransdatter. Everywhere in Europe some people were identified by a sobriquet such as One-eyed John or Regnaulde the Cripple.

In their choice of names, as in everything else, early modern people exhibited a wide diversity of practices which reflected their own cultural preferences. In the French Vixin, for example, until the teachings of the Tridentine Church finally caught hold around 1690, people much preferred to use archaic local names rather than naming their children after the saints to which local parish churches were dedicated. They also had a strong aversion to the name of Paul, perhaps because of St Paul the Apostle's rigorous views about the purpose and meaning of marriage. By way of contrast, in the 1650s in parts of Sussex Puritan parents gave their children odd names such as Praise-God and Much Mercy.

In some social groupings there was a tendency for parents to ensure that one particular first name would be borne by a living member of the family. At a time when infant mortality rates (death within a year of birth) were seldom less than 20 per cent and when less than half of the people born could be expected to reach maturity, two or three successive sons (the first perhaps being sickly) might be given the same or very similar Christian names. For example, one of my seventeenth-century ancestors living in the English colony of Salem was named Jonathan; his brother, an indicted witch, was named John. Among lineage conscious people who were concerned about the continuity of the family in the male line, the choice of a Christian name for a new-born child might reflect the parents' committment to the concept of the family as a continuum of people in time, rather than to any feeling that each child was a unique being.

In the centre of capitalist endeavour which was Renaissance Florence, patrician fathers often gave their newborn sons the name of a recently deceased relative. The assumption here, as is still the case in parts of Africa, was that the new arrival would bear the same personality traits as the revered deceased; 'father comes again' as the Yoruba would say. However, the Christian Church was undeviating in teaching that each human soul was individually known to God and after death rested eternally with Him, or his antithesis the Devil, or in the half-way house between heaven and hell known as purgatory. So according to the teachings of the Church, father could never come again. The tension caused by the discrepancy between lay practice and the Church was not the least of the dynamic forces at work upon early modern family practices as they changed through time.

The north-west European marriage pattern

Of far more fundamental importance, however, was the emergence of what John Hajnal in 1965 called the European marriage pattern, a phenomenon unique to that continent. Yet, in view of its timing and location within Europe, it would perhaps be better to call it the north-west European marriage pattern in order to distinguish it more clearly from medieval and Mediterranean patterns.

The north-west European pattern comprised three elements. Of these the one which Hajnal found stood in starkest contrast to the marriage patterns found in the rest of the world was the late marriage of women, with at least 30 per cent of women of 15 years of age still unmarried. In the north-west European pattern's most developed form, the average age of women at their first marriage was usually between 24 and 28 years of age.

Another element in the pattern was the late age of male marriage, with men generally older than their wives. However, when it comes to assessing the fertility of marriages, this latter factor is of no great significance since once men reach the age of puberty they remain fertile until they die. The third element in the north-west European marriage pattern transpires to be of overwhelming importance in establishing the nature of social relationships and of community population size. This was the presence of a high proportion of adults – perhaps up to 15 per cent – who never married and never produced children.

Before the north-west European marriage pattern came into being and the medieval pattern was still being followed, it seems likely that most women married and began having children soon after they reached puberty at the age of 13 or 14. In early seventeenth-century Pedalbra in Valencia, Spain, 50 per cent of all women were married by the age of 17. Depending upon their fertility and their bodily strength – which could be much affected by diet or disease – an ordinary peasant woman might be expected to bear fifteen or more children before she completed her family. Here the principal determinants which fixed the number of children who survived childhood were family income (richer parents had more surviving offspring than did poor ones) and, less economically selective, general mortality rates. Under the medieval scheme most ordinary people tried to have as many children as possible. Here, then, the forces which set the size of each particular family appeared to contemporaries to lie outside human control.

In marked contrast to this, the development of the north-west European marriage pattern meant that local people recognized that humankind *could* control its own numbers and, except during the most severe famines, always keep the size of the local population well below a level which would exhaust food supplies. The people whose decisions to adopt the new marriage pattern were most crucial were of course the women. In Normandy (where the medieval pattern had been followed as late as 1400) the impact of the decisions made by thousands of women to forgo the pleasures of sex and marriage until they were in their 20s, began to make itself felt by the end of the fifteenth century. By 1500, the average age of first marriage among Norman women had risen to 21 years; by 1650–1700 it was between 24 and 26 years. By

1650–1700 late female first marriage had also become the norm elsewhere in north-west France and in Aquitaine in the far south-west. In Geneva, a city which has often been considered as fairly typical of Rhineland and western German urban patterns, the transition occurred later than in Normandy. As late as 1586 most Genevan girls married before they were 21. However, by 1593 the average marriage age had jumped to 24–5, where it has remained ever since. The transition occurred later still in Altopascio, north of Florence. Here, as late as 1700 the average age of female first marriage was 21.5 years. Fifty years later the north-west European pattern had replaced the medieval Mediterranean marriage pattern in Altopascio, and the average age at marriage had risen to 24.2.

The demographic consequences of female late marriage were considerable. By and large the number of children a woman will have in her child-bearing years – say between the ages of 14 and 45 – is directly related to the age at which she finds herself a husband; the younger she married the more children she will have. This shows up clearly in data from Colyton in south-west England. Between 1646 and 1719 the mean completed family size of Colyton women who married under the age of 24 was five. Women who waited to marry until they were between 25 and 29 had an average of 3.3 children. For women who waited until they were over 30 to marry the average number of children was only 1.7. Thus, in general terms, a woman who waited to marry until ten or twelve years after she had reached puberty, even if she remarried after the early death of her husband, let slip the opportunity to bring four children into the world (assuming a long birth-interval of two and a half years).

A birth interval of this duration was not uncommon among peasant families. However, in aristocratic circles it was often considerably shorter since aristocratic women very often handed their babies over to wet nurses. This tended to shorten the mother's lactation period and with it the length of time before she could again become fecund. As a result, aristocratic women tended to have more children than did peasant women. The proliferation of children in aristocratic families was also a consequence of early marriage among aristocratic females. In England, at least, aristocratic women did not come to follow the north-west European pattern of late marriage until the late seventeenth century.

Birth control

Late marriage together with chaste behaviour outside the nuptial bed are themselves effective means of controlling the number of children born. But *within* marriage the situation in early modern Europe is much less clear. Most historians assume that the only technique available other than sexual abstinence was *coitus interruptus* (the withdrawal of the male before he expels his sperm) and that this was a technique which would not occur naturally to anyone who was about to engage in the sexual act. Instead, it had to be learned. This meant that it could be forgotten and ignored by whole populations during the long periods when they were not concerned about limiting their own numbers.

The first reasonably reliable evidence we have of birth control being practised within marriage in the early modern period comes from Saint-Denis near Paris. Here, between 1567 and 1670 most married women stopped bearing children by the time they had reached the age of 34. As it is unlikely that these French women stopped having sexual intercourse with their husbands at the age of 33, the conclusion which seems to follow is that these couples were using *coitus interruptus*. But in seventeenth- and eighteenth-century urban France, a far less humane form of population control was widely practised. Urban women of even quite modest means – wives of shopkeepers and artisans – who did not know how to control their reproductive capacity, gave their new-born children to ill-paid wet nurses in the countryside. Anywhere between half and three-quarters of these infants died of maltreatment or starvation. Obviously, these mothers did not know about birth control.

Yet on the eve of the early modern period – the years from 1300 to 1400 – there is considerable evidence that some ordinary Europeans either knew about *coitus interruptus* themselves and transmitted the knowledge from mother to daughter during pre-marital chats, or could figure it out from the prying questions which Franciscan and Dominican friars asked womenfolk during confession. Writing about the situation in her native city of Siena in north Italy, St Catherine (d. 1380) asserted that hardly one married couple in a thousand was not guilty of preventing the birth of children within marriage. Yet if *coitus interruptus* were used as often as St Catherine and the friars suggested, it is strange that this knowledge should disappear from the common consciousness and oral tradition for two hundred years or more.

Among fifteenth- and sixteenth-century prostitutes something may have been known about douches and primitive inter-uterine devices. Yet even prostitutes seem to have placed less reliance on such things than on the techniques necessary to induce abortions. These secrets were probably generally well-known among village cunning women and case-hardened midwives. Andrew Boorde, a Scot who was one of the first doctors to publish a guide book to health (in 1547) mentioned that there were certain medicines which could induce an abortion, but he refrained from saying what they were lest they be used by 'light women'. The only difficulty with early modern-style abortions – a belt tightened around the waist was a favoured technique – was that they were only slightly less risky for the mother than they were for the foetus to whom life was being deliberately denied.

By the early seventeenth century the authors of almanacs and other writers who catered for the popular market were not averse to giving hints about how to induce sterility or how to cool down the passions before they reached fever pitch. Men were advised to rub their sexual member with hot peppers, to take purges to induce vomiting, to submit to blood-letting (on the assumption that sperm was white-hot blood), or to take ice-cold baths. Yet in the last resort the only sure way that early modern spinsters and bachelors could prevent the birth of illegitimate children was to abstain from all bodily contact with people of the opposite sex.

Never-marrying lay people

In England, at least, according to evidence recently tabulated from several series of parish registers, this is precisely what people did. Ignoring periodic fluctuations, the general picture which emerges from the period 1550–1720 is that nearly 15 per cent of the population never married and never had children. One reason why all these English people repeatedly put off getting married until it was too late to do so was the culturally-derived expectation that each newly married couple should live in a house of their own and be able to maintain themselves as an independent economic unit unaided by their parents or by the community. This meant that there was a correlation between the cost of living and wage levels on the one hand, and marriage (nuptiality) rates on the other.

For reasons which are still not fully understood, there appears to be a thirty or forty year time lag between substantial changes in cost of living rates and corresponding changes in the nuptiality rates. The probable explanation for this is that following a drop in wages relative to the cost of a basket of food in the market, opportunities to grow food in the back garden and to pick up clothes and other items without entering into a market transaction gradually declined. Eventually young people of a mind to marry found they simply could not afford to do so. This decision not to marry, a self-imposed internalized control, meant that in the unit of the parish as a whole standards of living did not collapse following a period of economic hardship. This is not to say that individuals did not suffer.

Whether this English pattern – which was only fully unravelled in 1981[1] – might also hold true for selected parts of the Continent during the early modern period is at present unknown. But looking beyond our time period, we do know that in eighteenth- and nineteenth-century Norway and in certain German villages, farm labourers whose marriage prospects depended upon what they could save from their wages, consistently waited a year or two longer to marry – until they were 28 or 29 – than did farmers whose economic prospects were more secure. Here then, as in England after 1550, internalized control mechanisms were in evidence.

Celibate religious and other élites

In Catholic early modern Europe, among a committed minority drawn from the governing levels of society as well as from the upper strata of the peasantry, controls of quite a different sort were found. For monks and nuns (who lived in enclosed orders), for mendicant friars (such as the Dominicans and Franciscans), and for parish priests (the secular clergy) the state of celibacy was a precondition for entering the religious life. Acceptance of a life of celibacy was based on the ancient and medieval notion that the Deity paid special heed to the prayers offered up to Him by those who had vowed to forgo the pleasures of sex on His behalf. According to the teachings of the Christian Church after St Benedict of Nursia established western-style monasticism in the sixth century, such people played an important social role. It was through their mediation that society could be assured that God would continue to favour them with His benefactions.

The strength of this conviction, and the attraction which the enclosed religious life provided for well-heeled parents of adolescent girls, rose and fell in response to a complex of social factors. At the deepest levels, a family's choice of whether or not to send daughters off to a convent depended on their society's current attitude towards women. In most Mediterranean societies the woman-as-virgin ideal (based on the characteristics of the Virgin Mary) was held in high esteem. But coexisting with this ideal was the woman-as-mother ideal which was clearly expressed in the iconography of the Renaissance. Among the most favoured subjects chosen for portrayal by artists such as Iacopo and Giovanni Bellini were the Virgin Mary and her Holy Child.

In Catholic countries the enclosed religious life continued to be held in high esteem throughout the sixteenth and seventeenth centuries. Yet in some centres there was a marked decline in the number of *men* who chose the life of celibacy in an enclosed order (this excluded the mendicant Dominicans and Franciscans). In a survey made in Florence in 1552, nuns outnumbered monks by a ratio of nearly five to one (3419 to 750). How dedicated these nuns were to the task of praying for their families and city is open to speculation. According to a cynical sixteenth-century Venetian chronicler, twenty-five of the convents in the Venetian Republic were brothels and 'an afront to God'.

In Protestant lands after the Reformations, many intellectuals continued to adhere to medieval clerical values and held that the life of the mind was incompatible with marriage and a household overrun with small children. Until the nineteenth century tutors at colleges at Oxford and Cambridge

Universities were forbidden to marry if they wished to enjoy the benefits of lodging in the college and eating at high table. Students were also expected to be single. It is no coincidence that the first degree which university students receive is a bachelors degree.

Many of the greatest Renaissance artists, architects and sculptors were also bachelors by choice, among them Donatello, Leonardo da Vinci, Michelangelo and Borromini. All of these geniuses followed the injunction of St Paul the Apostle literally and devoted themselves to a life of transforming a vision of the Spirit of Man and of the Spirit of Universal Order into material substance, rather than concerning themselves with women and family.

Some other élite minorities also disdained to take wives and to contribute to the further growth of population. In Spain, a nation almost continuously at war with rival states outside its own boundaries or with rebels within (Spanish armies were in combat somewhere for seventy-two years in the seventeenth century), it was held that officers in the military should not marry. And partly because prostitutes were available, only a minority of the sons of the old patrician families in Venice took wives. As a bemused English contemporary of Shakespeare observed:

In Italy marryage is indeed a yoke, and that not [an] easy one but so grevious as brethren nowhere better agreeing yet contend among themselves to be free from marryage and he that of free will or by persuasion will take a wife to continue their posterity, shall be sure to have his wife and her honour as much respected by the rest, besyde their liberall contribution to mantayne her, so as themselves may be free to take the pleasure of women at large.... For in those frugall commonwealths the unmarried live at a small rate of expenses and they make small conscience of fornication, esteemed a small sinne and easily remitted by Confessors....[2]

As late as 1714 there were on the average four adult males in the households of the old Venetian élite; generally only one of them was married.

Servants

One of the most distinctive differences between the Mediterranean world on the one hand and southern and central England and some of the urban centres of north-west Continental Europe on the other, was in the composition and expectations of the servant population. In rural Italy most farmers kept their sons at home (the stem or joint family) and used family labour to cultivate their lands in preference to hiring outsiders. Though household servants were known in Florence – in 1552 they constituted 17 per cent of the population and were found in 42 per cent of the households – it is not clear whether they were married or saw service as a period preparatory to marriage as was the case in England.

In England, where at any one time 30 to 40 per cent of the youthful population between the ages of 14 and 29 were servants of one kind or another and at least a third of all households contained servants, the institution of service was closely linked to delayed nuptiality. In Lichfield, a reasonably representative English Midland town, a survey taken in 1696 shows the correlation between service and the age of marriage. The results are shown in Table 2.

Table 2 *The correlation between service and the age of marriage in Lichfield, 1696*

	Age	Percentage in service	Percentage married
Women	15–19	18	1
	20–4	42	8
	25–9	50	38
	30–4	12	59
Men	15–19	47	0
	20–4	24	8
	25–9	5	25
	30–4	1	73

Source: Peter Laslett, *Family Life and Illicit Love in Earlier Generations* (Cambridge; Cambridge University Press 1977), p. 44.

The same sort of correlation also held true in the French cloth town of Reims in the early fifteenth century. Here 42.4 per cent of the unmarried females between the ages of 20 and 24 were in service, with 20 per cent of those between 25 and 29 and between 30 and 34 similarly employed.

The connection between delayed marriage and service was especially apparent in the case of servants, male or female, who lived in the same house as their employer and were accounted as part of the family. During their time in service, these 'life-cycle servants' (the term is Peter Laslett's) expected to save up enough money to enable them to set up their own households by the time they were in their late 20s or early 30s. But while they were still in service, these life-cycle servants were expected to practise sexual abstinence. Because most employers rigidly enforced the rule that living-in servants should not marry and clutter up the household with more mouths to be fed – which was the reason why employers hired servants rather than having more children of their own – life-cycle service could not be a permanent condition. A female servant who was impregnated by her employer would be sent packing before she bore her illegitimate child or was married off to some poor man who undertook to maintain her and her child. In France perhaps a third of all illegitimate births were the result of such a confrontation between a servant girl and her employer.

In fifteenth-century rural England and again in the late seventeenth century (the rate fell in the interval) one farmer in four had one or two (seldom more) life-cycle servants living in his household. They were hired by a contract arrangement made at the annual hiring fair and generally served for a calendar year. The contract was enforcible by both parties in a court of law. The servants were to be provided with food, clothing and shelter and a lump sum in cash at the end of their term of service. They were also supposed to receive some training in agricultural techniques or in the craft or trade practised by their master. Living-in servants were regarded as dependants in much the same way as were the householder's own offspring and could be subjected to the same sort of discipline.

We know little about the emotive relationships between the young English servants who lived in enforced celibacy and their employers and the employer's wife and children. Court records from the seventeenth century, when Justices of the Peace were attempting to cut down the poor rates (taxes levied to support the poor) by compelling unwilling farmers to hire servants, suggest that in some cases employers starved or maimed their servants in order to persuade them to break their contract and leave. On occasion this disciplinary technique got out of hand and the servant died. At the Essex assizes held between 1560 and 1709, forty-five of the 431 victims of homicide were household servants. According to the bills of indictment, 41 per cent of these people were killed by a female household head or wife. So intent were juries and judges to see that household discipline was maintained that only five of the alleged murderers were found guilty. Yet considering that during the period 1560–1709 several thousand servants entered into contract arrangements with Essex employers, the termination of only forty-five of these in the violent death of the servant suggests that most employers treated their servants, if not well, at least tolerably.

As we have seen, in the fifteenth century most Italian farmers used family labour. Around 1500 an Italian observer of the English scene who was unfamiliar with life-cycle service asserted that 'the want of affection in the English is strongly manifested towards their children; for after having kept them at home till they arrive at the age of 7 or 9 years at the utmost [14 would have been more accurate] they put them out, both males and females, to hard service in the houses of other people...to learn better manners'. He went on to suggest a reason why the English were so unfeeling towards their children: 'being great epicures and very avaricious by nature [they] indulge in the most delicate fare themselves and give their household the coarsest bread, and beer, and cold meat baked on Sunday for the week…if they had their own children at home they would be obliged to give them the same food they made use of for themselves'.[3]

These insights suggest why it was that English people put up with life-cycle servants in their homes during periods when living costs were low and wages were high; it was cheaper than hiring casual labour during the planting season and harvest. As Timothy Nourse put it in 1700, when these conditions obtained and when living-in servants were regarded as indispensable, ''tis better to have work waiting for our servants than servants for our work'.[4]

The most favoured form of life-cycle service was to be taken on as an apprentice in one of the great chartered companies or craft guilds in a city or large town, generally for a term of from five to seven years. In England, where there was no great social stigma attached to trade (the contrast with France and Spain is instructive), lesser gentry and yeomen to say nothing of husbandmen were not ashamed to send their sons out to serve as apprentices. When economic conditions were favourable, this country-bred apprentice could expect to become a journeyman at the end of his term, preparatory to taking tests set by the craft guild and setting up as a master and as a married household head. In Frankfurt-am-Main in the German Empire and in many other cities as late as the eighteenth century, the only men who were accounted full citizens were those who had been promoted from an apprentice, to a journeyman and then to a master and guild member and had found themselves a wife.

If a man were a life-cycle servant in the English context, he had at least the potential of becoming a farmer or craftsman, especially if he managed to find a wife who still had the lump-sum payment she had received at the end of her own time of service. For both parties to the marriage the austerities they had endured as servants now paid handsome dividends. Since established family heads in England did not want non-related middle-aged people cluttering up their households, improvident men who during their term of service failed to save up enough money to set up a household of their own by their early 30s usually found it difficult to have their annual contracts renewed. Their only option was to become wage-labourers. A sizeable proportion of young people in the 14–29 age category not fortunate enough to become life-cycle servants also became wage-labourers. As Ann Kussmaul has recently put, it 'to become a labourer was to be a recognised failure'.

People who subsisted on wages lived on the knife edge of disaster, the potential victims of every downturn in the local economy. One sunny day they had a job; the next might find them unemployed and unable to buy their food and other basic necessities. If they were struck down by illness or disabled in a mishap and lived in a city where charitable institutions happened to exist, they might find help there. Otherwise their only alternative was to become beggars (see Chapter 6).

In urban areas in north-west Europe the possibility of working as a non-resident wage-labourer was open to women as well as to men. In Lyon in France, for example, women were to be found on building sites, helping with the construction of bridges and roads, town walls and mills. The only snag was that women's wages were generally only half or three-quarters those of men.

Non-resident wage-labour also seems to have been common in the seven northern provinces of the Netherlands, especially after the mid sixteenth century when Dutch farmers fell under the spell of specialization. For them, specialization extended not only to crops but also to social arrangements. Workers were seldom allowed to reside in the same village as their employers, to say nothing of living in their employers' neat nuclear-family dominated households. Instead, they were made to live in separate dependent villages. The squalor of these villages inhabited by wage-earners who were expected to work twelve to fourteen hours a day was not the sort of subject a fashionable painter such as Jan Vermeer chose to record for posterity.

Transfers between the generations

As we have seen, not all young early modern Europeans lived in localized societies where it was possible to work outside the family of birth in order to save up enough money to get married. In much of Italy, in southern and central France and possibly in Spain – areas where joint or stem families were the preferred household process – funds which would enable a man to get married and bring his wife back to the family home or to set up housekeeping for himself and his bride necessarily came mainly from his parents and his future in-laws. Even in regions where nuclear families dominated, for some people such transfers between the generations were also an important precondition of marriage.

Except for the very poorest, most early modern European parents had at least a favoured pot or pan, an axe or a saw, or a magic amulet or trinket which they wanted to pass on to one of their offspring. Although this small transfer was not the kind of fact known to history – it would not appear in any probate record – to the two parties concerned it was of no less symbolic value than the transfer of a hundred acres of good arable land. Thus, in Haute Provence in the early eighteenth century a father such as Jean Reboul could be expected to distribute, on his death bed, his favoured small belongings to each of his sons in witness of the affection in which he held them.

For parents who held land or buildings, this *real property* was generally the most important of the things involved in the transfer between the generations. According to most of the formal legal systems found in Europe (written customary law or written Roman Law as opposed to unwritten custom), property was considered to be something which was held by individuals. Aside from the Anabaptists, some of the patricians of capitalistic Genoa who were grouped into atypical family organizations known as *alberghi* and a few other minority groups, real property was seldom held in common by large loosely structured or tribal groups as it so often was in pre-Muslim, pre-colonial Africa.

The transfer of real property and, where they still existed, the use-rights associated with it (see Chapter 3) might take place all at once with the death or retirement of the parents and the succession of the heir or heirs designated by local custom. Or it might be a more gradual piecemeal process. The dowries (wedding portions) which girls received from their parents to enable them to marry a sinful mortal or the lesser sum needed to enrol them in a convent, and the portions received by young men who were leaving home were all part of this transfer process. In regions where the rights to property were most highly developed – England, the Netherlands and the German Rhineland – the young people who left their parents' home with their gifts in hand had no legal rights (other than those established in their parents' will) to other financial support from the parents or siblings they had left behind. However, in some parts of France custom allowed young men who left home to retain the right to be partially maintained with a bag of grain or two a year from their parents' farm even after it had passed to a sibling. If this core family farm were to be sold, they had first option to buy it.

In the narrowest sense of the term, *inheritance* was the last phase in the process of transferring property from one generation to the next. It might be either of two pure forms or, as was more often the case in practice, a combination of the two. One of the pure forms is known as *impartible* inheritance. Here the bulk of the older generation's land – the functioning farm – went to only one heir. If this heir were the eldest son, a specialized form of impartible inheritance, known as *primogeniture* was being practised. Following the other pure form, known as *partible* inheritance, the family lands and property were divided among several heirs, either among all the children or, as in Norman custom, among the sons alone to the exclusion of daughters. One heir might get the livestock, another the farming equipment and the third the house and land. Alternatively, the land itself might be subdivided into small farms for each of the heirs. Such practices were much used in Languedoc in southern France in the late sixteenth century and often resulted in farms which were too small to support a man and his family. Non-equalitarian though impartible inheritance might be, at least it served to maintain the heir without difficulty. For this reason it was much favoured by genteel families who wished to build up a substantial block of property.

Peasant cultivators to whom local custom and their seigneurs allowed some personal discretion in the matter often chose not to follow the written customs of their manor precisely (in France most oral customs were transferred into writing by the end of the sixteenth century). For some of the peasants who bypassed written custom, it was of central importance to maintain the essential unity of the family farm which they had inherited from their parents and which they themselves had enriched with the sweat of their brows. Other peasants in the same region, eccentric individualists, might be more concerned to make adequate provision for *all* of their children, both male and female. Such peasant parents hoped to build up suitably sized dowries for all of their daughters so that they could marry men of the same social status as themselves; in practice usually only the eldest daughter could be so favoured. These ambitious peasant parents also tried to provide all of their sons with the resources – and by the sixteenth century the formal education in literacy and numeracy – necessary to set them up as market-oriented cultivators or perhaps as respectable craftsmen or merchants, or as members of one of the professions – as bureaucrats, doctors or lawyers.

Yet, whatever his aspirations for them might be, a peasant cultivator could only provide for his children if he had a considerable surplus on hand and if all other circumstances were favourable. A small farmer who tried to follow the example of his wealthy yeoman neighbour and burdened his principal heir with the obligation to pay substantial dowries over a term of years, together with the portions due to younger sons when it came time for them to leave home, might compel his heir to borrow money to pay off these obligations. If the heir holding the core family farm were already hard pressed to pay for new stock and other equipment (other brothers having been given the father's stock and gear) and burdened with children of his own, the results might prove disastrous for him. In Cambridgeshire, where the results of parents' miscalculations have recently been studied, many small farmers lost their holdings to their creditors during the years of general economic hardship in the 1620s and 1630s.

Inheritance customs also had to make provision for widows who outlived their husbands and for the children – half-brothers and sisters – a man may have had by several successive wives. If local custom permitted, and many customs did, a widow might have a life-time interest in the family tenures and have her name entered accordingly in the records of the manor. So long as she remained chaste and unmarried until she finally died or decided to retire from the management of the farm, such a widow's husband's heirs could only be heirs in expectation.

One can never know how many Continental Europeans had marital careers similar to that of Aimé Piron, a wine-grower in Mogneneins, in Burgundy. Piron was born around 1652 and had three children by his first wife. One month after her death he remarried and had – or rather his second wife had – three stillborn children. After her death in childbirth, Piron remained a widower for ten months. Then he married a 24-year-old virgin (for most French and Italian men virgins were preferable brides) who lived for only three months. By his fourth wife, Pierretta, Piron had six children, five of whom were still alive when Piron died at the age of 52. Piron's widow lived on to the age of 75 in chaste widowhood so that she would not lose her inheritance rights.

Few inheritance customs written by lawyers could cope with a situation such as this without giving offence to some of the parties concerned (attempts to settle problems of this sort kept lawyers in business). In many areas of northern France the custom called for 'partage by marriage bed'. Had this custom been used in Aimé Piron's case his estate would have been divided into two, since two wives (his first and his fourth) had borne his eight surviving children. The three children of his first marriage would each receive a sixth of his estate. The five children who remained living with his fourth wife, Pierretta, would each receive only a tenth of the estate. Because of the imbalance in the size of their inheritances, it is likely that the two sets of children were not on friendly terms with each other. Yet one thing may have bound them together, their common hatred of Mother Piron, who as we saw survived her husband for many years and had a prior claim on the estate.

No open inter-family violence appears to have broken out in the family headed by Widow Piron but further south in Haute Provence there were several cases in the seventeenth century of widowed mothers being mistreated by their sons. For example, in 1686 Honorade de Pêrier, widow of Seigneur Antoine le Bon, complained that since the death of her husband her son, Jean-Baptiste, had frequently insulted and abused her. A second son, no friend of the other, had remained faithful to his mother.

The role of the patriarch

Wherever the dictates of the Roman Law held sway, in joint and stem families, all the men in the household, married as well as single, were dependants of the head of the household – the patriarch. No matter how old they might be, they could not establish an independent business of their own or enter into any kind of contractual agreement without the old man's permission. In Tuscany, at least, the household head was responsible for all the debts contracted by his dependants. Everywhere the authority of the patriarch was based on his legal right to control his wife's dowry and to determine which of his children should marry, which should be his heirs, and what the other children would receive as dowries in the case of girls, or as portions in the case of boys.

In a household where the paterfamilias was by law at liberty to beat his wife and children whenever he saw fit, drunk or sober, the reality of power was made apparent each time the family sat down together at dinner, an event which might only occur at festivals. At the head of the table sat the father. At his right side sat his chosen heir followed by other resident males including servants in descending order of rank. At the patriarch's left hand sat his submissive wife and daughters in order of age. Yet in some regions such as the Nivernais, peasant patriarchs never allowed women to join the menfolk at dinner. Instead, they expected them to stand behind the men's benches (chairs for lesser family members only became standard in the late seventeenth century), quietly ready to serve at the men's beck and call. Wherever the stem or joint family held sway, so long as the old patriarch survived with his faculties intact, family members made an effort to conceal their animosities and to keep their tempers under control.

The aged

From the point of view of the younger generation, old people often lived for a distressingly long time. For example in the rural areas around Florence in 1427, 17.5 per cent of the population were more than 57 years old. Here where a joint family was the preferred family type, most old men kept a firm grasp on the management of the family farm until they became senile or died. This meant that young potential heirs had to wait around until they were 45 or 50 before they could come into their inheritance and their wife could become the dominant female in the household.

In a world where elderly people who retained control of the means of production were in a position to frustrate the ambitions of youth, it was natural that the concept of the 'aged' should conjure up a dual image. On the one hand it was held that old people should be honoured. They were the people who knew the proverbs which were relevant for every occasion. They held the treasured memories of the community and were the custodians of oral history. Just as is the case in West Africa today, whenever there was a boundary dispute to be settled, or whenever the precise nature of local custom needed to be determined, the services of the elders were in demand.

Yet even before old people's wisdom had been replaced by the printed word and land surveyors' maps, and proverbs had come to be despised as irrelevant remnants of the past, there was another image of the aged which was much less favourable. The young and middle-aged men who, as in Cervantes's early seventeenth-century Spain, wrote plays for performance on street corners or farm yards during festivals generally caricatured the old as blundering, incoherent fools. What is meant to be old was summed up in 1614 by Sir Walter Ralegh in his *History of the World*. As he put it: when old, 'our attendants are sicknesses, and variable infirmities; and by how much the more we are accompanied with plentie, by so much the more greedily is our end desired, whome when Time hath made vnsociable to others, we become a burthen to our selues; being of no other vse, than to hold the riches we haue from our successours'.[5]

Just as Ralegh suggested, the strategies used when an elderly father was on the point of retirement frequently were a cause of bitter discord between the generations. For example, in many parts of Scandinavia the practice was for the old peasant farmer to sell his land and farm buildings to his heir at a standard market price and then to live out his days on the proceeds in a little house of his own. This was fair enough from the parent's point of view but far from satisfactory for the inheriting son. For, in order to find enough money to buy out the old man, he would have had to borrow heavily and probably to delay his own marriage. Years later he might still not have enough money to provide proper dowries for his spinster daughters.

In eighteenth-century Austria, where stem families were common, parents who were on the point of handing over control of the family farm to their co-resident heir made it clear that they could not depend on their child's sense of affection to provide for them decently. In that society, on their retirement hard-faced parents established air-tight legal rights to certain rooms in the family house with rights of access, the rights to stipulated parts of the garden and an allowance of food and ready cash. In sixteenth- and seventeenth-century England, contracts of this sort were also sometimes drawn up, though usually the beneficiary was a young widow of an old man. In Knebworth Harcourt in Leicestershire, for example, the widow of old John Carter secured the legal right to use three of the seven rooms of the house inherited by Carter's son and heir and stayed in possession of them for twenty years. However, in other instances English arrangements for retirement were less formal and for the old person involved, much less secure. In seventeenth-century Cambridgeshire a few old men and women were recorded as living with their married children not by legal right, but in the capacity of a sojourner or temporary visitor who at any time might be asked to leave.

Sexual practices outside marriage

Both in the Mediterranean world where late marrying men tended to marry chaste brides eight to ten years their junior, and in north-west Europe where *both* men and women tended to marry late (in England the age gap between spouses at first marriage was generally less than two years), males had to wait ten or more years after they reached puberty before they could enjoy sex within marriage. This raises a question; how did young men, and indeed women, relieve the exciting sexual pressures which were welling up within them during the long years after puberty? By the nature of things, there is little direct evidence with which to answer this question. However, evidence derived from hostile clerical sources suggests that many young people had recourse to solitary masturbation.

According to the confessional manuals used by Catholic priests around 1500, masturbation was a particularly odious sin. Since the auto-manipulation of the 'devil's own tools' (the sexual organs) gave people intense carnal pleasure it threatened the Church's redemptive scheme which was based on the concept that this world was a vale of tears and that the only pleasure worth striving for (through the mediation of the tithe-collecting Church), lay in Heaven; even there there was no sex. There was also the very real danger that frequent masturbation might encourage young people to regard marriage and legitimate procreation as unnecessary. As an early sixteenth-century moralist put it: 'There will be found some so enslaved to the filth of this sin, as is, most often the youth of both sexes, that the men will not want to marry, nor the women take husbands....'[6] Similarly, during the sixteenth and seventeenth centuries Calvinist clergymen who adhered to a strict interpretation of Saint Augustine's admonitions about sex regarded masturbation with horror.

Yet among ordinary lay people masturbation seems not to have given rise to feelings of anxiety. Indeed, the discharge of fluids through masturbation was regarded as no less natural than the passing of urine. In the years before 1700, the same attitudes prevailed among sections of the governing élite. For example, the medical doctor at the court of King Henri IV of France (1589–1610) who chronicled the physical and psychological development of Prince Louis (later Louis XIII) noted that on several occasions the infant fondled himself in public and received the approbation of bemused courtiers.

Masturbation appears first to have come under lay attack in a pamphlet published in England in 1710. But the full-scale campaign against the practice had to wait until 1764 when Dr S. A. Tissot used pseudo-scientific evidence to support his claim that masturbation caused blindness, physical deformities, stunted growth and a host of other terrors. During the sexually repressive nineteenth and early twentieth centuries it was fables of this sort which parents and teachers drilled into the heads of their children.

Another sexual practice which in lay élite circles at least was widely tolerated at the beginning of the early modern period only to fall into disrepute later, was homosexuality. Before about 1500, Florence was one of the most publicized centres of this practice. Here, where most patrician males married girls fifteen or twenty years their junior, they were already old men before their sons entered adolescence and were almost useless as virile role models for the young. As a result young men living at home were much under the influence of domineering mothers who were still young enough to be sexually attractive. The followers of Sigmund Freud (the early twentieth-century Viennese founder of psycho-analysis) claim, with scant justification, that such home environments are ideal nurseries for male homosexuals. What was more likely to have been the case was that Florentine élite culture as a whole was passing through a period when homosexuality was regarded as no less fashionable than the richly embroidered velvet clothes which emphasized the relevant parts of the male anatomy. During this period Sozemene de Pistio, a professor at the University of Florence, took some of his stylishly dressed male students aside and asked them if they were looking for wives. When they all replied in the negative, de Pistio is said to have remarked that in that case they must all be looking for husbands.

In England at the Court of Elizabeth I, the Virgin Queen who frowned upon courtiers who married, homosexuals were also common. They were even more in evidence in the next reign. The new king, James I (1603–25) was himself a homosexual (his lovers didn't seem to mind that he never bathed), and during the last half of his reign allowed important decisions of state to be taken by his favourite, the bi-sexual Duke of Buckingham. In the late seventeenth century a few aristocrats who were unfaithful to their wives, men such as John, Second Earl of Rochester, were also game to have a fling with a boy. As Rochester put it: 'And the best kiss was the deciding lot; Whether the boy fucked you or I the boy'.[7]

In early centuries the Christian Church was not open in its opposition to homosexuality. Indeed, before the twelfth century, several suspected or known homosexuals were canonized as saints. But by the eve of the Reformation, sexual intercourse between males had joined other moral offences which the Church classed as 'sins against nature'. According to Jean Gerson, a famed early sixteenth-century French moralist, these detestable sins called down 'divine vengeance – famines, wars, plagues, epidemics, floods, betrayal of kingdoms, and many other disasters more frequently, as Holy Scripture testifies'.[8] By the 1550s or 1560s most states had made homosexual practices, or at least buggery (anal entrance), a capital offence. In the Calvinist citadel of Geneva more than fifty homosexuals, many of them Italian immigrants, were put on trial and half of them executed between 1555 and 1678. In the 1670s and 1680s the central law court of appeal serving the northern third of France, the Parlement of Paris, also condemned several homosexuals to be burnt to death at the stake.

At the village level there is very little evidence, one way or another, about homosexual practices. Before the end of the early modern period and the partial acceptance of the reformation in manners, most ordinary people slept nude four or five to a bed (one bed was all most families could afford) and anything might have happened. In the Mediterranean world it appears that most people had no strong feelings about bi-sexual behaviour and expected that the boys who gave men pleasure would later marry and prove themselves to be proper husbands. In English village societies, however, if the situation in sixteenth-century Essex is anything to go by, most people insisted on maintaining the normal sexual order. Homosexuals who could not control their passions were persuaded to go off to London where they could meet others of their kind and lose themselves in the comparative anonymity of the city.

Or perhaps it was simply a case in England and other parts of rural north-west Europe that homosexuals would be quietly tolerated if in all other respects they met the requirements of neighbourliness. This a person such as George Andrews of Westonbirt in Gloucestershire failed to do. Not only was Andrews a homosexual – he buggered Walter Lingsey, a young servant from Gloucester, in August 1617– he was also a principal agent of the London property holder, Sir Richard Holford. For several years Holford had been attempting to civilize his Westonbirt tenants by teaching them good manners and prying into their private lives. This meddling was much resented by local people. Here then two cultures were in conflict; the popular rural and the city-based élitist. The Westonbirt people had no quarrel with the buggered boy, Lingsey, but only with farmer George Andrews and Sir Richard. As a means of showing their displeasure and ridiculing the moral reformer and his resident agent, a hundred or more local men and women held a mock lying-in at which young Lingsey, dressed in women's clothes, gave birth to a baby made of straw.

In Florence the campaign against homosexuals was already underway by the early fifteenth century. By 1432 a night watch had been created especially to search under bridges and other secluded public places for prowling homosexuals. But a more positive step was to establish municipally supported brothels where young men might be tempted to assuage their passions with a female prostitute. However, the prostitutes – aliens from Germany or the north of Italy – soon found that the only way they could attract customers was to attire themselves in male dress (transvestites) and to submit to being buggered. Yet gradually non-citizen males in Florence became accustomed to use the brothels for the purposes for which they were originally intended, with the man on top and woman beneath, face and breasts upwards. By the 1490s, when Savonarola, the fiery popular preacher, was denouncing the immorality of Florence, prostitution was the sexual vice to which he objected most; he had already ensnared most patrician boys in his zealously anti-homosexual evangelical squads. Yet efforts to force prostitutes to live in only one quarter of the city – the Mercato Vecchi – and to cut down their numbers were only moderately successful. A survey made in 1560 showed that there were still 200 prostitutes, many of them licensed, to serve the 15,000 adult males in Florence.

Brothels

At Avignon, Lyon, Zwickau and many other cities in the Germanies, France and Switzerland, brothels were similarly subsidized by municipal governments. In all these cities shrewd fathers realized that the middle-aged men who had lost their wives in child-birth or some other mishap almost always chose their second or succeeding wives from among the pool of young marriageable virgins. By reducing the size of this pool, these older men thus curtailed the chances of younger men who had served their apprenticeships and wanted to marry. Quite clearly, it was a question of poor young men pitted against considerably wealthier older men who could serve girls as father figures as well as spouses. By making provision for municipally sponsored brothels the city fathers hoped, in the interests of civic harmony, to dampen the latent hostility between the two age groups. Accordingly, there was an unwritten convention that the brothels should be reserved solely for the use of the young men. Older men or priests (celibate in theory only) who too often frequented these establishments were reported to the city authorities by the respected – but not quite respectable – Madames who ran the brothels.

Before the 1550s, official toleration of the sexual exploits of young unmarried apprentices, labourers and servants often went further than this. In Dijon and other cities in south-east France and in southern Italy and Sicily gangs of men were covertly allowed to engage in mass rape. A series of cases studied in late fifteenth-century Dijon shows that the young mass rapists were often associated in an occupational grouping or in an informal neighbourhood street gang. One of their number was generally a married man in his early 30s; the rest were raw youths who were being initiated into sex with a woman for the first time. Their victims were usually girls who were reputed to be concubines or girls who were about to be married and had perhaps lost their virginity to their intended husbands. When a mass rape was in progress the neighbours seldom made any attempt to intervene, though in the town of Catane in Sicily the gentlemen who raped a girl in the presence of her mother in 1505 first took the precaution of blocking up the neighbours' doors! In the honour-conscious Mediterranean world, and apparently in the Germanies as well, after a girl had been raped her reputation was irretrievably shattered. If one of the rapists could not be persuaded to marry her, she had no other option but to leave her home area and join the sub-culture of full-time prostitutes in a distant city.

Superficially all of this was changed by the reformation of manners which the godly city-based élite attempted to impose on their social inferiors in the towns and countryside. At Zwickau in Saxony, for example, pastor Nicholas Hausmann and burgomeisters Herman Mühlpfort and Laurentius Barensprung succeeded in closing down all the town brothels in 1526. Between then and 1560 most of the municipalities in western Europe had taken similar action. Yet during the rest of the early modern period clandestine prostitution continued to flourish in ale houses and taverns – in the 1650s the Bear Inn in Wells in Somerset had a reputation for providing bed-time comforts – and in market towns and fairs and wherever men with money in their pockets gathered for relaxation and forbidden pleasures.

All this was not without its risks. Ever since 1497 (with the return of Columbus and his Genoese and Spanish crew from the West Indies) men who were not careful in their choice of prostitutes might find themselves the victims of syphilis, a noisome, debilitating and ultimately fatal disease.

The dual standard

As our discussion of prostitution shows, among respectable and élite Europeans after 1550 a double standard was in force. Following the teachings of the Christian Church – the self-appointed moral arbiter of Europe – women were expected to remain pure until they were married or risk losing their inheritance or dowry as well as their honour. Respectable married men also agreed that once married, women must be content with whatever sexual embraces their husbands chose to bestow upon them, so long as they were natural (navel to navel). A woman who committed adultery with another man was liable to heavy punishment. In Sicily, she could be banished or sent back to her parents; elsewhere a husband was free to beat her nearly senseless or take whatever other steps he saw fit.

Yet for the respectable men who so adamantly insisted that their own wives and daughters remained chaste, almost anything was permitted. Parting company with the teachings of the Church whenever enthusiasm for religion was not at fever pitch (i.e. in France before c. 1640 and after c. 1700), many respectable laymen held that they could have sexual intercourse with any woman who took their fancy; servant girls, lonesome widows, or wives of husbands who were away from home for more than a few days. Except during periods of rabid anti-clericalism – in the 1520s in the Germanies for instance – laymen did not think ill of a theoretically celibate priest who had a housekeeper who did more than sweep the floors. Even Erasmus, the humanist from Rotterdam who in the 1520s was in the vanguard of the movement to reform morals and manners, thought it but a light fault if a respectable man kept a mistress. Gentlemen's freedom of action was based, of course, on the tacit understanding that they should not create a public

Table 3 *Illegitimate births in Talavera
de la Reina, Spain, 1570–1609*

Year	Percentage of illegitimate births
1570–4	6.0
1575–9	6.6
1580–4	6.3
1585–9	6.5
1590–4	5.2
1595–9	5.8
1600–4	4.5
1605–9	3.7

Source: Peter Laslett, Karla Oosterveen and
Richard M. Smith (eds.), *Bastardy and its Comparative History: studies in the history of illegitimacy and
marital non-conformity in Britain, France, Germany,
Sweden, North America, Jamaica and Japan* (London: Edward Arnold 1980), p. 25.

disturbance while fornicating and that they should provide for the
maintenance of any child who happened to be conceived during this process.

Illegitimacy

Among ordinary people, however, the situation was rather different. During
most decades of the early modern period for which parish registers exist, the
number of children who were born out of wedlock or less than eight months
after marriage was less than one in ten. Fairly typical was the situation in
Talavera de la Reina in Spain between 1570 and 1609, as set out in Table 3.

In seventeenth-century France, where country people appear either to have
been taking the lessons taught by the Counter Reformation Church to heart
or to have avoided having the results of their sexual activities recorded, the
percentage of known illegitimate births was even smaller. In Beauvais it stood
at 1 per cent; at Ploudalmezeau in Brittany it was only 1.6 per cent, with a
peak of 4.5 per cent during the decade 1646–55.

Wherever Mediterranean family patterns held sway, as they did in Altopascio in northern Italy, there would appear to be a *direct* correlation between the rising age of first marriage of women – from 16 to 17 rising to 20 to 22 by the early eighteenth century – and rising rates of illegitimacy. Here local girls and youths were not prepared to wait until they were – in their own eyes – married before they engaged in sexual intercourse. But the reverse situation held true in England, where the north-west European marriage pattern was most firmly established. Here, throughout the whole of the parish register period – from 1538 to 1800 – young men and women who were not yet prepared to marry refrained from sexual congress in more than nine cases out of ten. This then was an *inverse* relationship; the higher the age at first marriage, the lower the illegitimacy rate. The system could only work if there was a firmly grounded network of social controls.

Wherever north-west European marriage patterns held, as they did in England, the majority of the women who gave birth to illegitimate children were within a few months of the local mean age of female first marriage. In common with other women who were more lucky, such women had waited until they were in their mid 20s to single out the man they wanted to marry. When arrangements between the two seemed to be fixed they allowed themselves to engage in carnal love. Then some disaster struck; for example, a local downturn in trade resulted in the man being thrown out of work. Deciding that the time was not propitious for marriage, the lover absconded and left his intended wife to fend for herself and the bastard child she would bear.[9] It was a man's world.

The ease with which the man absconded was closely related to the high mobility of English servants and wage-labourers. A sizeable grouping of transients – the percentage would vary very much from one parish to the next – sought out sexual companionship in alehouses, and taverns. In England these meeting places were supposed to be licensed by J.P.s and if unlicensed they could be closed down. A proliferation of alehouses was a possible reason why one parish might have a far higher rate of illegitimacy than another in which controls were more strict. In Branfield in Suffolk, for example, where local JPs had not taken order with unlicensed alehouses, the number of illegitimate children born in 1539 stood at 14 per cent of all recorded births.

Yet in England a sizeable minority of bastards (in some parishes 40 per cent) were born to women who had been born in the village and were bastards themselves. These bastard-prone people were frequently related to each other by blood and when they did marry, found their spouses from other bastard-prone families. Around the Lancashire village of Hawkshead, for example, the Atkinson, Dixon, Satterwaite, Tayler and twenty other families, out of the several hundred resident families, consistently bore or sired bastard children on each other during the parish register period. Here, as elsewhere, the bastard-prone families were not the most destitute families in the village, though they could scarcely be counted among the most respectable. In several of the German cities, as well, there was a suspicion in the minds of city councillors that people who were themselves bastards tended to be of loose morals. Thus, in 1536 the city fathers of Zwickau in Saxony ordained that: 'No master may have in his house apprentices, journeymen or carders of illegitimate birth, in order that this same whoring and other public blasphemy will not be tolerated'.[10]

Our knowledge of illegitimacy patterns depends very much on the availability and reliability of parish registers and other record sources. If the fact of an illegitimate birth were not recorded we have no way of knowing of its existence. Thus, in early fifteenth-century Artois there may well have been a substantial number of children born to parents who were not married to each other. Here village wisdom held that the child of two parents who lost their virginity to each other was sure to be mad or deformed. Accordingly, mature village matrons made it their business to entice young males of the community to lose their virginity. Whether the offspring who resulted from these lessons in sex were accepted by the matron's husband as his own cannot be known; there are no parish registers for Artois from this period.

In France – where officially recorded illegitimacy rates hovered at around 1 per cent until they shot upwards in the eighteenth century – hundreds of thousands of children were simply abandoned by their mothers and left to die, presumably unbaptized. In Rennes, the chief city of Brittany, visitors in the seventeenth and eighteenth centuries frequently saw corpses of babies in city streets and ditches. Though the city had a foundling hospital, an ordinance of 1717 forbade admission to babies born of parents from outside the city. These alien parents were doubtless the source of most of the infant corpses found on city streets.

Yet even among the resident citizenry of Rennes, the number of abandoned infants was sizeable. In this provincial city of between 32,000 and 34,000 some 3600 abandoned infants (most of them alive on arrival) were left at the Rennes foundling hospital between 1722 and 1741. If one assumes that all of these abandoned infants were illegitimate (though they may simply have been family surplus) this works out at an illegitimacy rate of 21 per cent over these nineteen years.

One probable reason why French parents secretly abandoned thousands of infants was that after 1556 infanticide (child murder) was a capital offence. There is considerable evidence to suggest that the new law was rigorously enforced by the uncomprehending élites who controlled the courts. Typically, Jean Bodin, one of the foremost philosophers of order in the sixteenth century, claimed that a woman who killed her own child was devoid of 'all natural and human affection and piety'. To his mind, such an act was only possible if the woman had a pact with the Devil. In the two centuries after 1556 people found guilty of infanticide counted for between 10 and 20 per cent of all the executions which were ordered by the Parlement of Paris. All told, in Paris and in all other jurisdictions of France more than 5000 women were executed for this offence, a greater number than were executed for witchcraft during the great witchhunt of 1560 to 1680.

Choice of spouses

According to the teachings of the Catholic Church, as set forth soon after the Council of Trent, the primary purpose of marriage was to create a partnership between two people of the opposite sex contracted 'in the hope of mutual help so that one aided by the other may more easily bear the discomforts of life and sustain the weakness of old age'. In this Catholic scheme (there were others), in second place were the purposes of procreation 'not so much that heirs and property and riches be left but that worshippers of the true faith and religion may be educated'.[11] Few Protestants would have quarrelled with this idealistic formulation. Yet in practice the marital arrangements which many people entered were rather different.

For a start because of high mortality rates among married couples (along with everybody else) a high proportion of marriages were for one of the partners a second or third marriage. Thus in sixteenth-century England, where widows had a reasonable chance of finding a new husband and the age spread between partners was usually only two or three years, about one marriage in seven was a second or third marriage for one of the partners. A century later in the Ile de France, the proportion was nearly one in three. In contrast to the English and northern European situation, in many parts of central France and in most of the Mediterranean world the tendency among widowers who were looking for new wives was to shun widows and instead to find a bride who was still a virgin. Thus in Sennely-en-Sologne in 1709 Jean Richard, aged 74, married Françoise Cochin, aged 24, his previous wife having died in October 1708 aged only 18. Here, where the virginity of the bride-to-be was of prime concern, it would be folly to think that a true partnership of equals in the Tridentine sense was established, or indeed that the young brides had had much choice in the matter.

In those parts of the Continent where seigneurial controls continued to be enforced, one's choice of a marriage partner might be restricted to the territory which one's seigneur controlled. In France seigneurs had the right to prevent young women from leaving a fief held in fee from the Crown to marry outsiders. Thus, in 1678 the seigneur of Sainte-Mère-Église in Normandy reminded his estate agent not to permit his men to allow their daughters to marry outside the parish without his permission, which was to say, without first rendering a monetary payment. In Swabia in the Holy Roman Empire lease contracts in the sixteenth century clearly stated that any man who married outside the overlord's territory would either lose his farm or lose the right to inherit a farm from his father. The same sort of controls were found in Italy in the lands of the Dukes of Tuscany. Here, in the course of the sixteenth century several sons of ducal tenants were expelled from the territory because they brought in wives without the duke's permission. Further north and east, in the Baltic and Balkan regions, where from the 1550s onwards the second serfdom was tightening its grip on subject populations (see Chapter 4), overlords were even more adamant in enforcing their controls over marriage partners than they were in western Europe.

Parental controls over who a young person could marry were also of considerable importance in some geographical regions and among certain social groupings. In the south of France and in other parts of the Mediterranean world where stem and joint families and the revitalized Roman Law held sway, a father had the undisputed right to choose which of his children should marry and whom they should marry.

Typical perhaps of the situation in several upland areas in south–central France was that found in the parish of Ribennes in the Gévauden, as described by P. Lamaison. Here, on the 'roof of France', stem families were the norm, and the concept of the *ostal* (the house, family lands, herds and possibly the ancestors' nail clippings) was still a living reality just as it had been in fourteenth-century Montaillou. Cautious parents generally waited until near the time when they would retire from active farming before appointing their heir (they did not trust their children). As part of the process of transferring control of the *ostal*, this son or, in one case out of three, daughter, would then be joined in marriage to the son or daughter of another carefully selected *ostal*. In the Ribennes system, where parents worked things out in collaboration with other parents, the heirs of two *ostals* were seldom permitted to marry since that would increase the wealth of one *ostal* at the expense of others in the parish. Here, where it was considered imperative to preserve the status quo in wealth and social standing, things were so managed that over the generations, heirs and non-heirs would be exchanged on an equal basis between all parts of the region. Because the population of Ribennes and the neighbouring inter-marrying parishes was small, at any one time it was likely that there was only a handful of possible partners from which prospective in-laws could choose. It was of no great importance to either set of parents if the intended bride and groom could not stand the sight of each other. The only thing which mattered was the well-being of the *ostal*. Yet in most cases the marriages lasted.

Similarly, in Haute Provence (just east of the Gévauden), where fathers also exercised strict control over the choice of spouses, less than 3 per cent of all marriages contracted in the 150 years after 1640 ended in a rupture. In those few cases which did, the rupture usually occurred after the heavy-hand of the father had been removed by death. Such a rupture, confirmed by a notary, required that the girl's dowry be returned to her parents. This last transaction upset several other parties. Sisters of the ex-husband, who had counted on the ex-wife's dowry as a source of funding for their own dowries were now left in the lurch.

In Protestant Basel (Switzerland), where nuclear families were the norm, parental consent was also a necessary preliminary for marriage. Here, with typical Swiss thoroughness, the ordinance of 1533 made it clear that even in the case of a second or third marriage for one of the parties, both sets of parents had to give their approval; without it the bride and groom would lose their inheritance rights.

Among the European and English aristocracy and gentry, arranged marriages which put the welfare of the family group before considerations of individual happiness were also common. In France, parental control over marriage was supported by local written and unwritten custom as well as by royal decree. In 1556 and again in 1637, French kings, acting with the advice of aristocratic parents who feared that the honour of their noble houses would be tarnished if their offspring married spouses of their own choosing, ordained that all sons under the age of 30 and all daughters under the age of 25 were dependants of their parents. Legally, they could only marry with their parents' permission.

Yet in some parts of northern France, parents of peasant status ignored the royal decree. In Normandy, where local custom held that daughters could not inherit if there were sons in the family, in practice girls often chose their own husbands. When speaking of his daughter's intended marriage, Julien Fleury, a *laboureur* of Couville, affirmed that he had allowed his daughter a free choice, knowing that in such matters she was incapable of making a bad decision. Even if she had, it would not have harmed the inheritance prospects of her brothers. In Troyes, in the Champagne, some daughters of the bourgeoisie simply ignored their parents altogether. Thus, in 1484 a girl named Bernarde told her friends that she was engaged to the man she loved and that she didn't care what her father said. In any case she assumed that he would soon calm down and accept the marriage as a *fait accompli*.

In non-élite England, where marriage was less closely tied to inheritance than it was among the aristocracy or among the more static societies on the Continent, young people might voluntarily consult their parents about the suitability of the person they loved. Yet in the last resort, they had a free hand.

Perhaps typical of many respectable English families of the middling sort was Ralph Josselin of Earls Colne, Essex. Although Josselin spent a large proportion of his life-time earnings in furthering his children's careers, he never successfully influenced their choice of partners. Indeed, in England those parents who did attempt to do so sometimes found themselves brought before a court of law on an apparently unrelated charge cobbled together by the offended offspring.

Community controls

In the many regions where village solidarity was held to be of utmost importance (for a discussion of immobile as opposed to more fluid village structures see Chapter 3), the entire peasant community was concerned about which boy should marry which girl. In northern France the mechanisms which controlled young children's later mating patterns probably first came into operation at the *veilles*, the spinning and sewing sessions at which village women met during the long, dark winter evenings. While chattering over their work by the light of a few candles, the women discussed the marriage prospects of each of the girls and pre-adolescent boys who were playing at their feet. Once a community consensus was reached the boys and girls concerned were informed and given to understand that no one would think ill of them if, on some later festive occasion or young persons' pilgrimage to a religious shrine, they chose to explore each other's anatomy more closely.

One of the most important of the festive occasions at which adolescents and young men and women in their 20s might come to know each other more intimately was on the night of St John's Eve, on the summer solstice of 24–5 June (see Chapter 5). Another was on May Day (1 May). Though customs varied from one village to the next, the usual practice was for young men to plant a tree (an obvious phallic symbol) before the door of every marriageable girl in the village. Ill-favoured wenches were rewarded with a dead branch or other token of barrenness. In the course of gathering the greenery from nearby forests or wastes, young men and women who had been marked out for each other by their elders perhaps got to know each other a little better. On a number of other festive occasions as well young people mingled together freely. Some of their meetings were at the impromptu *veilles* at which men were present as well as women. These affairs were given over to dancing, storytelling and, by the seventeenth century at least, to listening while a literate villager read aloud tales about knights, dragons, fairies or saints. At other meetings, sex-play followed a set form. In northern France and in several other parts of the northern world, the Feast Day of the Holy Innocents (28 December in the Christian calendar) was given over to what respectable people after about 1550 referred to as lewd dancing. On this day naked or nearly naked youths chased nubile girls around the local parish church to the cheers and boos of the onlookers. The girls retaliated by throwing ashes into the faces of their pursuers. These rowdy community occasions – which in the urban Mediterranean world had their parallel in Carnival just before Lent (see Chapter 5) – were intended to ensure the future continuance of the local population by propitiating the spirits which controlled fertility. They in no way jeopardized the community consensus about the pairing off of young people.

In many of the German-speaking lands the village people who were most in evidence in controlling the choice of spouses were the unmarried young men themselves. It was they who supervised the practice known as 'night courting' or bundling. Early in the 1730s, when the practice first became known to the written record, J. F. Osterwal, the pastor of a Protestant parish in Switzerland could scarcely control his rage when he wrote: 'I am compelled to report a shocking disorder here which is very common in certain places…and which ought not to be known in a country where they profess to be Christians….' As summed up by the folklorist Arnold van Gennep,

this custom which was openly approved by all the youths of the village and by the interested families [non-villagers were rigorously excluded] allows the girl on certain nights, especially Saturday, to open the window or door of her bedchamber or the common bedchamber of all the nubile girls of the house successively to different gallants. The man chosen for that night rests completely clothed or partially clothed so that the principal act of love could not be accomplished. The night is spent in talking about the events which have taken place in the village or sleeping in each other's arms until early morning. Then the boy returns to his home or work. It is the girl who decides which gallant she will receive in her bed. These gallants are not necessarily amongst those from whom she will choose a fiancé. The *kiltgang* [the German term for night-courting] is neither a trial coupling nor a way to give preference in marriage. More important it is only exercised between boys and girls from the same village; rarely from the whole parish.[12]

In addition to Switzerland and the German Empire, night-courting was also practised in Scandinavia, in Celtic Scotland and Wales and also in the Vendée and the Savoy. Because it was unsupported by any of the writers of the Christian New Testament, it was one of the many folk customs which reformed clerics of both the Catholic and the Protestant persuasions did their best to eradicate. In Catholic Savoy in 1609 night-courting was made grounds for excommunication (this meant that the culprit could not receive the holy sacraments). In Champagne a similar ordinance went into effect in 1680. Yet, especially in Protestant lands where the hold of official religion over ordinary people was far from secure, night-courting long continued to be part of the traditional ritual of courtship.

Community involvement in the choice of marriage partners was most pronounced in villages where endogamous marriages (the choice of marriage partners from the same village) were the norm. In northern France where at no time in the early modern period did more than 10 per cent of any village population voluntarily leave the village of their birth – 5 per cent was probably closer to the usual rate of out-migration – marriage between near neighbours and close cousins was the rule. For instance, in the town of Chilly, which was only 30 kilometres from the rapidly growing metropolis of Paris, of the 325 marriages celebrated in the local church between 1608 and 1662, 86 per cent of the partners came from Chilly or a nearby hamlet. Further south, in Rosier-sur-Loire in Anjou between 1661 and 1700, 93 per cent of the partners came from the village in which they married.

In the relatively closed worlds of seventeenth-century Chilly and Rosier-sur-Loire, the overwhelming majority of men married daughters or widows of men in the same occupation as themselves. Wine producers found their spouses from other wine-producing families; artisans married the daughters or widows of artisans. In both cases the wife-to-be required no training in her future husband's work. However, in some parts of the Massif Central, it was the two families' social standing rather than their occupation which mattered most. Here it was not uncommon for men whose main source of income came from arable farming to marry girls whose families herded sheep or cattle. Yet, as a general rule throughout the whole of rural Europe, the higher a man's social standing the less likely it was that he would choose a first wife from a family of lower social standing than his own. In a word, for a woman marriage to a previously unmarried husband was seldom the path to upward social mobility.

The weakness of community controls in England

Of all the regions of Europe, community involvement in the choice of spouses was *least* in evidence in lowland England. This was both because of the mental attitudes of ordinary village people and because of the institution of life-cycle service. By its very nature service encouraged both short-term and permanent geographical mobility. For example, of the sixty-seven living-in servants in Clayworth in Nottinghamshire in 1676 only one, Anne Bingham, was still to be found in the village twelve years later; even she had changed her employer at least once. Though English teenagers leaving home for the first time might work for a year or two under some near neighbour, in later years they tended to travel farther afield. Some migrants went only 15 or 25 kilometres, to the next parish, but a substantial minority crossed over several parish boundaries to go to the nearest large city. With its population of 200,000 in 1600 and 550,000 in 1700, London obviously exerted a particularly strong pull on migrants. (Without immigration no early modern city could maintain its own numbers, let alone grow.) Apprenticeship records from some of the great London companies show that before 1640 and the crisis of the Civil War, 30–40 per cent of the apprentices had come from places 300 or 400 kilometres away. After the Civil War long-distance north–south migration slowed down as migrants from the north of England travelled shorter distances to York and to the northern towns which in the eighteenth century would become centres of industrialization (a fate which York was spared). Other northerners from the lowlands took up proto-industrial by-employments in northern upland regions (see Chapter 4).

In England, mobility was not limited to life-cycle servants or wage-labourers. Indeed, by 1600, if not by 1500, two English people out of three changed their village of residence at least once in the course of their lives; as we noted above this trend continued into the eighteenth century. One reason why pre-industrial English people who had at least a small store of savings could be atomistic individualists was the flourishing market in land. In contrast to, say Tuscany in 1427, English farmers in the fifteenth century and later could rent, lease or buy arable and pasture as the need arose and then sell it off when it was no longer required. This made it unnecessary for the less substantial farmers to stay in one place. Instead of remaining in the village of their birth where the larger farmers had used fair market means to win control of the best land, lesser farmers could sell off their properties and move to another locality where the going price for land was lower.

Such people – in most villages the majority of the landholding population – did not have a highly developed sense of place – this house, these trees, these family acres. These sentiments were the monopoly of the top 5 to 10 per cent of the village landholding population, the men and women who, in the years after about 1590 in a village like Terling in Essex, came to form the village élite very often remained in the village of their birth to build up little family dynasties. In contrast to such people (the record-generators best known to history), the less substantial farmers did not feel the need to live with the same tightly-knit group of people who shared common ancestors and a common 'life-world' in the Habermas sense (see Chapter 3). For these people the concept of family lands to which one could always return was meaningless. So too was the concept of a home village to which one could remit part of one's wages in the expectation that one would eventually return to die and be buried among one's ancestors. It was people of this sort who in the years before 1660, in their tens of thousands, migrated either as farmers or craftsmen or indentured servants to the new lands in Virginia, Maryland, Carolina and New England.

But if English men, and to a slightly lesser extent English women, did not feel themselves tied to any one village, they did at least feel a continuing sense of loyalty to their own parents and to their 'country'. This 'country' consisted of the geographical region where most of the ordinary folk spoke the same dialect (gentlemen, in contrast, were at least aware of standard English after about 1550), used the same building materials for their barns and houses (there are a dozen or more principal vernacular housing styles in England), and did other things in more or less the same way.

These perceptions of one's 'country' were reflected in ordinary English people's choice of marriage partners. So also was the fact that people who had served as household servants, servants in husbandry or as casual wage-labour-ers in several villages had a considerable range of marriage partners from which to choose. In the village of Terling in Essex in the years between 1590 and 1629 only 19 per cent of the men and 34 per cent of the women married in the local parish church in which they had been baptized. However, the more common pattern was that about 40 per cent of the marriages celebrated in a village church were between a man and a woman from that parish and another 20–30 per cent from nearby parishes. This suggests that many of the people who had left home earlier to enter service were on the lookout for spouses from the same general geographical area. When they completed their time in service, pooled their savings and married, they first set up housekeeping in a village which was nearby but not necessarily the same as either of the villages in which the man and his new wife had been born.

Charivari

In England, no less than on the Continent, the controls which a village or neighbourhood population exercised over the choice of marriage partners was sometimes expressed in a noisy demonstration known as a charivari. The charivari was a complex many-faceted phenomenon which operated when the organizers/participants felt that the normal social relationship between the sexes was being threatened. In some social systems they were a means by which the young men of the village showed their displeasure if an outsider married a local girl. In a particularly violent demonstration which took place in October 1588, the chaplain and curé of Ames in Artois barely escaped with their lives after they had joined a local girl in marriage to a man from the nearby village of Pernes, a 'foreigner'.

Charivaris might also express community displeasure if two partners greatly different in age married; an old man with a young girl or an older widow with a local youth. Participants in the charivari held that both sorts of pairings were an inversion of the normal social order, though as parish registers show marriages between winter and spring were common enough. One recalls the marital career of old Jean Richard of Sennely-en-Sologne (see p. 69). In some social systems charivaris directed against aged remarrying widowers came into prominence (i.e. entered the written record) just at the time when the average marrying age of local women was rising. This rising age level meant that the size of the pool of marriageable girls from whom young men who had just finished their apprenticeship could choose brides was perceptibly shrinking. Thus, in Dijon in Burgundy charivaris directed against widowers and their young brides became particularly common after 1550. Here the age at which women were deemed marriageable had risen to over 21; a century earlier, in 1450, it had been less than 20.

Yet the reasoning behind a charivari was not always readily apparent. Thus, more than fifteen of the charivaris known to have taken place in Moderna in north Italy between 1527 and 1547 were protests against the marriages of widows and widowers who were of much the same age. Perhaps what troubled Moderna youths and recently married men most was that by virtue of their widowhood, the women were at law free to choose their marriage partners without consulting anyone. Such women and their new spouses probably felt that it was unnecessary to follow the customary requirement of regaling local people with free food and drink. The organizers of the charivari retaliated for this breach of custom by hurling dead animals and animal and human excrement at the couple and serenading them with terrifying noises produced by drums, trumpets and more make-shift instruments. The victims' only recourse was to leave town and make a new residence in a place where they were not known.

Though most of them were unrecorded, in many of the villages of Europe charivari or some other form of 'rough music' probably often came into play against a wife who had cuckolded her husband; men considered that female adultery was an inversion of the normal social order. In England a frequent practice was to require the man who lived next door to the cuckolded husband – a neighbour who had obviously fallen short in his surveillance duties – to put on women's clothes and ride back to front on a mule through the village. In his hands he was made to carry a distaff, an instrument of phallic form used by women in spinning thread. An alternative form of charivari took place if a man had beaten his wife once too often. Here it was the wife-beating husband rather than the neighbour who was made to endure the 'rough music'. Similar community intervention to force men to deal more leniently with their wives has also been noted in sixteenth-century Dijon.

What was marriage?

In early modern Europe there was no one generally agreed upon way to enter into matrimony. In some localized social systems – which might differ from one village to the next – some people followed the old Roman Law custom and held that the engagement, or as the French termed it, the *fiançailles* (hence the English word fiancé), was the most important part of the procedure. One such engagement/marriage was contracted at Christmastide in 1483 in or around Troyes in the Champagne. The process began when Jean Binet appeared at the house of the father of Henrietta Lagouge, a widow, seeking permission to marry her. Queried by her father, Henrietta agreed that she wished to marry Jean if that would please her parents. All the adults in the household then sat down at a table and the widowed bride-to-be's uncle asked her to give Jean a glass of wine 'in the name of marriage'. After drinking the wine, Jean kissed Henrietta, saying: 'I would that you receive this kiss in the name of marriage.' To which the father and the other men replied: 'You are engaged, the one to the other.' In the eyes of everyone present and of the community, the couple were now free to live together as man and wife.[13] This custom was still being followed by people in the area around Gatteville in Normandy nearly 170 years later. In 1650 a Catholic missionary reported that 'one is still obliged to preach strongly against the ignorance which one finds amongst the majority of those who are engaged [who] imagine that all is permitted from that moment'. Gatteville people had still to learn the Church's definition of 'sin' at least as far as premarital sex was concerned.[14]

In the north-west of England, in Scotland and in some parts of Scandinavia an old Nordic custom known as hand-fasting continued to be practised in the sixteenth and seventeenth centuries. This custom allowed the couple to live together for several months. If the woman became pregnant, they would celebrate a public wedding. But if she proved barren – in folk mythology no *man* was infertile – the relationship could be broken off with no hard feelings on the part of the woman's feud-prone kin.

Another way of contracting what community elders recognized as marriage was based on an old mainland Germanic custom. This held that a man and a woman were bound together in marriage from the moment when the man promised to take the woman as his wife and had cemented his promise with a full sexual embrace. In some regions he had also to give her a ring or a piece of silver, which was broken so that the two pieces could later be matched. Well into the nineteenth century consensual marriages entered into by two parties acting on their own were much favoured by vagrants who ignored the norms of settled respectable folk.

Consensual unions were not much approved by parents who had even a small amount of property to transfer to their offspring and the new spouse. In areas such as Renaissance northern Italy, where the utility of the written record was known, even quite poor parents insisted that their son or daughter's marriage be witnessed by two or three respectable people whose word would stand in a court of law. More often than not, one of these witnesses was a notary. Prosperous Italians who used marriage as a way of forging alliances between families commonly had recourse to a notary three or four times during the marriage-making process; once when the couple were formally engaged, once when the two families agreed to the terms by which the dowry of the woman would be paid over to the groom or his father, once at the public wedding and once again when the last portion of the dowry was finally paid over, perhaps five or ten years after the formal wedding.

The role of the Church

During the early part of our period priests were not regularly involved in the making of a marriage. This may seem strange to some late twentieth-century Christians, but in fact it was a consequence of a Church tradition which had been established as early as the sixth century. When Pope Gregory the Great (590–604), the author of a guide book on pastoral duties used all through the Middle Ages, sent his missionaries to bring the gospel to the pagans of Anglo-Saxon England, he ordered them to tolerate all local moral practices and customs which did not run directly contrary to the central teachings of the Church. The principle of accommodation, established by Gregory, was followed in the next century when English missionary priests in their turn brought the Word of God to the pagan mainland Germans. The same principle continued to be followed by missionary priests at work in Europe throughout the Middle Ages and only came to be seriously challenged after about 1550 when priests became leading instruments in the reformation of manners. Even then it continued to be used by Jesuit missionaries in China.

The early missionary Church's policy on marriage had consisted of three quite simple points. First, both the man and the woman had freely to give their consent to the union and must not be forced into marriage by their parents. Volition could most readily be assured if the marriage was witnessed by any two or three oath-worthy people, who need not necessarily be priests. Second, the Church insisted that no person should be married to more than one spouse at a time. Last, it held that marriages were made in heaven. They were only broken when God allowed the angel of death to carry off one of the partners. Thus, according to Catholic logic, divorce was impossible.

The Church did not enlarge upon these three cardinal points for several centuries. Then in 1439, at the Council of Florence, it decreed that marriage should be recognized as a holy sacrament in much the same way that baptism and extreme unction were sacraments (extreme unction was the priestly anointing with holy oil of a penitent who was on the point of death). In itself this decree of 1439 did not make it mandatory for a priest to be present at a wedding, but it was a step in that direction. The Church further tightened its hold over marriage-making at the Council of Trent. There, in 1563, the Tridentine Church affirmed that consensual unions, including those contracted by people who were under age and who had not received their parents' consent, were valid in the eyes of God even though they might be illegal according to secular law. However, the Tridentine Church now insisted that a cleric be present at a marriage ceremony, if only in the capacity of a witness who ensured that the two people married of their own free will.

Supported by the decrees of Trent, in one Italian diocese after another Catholic clerics began to make themselves an indispensable part of the marriage ceremony. They persuaded people that a priest's blessing (a ritual formula of words said while making the sign of the Cross) was much more likely to be heeded by supernatural powers than any blessing pronounced by a lay person. Two of the priest's blessings were thought to be of special mystic importance. The first was said at the time when the groom gave his bride the ring which sealed the marriage (an old Germanic custom taken over by the accommodating Church). Mindful of the use which polygamous German chieftains had made of rings in the second century AD during the time of Tacitus, wary priests took care to bless only one ring. If a cleric had accidentally blessed two or more rings, the groom might later go out and claim other wives on the strength of these sanctified talismans. At some stage in the process of transferring the blessed ring from the groom to the bride it had either to be dropped (a custom mentioned in 1536), or not dropped, as local custom required, in order to ensure prosperity for the new couple. Prosperity, happiness and fecundity were also assured through the second of the priest's blessings; that which he bestowed on the now married couple at their departure from the ceremony.

Ever mindful of local custom (good Pope Gregory again) the Church professed itself indifferent to where the marriage was actually performed. It might be held in the square in front of the church (as the French put it 'in the face of the church'), in the church building, in one of the parents' houses or wherever else convenience required. Yet, wherever the ceremony was actually performed, one thing was certain; by the late sixteenth century Catholic priests had made themselves principal actors in the drama in all the lands where the decrees of Trent were accepted.

They were not accepted everywhere even in the Catholic world. In France, where aristocratic alliances were cemented through marriages, men of birth did not take kindly to the Tridentine insistence that the bride and groom should be publicly asked whether they consented to the union; the parents would be humiliated if they happened to say: 'non, jamais'. Partly for this reason (inter-state rivalries were involved as well), until the early seventeenth century the king of France and the provincial parlements (law courts) refused to register the decrees of Trent or to regard them as binding. Thus for more than two generations, in the absence of a central state-supported policy, it was left to the discretion of each of the 120 or more French bishops (themselves sons of aristocratic families) to decide which Tridentine decrees to enforce and which to ignore.

Propagated in response to the Protestant Reformations (see Chapter 5), the decrees of Trent were, of course, held to be entirely irrelevant in Protestant lands. For his part, Martin Luther denied that marriage was in any way a sacrament. Yet, by the 1520s respectable German Protestant clerics and lay magistrates had come to abhor popular-style consensual unions and accordingly gave city magistrates full control over the making and dissolving of marriages. The situation was less clear in England. There Anglican Church officials were unwilling to cut themselves entirely adrift from Catholic pre-Tridentine matrimonial doctrines. For this reason the Church of England (which had broken from Rome in the 1530s over Henry VIII's divorce and again, more permanently, under Elizabeth I in 1559), continued to affirm that an engagement constituted a binding contract; 900 years later Pope Gregory's principle of accommodation still held. Yet at the same time, the Church of England strongly encouraged people to be married by their priests after banns had been read in the parish church on the three preceding Sundays. Respectable English Protestants, particularly among the growing groupings of acquisitive merchants and town-dwelling pseudo-gentry, laid great stress on the virtues of holy matrimony and usually used the services of the Church. Historical demographers, who are dependent upon parish registers when calculating marriage and fertility rates like to assume that most ordinary people also got married in a church. However, nobody was under any legal compulsion to marry in a church until the passage of Lord Hardwicke's Marriage Act in 1753. By that time so many dissenting churches which were lax about keeping records had been established – Quakers, Presbyterians, Baptists and the like – that it became almost impossible to verify whether each and every couple who claimed to be married had actually been married in a church.

The changing role of the populace

In most of the social systems of fifteenth- and early sixteenth-century Europe the whole of the male moral community along with some of the women insisted that they should play a conspicuous role in the making of any marriage which was not a privately contracted consensual union. Community members saw themselves both as sponsors and guarantors and, if the marriage proved fruitful, as the ultimate beneficiaries of the union. In northern Italy, Switzerland, the Low Countries and several other regions, when a girl left her father's house for the last time she was accompanied by a great throng of men and boys beating loudly on drums, blowing bagpipes and trumpets and firing off guns. Surrounded by all this joyful and tuneless din, no person in his or her right mind could doubt that a rite of passage was taking place.

In the Mediterranean world and in Celtic lands, a crowd of villagers surrounded the small group of family intimates and officials who witnessed the central drama at which the bride's father or a surrogate father (perhaps one father in three had died long before his daughter's wedding) formally handed the woman over to her new master, her husband. While this was going on, the crowd continued in the noise-making. Their purpose now was to drive away the lurking malevolent spirits which might otherwise harm the new couple. More popular rituals followed. After the wedding, sometimes weeks later if it had taken that long to collect the first portion of the dowry from the bride's parents, the newly weds were accompanied to their own house by another procession of fiddlers, drummers and other noisy demonstrators; all of these people had to be paid off with food, drink or money before they would go away. In the mountainous areas between Switzerland and France known as the Jura, in the weeks which followed the wedding, further processions carried the newly weds to all the villages in the region. These visits were designed to allay all lingering doubts in the minds of discarded suitors that the new householders had forever altered their status and were now man and wife.

Although certain prosperous Continental regions such as the urban centres in the Low Countries ran a close second, far and away the most elaborate celebrations in which the whole of the populace participated were those which took place in Renaissance northern Italy. Among the patricians of Pistoia and Florence, the cost of the processions and the lavish wedding feasts which the new couple were required to provide might exceed the annual wages of half a dozen honest craftsmen. Years later the burden of paying off the costs of this entertainment might still be reflected in the paucity of the furnishings of the couple's private rooms; theirs was certainly not the Protestant ethic of worldly asceticism. Yet patrician Italian families considered that this money had been well spent. They or their humanist spokesmen – men like Leonis Baptiste Alberti – saw these public rituals as necessary flights of fancy and as a release of social tensions. Through them they momentarily escaped the grim reality of the everyday world. No less important, it was at these great public spectacles that the links between the ruling levels of society and their dependants, clients, friends and hangers-on were strengthened and renewed. In the more humble but no less exuberant celebrations which took place at the village level in all parts of Europe at a public wedding, the bonds of local solidarity were similarly strengthened and the burdens of ordinary life temporarily forgotten.

Changing standards of decency

Early in our period it had not been thought improper if close friends were present during the most intimate parts of the making of a marriage. In Zwickau in Saxony, for example, the custom was for the bride and groom to bathe together and to distribute food and drink to their friends while still dripping wet and naked. Friends were also present in the bedchamber when the marriage was actually consummated. In Brittany, Normandy and the Savoy and in some other regions this final act of marriage did not take place until one night after the marriage itself. During the 'night of Tobie' which followed directly after the wedding, village women hurriedly taught the new bride what little they knew about the facts of life. The menfolk sat apart with the groom, drinking and stirring up his passions with lewd stories. The next night the new couple were put to the test. After the cosy bedroom scene where the bride lost her cherished virginity a score or more people would be able to testify that she had been truly impregnated by her lawful husband; the legitimacy of their offspring could not be in doubt. Once again community controls had triumphed.

All this changed in the years after about 1550 with the spread of the reformation of manners. Although as late as the early seventeenth century King James I of England interested himself in what newly married courtiers did on the night of their marriage, such concern about other people's sex life was regarded with horror by the ever growing minority of prudish people, including James's son, Charles I. Typically, at Zwickau in Saxony an ordinance of 1540 forbade the practice of holding public nuptial baths. Indeed, among respectable people everywhere nudity except in the arts came to be regarded as unseemly. Under no circumstances were men or women to be seen defecating or urinating in public. Even in York in northern England, a region which was generally a generation or two behind developments further south, in 1600 the city corporation finally got around to placing a screen around the privy in the council chamber. For these town fathers in common with the respectable vandals in the Vatican who ordered that the privy parts of all the antique Greek and Roman statues in the Vatican Museum be covered with stone, the human organs which performed the reproductive functions or through which excrement was channelled had become objects of shame.

Yet it was many years before these élite notions became firmly fixed in the minds of ordinary village people. In Somerset in England as late as the 1650s – the decade which was supposedly dominated by the harsh moral code of the Puritans – a village matron such as Mary Combe, an innkeeper's wife, could parade around her town naked and loosen the drawstrings of men with whom she wanted to copulate. After sifting all the evidence G. R. Quaife has recently concluded that most of Mary Combe's West Country neighbours were quite prepared to tolerate her eccentric behaviour.

It was with similar mixed success that prudish people who took the precepts of the reformation of manners to heart tried to prevent obscene revels from taking place during the public portion of a marriage ceremony. To their mind public participation was a legacy from the pagan past and unworthy of a Christian society. Typically, in the Saxon town of Zwickau an ordinance of 1540 decreed that nobody other than the parents and siblings of the bride and groom, or in their absence one friend of the groom and one friend of the bride, should accompany the new couple home. Everywhere the godly people who controlled the magistracy and other instruments of repression did their best to stamp out public participation in the making of a marriage. Changes in social habits do not occur all at once, yet in many regions the work was complete by about 1750. Village weddings had now become tame affairs. If the populace were present at all they were merely passive observers.

The home environment

Several sorts of material, none of them infallible, have been used by historians in their attempts to recapture the essence of the home environment known to ordinary married early modern Europeans. Of these the most ambiguous is the evidence left by surviving examples of vernacular architecture and by the inventories of the goods left by people at the time of their death.

In most parts of the Mediterranean world peasant houses at the end of the early modern period still consisted of only a room or two with part of the ground floor used as a shelter for livestock and chickens. The furniture was rudimentary; a rough wooden table and benches and straw mats for sleeping. Such houses provided individuals with little privacy and can scarcely have encouraged any person to stay in the house except to sleep. In a nucleated village where extended family members and the neighbours were usually within earshot of one another, there was likely to have been little sense of intimacy or affection between a man and his wife or between the parents and their children. Here, the bedrock of social solidarity was the extended family and/or the village rather than the conjugal family.

Rather different was the situation north of the Alps, in the Low Countries, in southern and central England and in the more prosperous parts of northern France and the Rhineland. In all of these regions by the late sixteenth century house-types and furnishings were beginning to make it possible to convert a mere house into a home. Here, houses of even quite modestly-placed peasants were being built with special purpose rooms including separate chambers for the parents and for the children and servants. To heat these houses two or three fireplaces and chimneys had come to replace the old single hearth. To make the houses more light and airy, glass windows were inserted into the stone or wattle and daub walls. And to make them more suitable retreats from the cares of the world outside, an increasingly high proportion of the family's disposable income was spent on bedsteads, feather-down mattresses, linen sheets and warm blankets. In England, by the early seventeenth century, nearly a third of an ordinary rural family's expenditure on household goods was for bedsteads and chamber fitments. Yet, whether these bedchambers served merely as havens for disgruntled individualists, or as centres of a new sort of affective intimacy between husbands and wives can only be a matter for speculation. Not until the tail-end of the seventeenth century was a sizeable proportion of the family's expenditure on household goods used for tables and chairs, pewter dishes and utensils. This movement to provide solid, long-lasting furniture for the family's main living area might be taken to suggest that ordinary families were beginning to spend more time together over dinner and in the evening hours.

The introduction of tea drinking in the late seventeenth century (an innovation brought from the Far East) provided menfolk as well as women with a beverage they could easily prepare at home without the need to go out to join the neighbours in the alehouse or tavern. Yet some men still preferred the company of other men and the odd prostitute at a tavern to staying at home with their nagging wife and screaming children. As Jean Charles Houzea of Cambrai put it when he was accused of drunkenness in 1692: 'Where could you find a man who has never gone to a *cabaret*?'[15]

Anti-feminism

A second source of evidence about the affective relationship between men and their wives derives from the writings of the élite who were educated in the classical traditions of ancient Greece during the time of Plato and Aristotle (Athenian democracy did not extend to women) and from official and semi-official government pronouncements. In France, for example, a document drawn up in 1670 on the order of Jean Baptiste Colbert, Louis XIV's finance minister, made it clear that families created by state-approved forms of marriage (i.e. not consensual unions) were the fundamental unit of the hierarchy of orders over which the king liked to think he presided. Within this notional family wives were second-class citizens and in all things were to be obedient to their husbands.

Writing more than a century earlier, the French satirist, François Rabelais (died *c.* 1553) made it clear that the subordination of women to their husbands, fathers or brothers was essential for the well-being of civil society. Drawing directly on Plato's *Timaeus*, Rabelais held that women were incapable of reason and that their actions were motivated solely by the sexual passions which were seated in their wombs. As he put it:

For Nature has placed in a secret and interior place in their bodies an animal, an organ that is not present in men; and here there are sometimes engendered certain salty, nitrous, caustic, sharp, biting, stabbing and bitterly irritating humours, by the pricking and painful itching of which – for this organ is all nerves and sensitive feelings – their whole body is shaken, all their senses transported, all their passions indulged, and all their thoughts confused.[16]

Similar sentiments about the irrationality and sex-driven nature of women were held by the Englishman Robert Burton. In his *Anatomy of Melancholy*, written in 1621, Burton asked 'what country, what village doeth not complain...of women's unnatural, unsatiable lust?'[17]

Two movements contributed to this élitist male notion that women were imbeciles whom a husband could only trust, to say nothing of love, at his peril. In an earlier period husbands in their 20s or 30s who married first wives who were only 18, or younger, could expect to control them in much the same way as they could control a child. But when new first wives on an average came to be 24 to 28 years of age, husbands who were not much older than that themselves suddenly found themselves confronted with somebody who was their intellectual equal if not their superior. To compensate for this new balance in the household, husbands in the upper level of society had recourse to the myth of feminine inferiority. In regions where the Roman Law prevailed and in aristocratic circles everywhere, this myth was given the full support of the courts. Earlier in this chapter, when discussing stem and joint families in Roman Law regions, we saw how thoroughly the family patriarch dominated the activities of every member of the household including his wife and his daughters-in-law. Seemingly in such families there was little room for what Lawrence Stone termed affective individualism in the relationship between husband and wife and parents and children.

The other movement which encouraged the male élite to think that most normal women were sex-starved half-wits was the reformation of manners. Before this movement had begun around 1550 and before oral village wisdom was contaminated by printed works devised to be read by simple folk – beginning in the German Empire in the 1520s (see Chapter 6) – the older village women assembled at their *veilles* had been the transmitters of the semi-pagan customs of the local folk. To the élite way of thinking, if the reformation of manners was to make any headway, the oral traditions which women transmitted had to be eradicated. Accordingly, an order was given to prohibit the meeting of unsupervised *veilles*. Around Chartres in the Beauce, for example, priests were instructed in 1687 to teach that *veilles* were meeting places with the Devil.

Similar attempts to downgrade the standing of women were taken in the schools, the preserves of the middling sort and of their social superiors. Although in the early years of the sixteenth century humanist educators had been willing to teach girls the same range of subjects as boys – history, logic, philosophy, Latin and modern languages – by the last years of that century these subjects were no longer considered appropriate for females. Instead, they were sent off to sexually-segregated schools where they were taught to be homemakers and dull-witted foils for their better educated (though not necessarily more intelligent) husbands. As Richard Mulcaster, the English pedagogue put it in 1581, because of their natural weakness women should content themselves 'to be the principal pillars in the upholding of households…to look to her house and family, to provide and keep necessaries though the goodman [the husband] pays, to know the force of her kitchen for sickness and health in herself and her charge'.[18]

Through the printed word and through officially sponsored pronouncements at church or in schools, women after 1550 were taught to regard themselves as inferior beings. This process was of central importance in the moral reformers' programme of cultural coercion; internalized self-denigration is the most effective of all the instruments of oppression. At a time when clerics were being pushed into the background and many new professions were opening their doors to laymen, laywomen were being excluded. No women were to be found in ministries of state, in attendance at the universities, in the church serving as churchwardens, or as town constables or bailiffs. Though newly widowed women might continue to carry on their husbands' business and keep on the servants and apprentices already in the household, in most parts of Europe they were forbidden to hire new apprentices. This meant that as soon as the existing apprentices finished their term of service, the business would have to be wound up unless, in the meantime, the widow found herself a new husband. Unfortunately, the male preference for virgins – especially on the Continent – made remarriage difficult for all but the most determined widow.

In cities such as Nuremberg in the German Empire women were altogether forbidden to carry on full-scale business of their own. They were, however, permitted to serve as petty traders, as appraisers of dead people's property (here their personal experience as housewives and consumers stood them in good stead), and as employment agents, a job which local men apparently held in scorn. Prevented from entering the primary market sector in their own right, Nuremberg women at least had virtual control of the secondary economy. In rural areas in most parts of Europe the same sort of dichotomy between the sexes held. Women assisted their menfolk, the primary producers, with work in the fields at harvest and haying, and had to earn their own pin-money by selling eggs and garden products. Thus, in practice as well as in theory, most married women's principal place was in the home.

Marital breakdown

The third source used by historians are the records of the court cases which were initiated because a marriage had broken down. These, together with pamphlet literature about specific cases of marital disorder are, of course, entirely concerned with disfunctioning families. Only indirectly can they tell us about the operation of the millions of ordinary families which never appeared in the records of a court and which only broke up because of the death of one of the leading family members through a cause other than being murdered by a spouse, child or servant.

In most parts of the Continent, systematic study of court cases concerning family breakdowns is still in its infancy. However, a small handful of local studies do exist. Thus, we know that in the jurisdiction of the Parlement of Toulouse, 28 per cent of the murder cases which came before the court between 1690 and 1728 involved the murder of one family member by another; about half of these murders had clearly been premeditated. In a society where women were thoroughly cowed, most victims and murderers were fathers, sons or male siblings. This suggests that male non-heirs who could no longer tolerate the aloof behaviour of the father's appointed heir, and heirs who felt that they could no longer wait for their father to relinquish control of the household by retiring in the end had recourse to a gun, knife or poison.

A study of Haute Provence, a region 200 kilometres east of Toulouse, shows that among local stem and joint families there was a remarkably low level of household murder in the seventeenth and eighteenth centuries. Though non-inheriting brothers in this region had no reason to love their inheriting siblings, in most cases the two parties stopped short of murdering each other. Moreover, during the life-time of the family patriarch more than 95 per cent of the families whose creation was recorded by a notary remained firmly together with sons and their wives meekly obeying the dictates of the patriarch and his wife. One of the rare occasions of a rupture between a father and a son occurred in the Féraund family in 1715. A year earlier, on 3 January 1714, the widowed father had remarried and chose as his bride the sister of the woman (Anne Barbaroux of Colmars) whom his son and heir had married on the same day. Here tensions between the father's new wife, Marie Barbaroux, the nominal dominant female in the household, and her stepson's wife, Anne, proved too great for any of the parties to bear. They took the case to a notary who arranged a separation for the feuding couples on 20 December 1715, just less than two years after the new menage had been formed.

In the English county of Essex, as J. A. Sharpe's pioneering study of family violence shows, disputes which resulted in the death of a family member constituted only 14 per cent of all the homicide cases which came before the courts between 1560 and 1709. Even if one includes the non-related household members (living-in servants) who were the victims or perpetrators of murder, the proportion rises to only 24 per cent. This is less than half the modern English rate; in 1957 more than half of all recorded homicides were the result of violence within the co-residential family. In Essex there were only 431 murders recorded during the whole of the 250 year period, when the county's population was about 80,000. This suggests that the ordinary early modern English family lived together in a degree of harmony that was perhaps even greater than that known to modern families which, according to Edward Shorter and Lawrence Stone, have undergone a revolution in sentiment and are bound together by close affective ties which exclude their neighbours and everybody else who is not a part of the inward looking nuclear family.

In the early modern English household murders which did occur women figured prominently. Fed up with being kept at home with the children and servants while the husband was out at work on a neighbour's farm or in a shop, women in the Essex case study were responsible for nearly 42 per cent of all household murders. Here and in other counties a few of the victims were spouses. Thus in 1592 Alice Arden of Faversham in Kent hired a professional killer to rid herself of her unwanted husband so that she could marry another man. But most of the victims of a housebound woman's rage were either her own children or living-in servants.

Affective bonds with children

A want of affection between mothers and their children is scarcely the impression one receives from looking at the totality of the available evidence, despite the conclusions reached in the last section. Perhaps typical was the wife of an Essex wheelwright who, according to a pamphlet published in 1607, on the night that she was murdered by her husband prepared her children for bed 'like a loving and natural nurse'. Later that night the children awoke and 'missing the company of their kind helper (who was wont to give them as loving a good morrow as she had, at her last parting, given them a kinde good night) beganne to call and cry for her'.[19]

Similarly, although their play ended in tragedy, no want of affection was in evidence between Richard Terry, a Hertfordshire tailor, and his young son. One day in 1617 Terry was at home playing shuffleboard with his son. Then all at once the son cried out that his father had cheated. Insulted, Terry ordered the boy to leave the house and struck him when he refused to go. In the scuffle which followed, some coins dropped out of the boy's pocket (how many parents allowed their children spending money?). When the lad bent over to pick them up, his father kicked him in the rear end. Heedless of what he was doing the boy picked up a jug and hurled it at his father. As a result of this blow, Richard Terry died sixteen days later.

Although the evidence about relationships between parents and children too young to be sent off as life-cycle servants is at best patchy, it would appear that in many English lowland regions where arable husbandry was practised, ordinary parents appreciated children's need for play. For example, Ralph Josselin of Earls Colne seems never to have expected his young children to help about the farm; this work was done by servants in husbandry or by wage-labourers. Psychologists tell us that play and playful fantasizing are important elements in character formation. Innovative, interesting individualists of the sort Alan Macfarlane sees everywhere in Tudor and Stuart England did not become that way by being used as drudges as soon as they could walk. No less important, ordinary English lowland parents regarded each of their children as distinctive beings who needed to be understood on their own terms as they passed from infancy to childhood and then on to full adulthood. The time and financial resources which in the early modern Mediterranean world parents frittered away on extravagant family reunions and festivals were in England devoted largely to educating the family's children in preparation for adulthood. Thus equipped, ordinary English children were better prepared than most of their peers on the Continent (possibly excepting only the Dutch Republic) to be upwardly socially mobile.

Love in marriage

Relations between parents and children is one of the cores around which an affective family can be built; the other, of course, is the relationship between husbands and wives. Once again the evidence is at best patchy. This is largely because the conjugal relationships of ordinary people whose marriage was not on the point of collapse was not of any concern to record keepers. However, there are occasional hints that ordinary people expected to be able to love their spouses. Thus, in the 1520s Grégoire Espérandieu of Languedoc gave direction that prayers should be said for the soul of his wife who during their married life had 'performed so many, so pleasing, untellable and free services for him'.[20]

During the same period several sets of Languedoc men and women established their households on the basis of a notarial contract which stated that they would be at each other's beck and call 'like brothers'. Less ambiguous in its sexual overtones than either of these two examples are the words of a neighbour of the brothel keeper, Margaret Ferneseede, whose husband was found murdered in Peckham, London in 1608. Hearing that the new widow was unconcerned about her husband's death, the neighbour woman exclaimed: 'For mine own part, had such a mischance falne to my fortune, I should have wept mine eyes with sorrow'.[21]

Divorce

In many parts of Europe, couples whose marriage was in a state of collapse were not at law permitted to divorce. However, wherever the Catholic

Church retained effective control of such matters, couples whose marriage was in difficulty were permitted a legal separation, an agreement which did not permit either party to remarry. According to the Church, such a separation was possible if both parties decided to renounce the world and join holy orders, if one party were a heretic or apostate, or if a husband so mistreated his wife that her life was in danger. A separation was also possible if either of the parties had committed adultery. Yet these teachings were not universally accepted in the Catholic world. In France, where the State in its quest for Absolutism insisted that it alone (rather than the Church) had full control over the institution of marriage, the official doctrine put forth in 1670 held that adultery was only punishable if it was committed by the wife. According to French law a husband who committed adultery was held to be blameless. No clearer expression than this could be found of the 'dual standard'.

In the Cambrésis, an area of Habsburg territory which was added to the French realm in 1677, the accidents of diplomacy allowed the Church to continue to exercise its old-style jurisdiction over marriage and divorce. Here in the seventeenth and eighteenth centuries (earlier records do not exist) the most common cause of a request for a separation was the husband's mistreatment of his wife. Four-fifths of all the cases begun by women were of this sort. Typically, as in the case of Jean Charles Houzea (1692), discord between the husband and his wife encouraged the man to spend most of his free time (and perhaps part of his wife's dowry) drinking in the *cabaret*. Coming home drunk and distempered he beat his wife on several occasions. In the end the poor woman asked for a legal separation.

In Protestant Zwickau in Saxony, where in theory it was possible to obtain a full divorce with the privilege of remarriage after a period of years, wife beating following a night of drinking in a tavern was also a common cause of recourse to the morals' court. Yet here the city fathers were loath to interfere with what they took to be a man's prerogative to beat his wife whenever he chose. There is the case of Hans Barbirer who in the laconic words of the records from 1540 nearly killed his wife 'again'. Because Hans and his wife could not agree on how their property should be distributed, the court formally ordered them to live together once more in the same house. Whether Frau Barbirer survived to die of causes other than beating is unknown.

In Zwickau, as in the Catholic diocese of Constance in the German Empire in the sixteenth century, or in seventeenth-century France, there was scant justice for the ordinary married woman. In all these regions élite judges, whether in the employ of the Church or the State, expected that ordinary men would beat their wives. Judges normally only took action to terminate a marriage when the parties were of high birth. Such a course seems to have been taken in the case of Antoine Poireau de Rabecque, secretary to the Prince of Nassau and Orange, Stadtholder of the Netherlands. In 1722 he beat and tortured his pregnant wife so severely that she aborted.

Unable to secure a divorce in the courts, in many parts of Europe ordinary people continued to take justice into their own hands. Most marital disputes which necessitated outside intervention probably first came to the attention of village elders or priests. Taking one or the other of the partners aside, they would attempt to persuade them to mend their ways. In England, church courts served ordinary people in much the same way. An alternative form of intervention whenever community norms seemed to be threatened was a charivari or some form of 'rough music'.

Wife sales

In regions as far apart as Italy and England ordinary people who had yet to fall prey to the reformation in manners and who wished to divorce their spouses had recourse to the sale of wives. This practice was first recorded in England in 1553, but undoubtedly arose at a much earlier date; most folk practices found in sixteenth-century England were clearly there in the fourteenth century. Wife sales enabled a man and wife to break off their marriage and marry other partners, something which the Church would not allow them to do.

As practised in the sixteenth century in Essex, Hertfordshire and in London, and in the seventeenth century in Oxfordshire, Warwickshire, London and southern Scotland, the sale of a wife took place on a market-day in full public view. It being a man's world, the established ritual was designed to show that it was the man who had been the aggrieved party, whatever the actual facts of the case may have been. Accordingly, the woman had to submit to being led into the market with a rope around her neck as an ox or a cow might have been. Alternatively, she might be made to ride to market seated backwards on a mule, again with a halter around her neck. When the procession came to the centre of the market, the husband or his agent offered the woman up for auction to the highest bidder. Bidding might be free, but to save embarrassment all round (suppose nobody bid for the wife at all), it was more usual for the whole thing to be arranged beforehand with the man of the *woman's* choice. Although other men might make bids, by prior arrangement this man's bid was the highest. When the offer had been accepted the purchaser would ceremonially remove the halter from the woman's neck. In the eyes of the bystanders he and the woman were now man and wife. The former husband was free to find another partner and live his own life as he saw fit. During the final act of the ritual popular ideas of fair play were also in evidence. The lucky bidder took the former husband off to an inn and treated him to all he cared to drink.

With the public sale of a wife and the establishment of a new and presumably more harmonious family we have come full circle. Our task now is to look more closely at the structures of rural society which lay beyond the confines of the family.

Notes and references

1   E. A. Wrigley and R. S. Schofield, *The Population History of England, 1541–1871: A Reconsideration* (London 1981).

2   Quoted by Carlo M. Cipolla, *Before the Industrial Revolution: European society and economy, 1000–1700* (New York 1976), p. 148.

3   Quoted by J. Ross and M. McLaughlin (eds.), *The Portable Renaissance Reader* (London 1977), p. 222.

4   A. Kussmaul, *Servants in Husbandry in Early Modern England* (Cambridge 1981).

5   Sir Walter Ralegh, *The History of the World* (1614), edited by C. A. Patrides (London 1971), p. 128.

6   J.-L. Flandrin, *Families in Former Times: kinship, household and sexuality*, translated by R. Southern (Cambridge 1976), p. 190.

7   A. Bray, *Homosexuality in Renaissance England* (London 1982).

8   R. Trumbad, 'London's Sodomites: homosexual behaviour and western culture in the eighteenth century', *Journal of Social History*, 11 no. 1 (1977), p. 188.

9   P. Laslett, *Family Life and Illicit Love in Earlier Generations* (Cambridge 1977), p. 179.

10   S. Karant-Nunn, 'Continuity and change: some effects of the Reformation on the women of Zwickau', *The Sixteenth Century Journal*, 13 no. 2 (1982), p. 24.

11   H. Lantz, 'Romantic love in the pre-modern period: a social commentary', *Journal of Social History*, 15 no. 3 (1982).

12   Quoted by P. Caspard, 'Conceptions prénuptiales et développement du capitalisme dans la Principauté de Neuchâtel, 1678–1820', *Annales E-S-C*, 29 (1974), pp. 994–5 (my translation).

13   A. Bourgière, 'Le rituel du mariage en France: pratiques ecclésiastiques et pratiques populaires (XVIe–XVIIIe siècles)', *Annales E-S-C*, 33 (1978), p. 642.

14   Quoted by Caspard, 'Conceptions prénuptiales', p. 196.

15   A. Lottin, 'Vie et mort du couple: difficultés conjugales et divorces: dans le Nord de la France aux XVIIe et XVIIIe siècles', *Dix Septième Siècle*, nos. 102–3 (1974), p. 70.

16   R. Rabelais, *The Histories of Gargantua and Pantagruel*, translated J. M. Cohen (London 1955), p. 378.

17   R. Burton, *The Anatomy of Melancholy* (London 1932), p. 56.
18   D. Cressy, *Education in Tudor and Stuart England* (London 1975), pp. 110–11.
19   Quoted in J. A. Sharpe, 'Domestic homicide in early modern England', *Historical Journal*, **24** no. 1 (1981), p. 46.
20   F. R. Du Boulay, *An Age of Ambition: English society in the late middle ages* (New York 1970), p. 127.
21   Sharpe, 'Domestic homicide', p. 46.

3 *The structures of rural society*

This toiling mass of peasants, cottars and herdsmen is the Fourth Estate, whose housing, life, clothing, food and way of life one knows well. A very hard-working people, that is everyone's whipping boy, and heavily overburdened with services, duties, for which they are in no wise the more devout. Also they are not united but a wild, seditious and untamed people whose activities, customs, worship and thoughts are well known to everyone, yet are not everywhere the same, but instead vary according to the customs of each and every district.

Sebastian Franck, 1552[1].

In this quotation Sebastian Franck identifies one of the great problems confronting any student of early modern society; its great diversity, 'not everywhere the same'. No less difficult is the problem of explaining why some regional societies underwent dramatic changes in the years between 1450 and 1720 while others remained essentially immobile and unchanged.

As a first step in bringing order to the complexities of the real world in times past, historians in the social science tradition often find it useful to create models. A specialized model much used by Max Weber and other early social scientists is a construct or 'ideal type' of, for example, the peasant. In this chapter this peasant ideal type will serve as a point of departure when considering changes and continuities in rural society. Here, too, an attempt will also be made to synthesize the interpretative structures created by rival schools of historical scholarship. Two of these schools, the neo-Marxist and the neo-Malthusian neo-Ricardian, clearly work within parameters set by ideology (although neo-Malthusians would deny this charge). The third school or, more correctly, loose grouping, is part of the open-ended empirical

Detail from 'Summer' by Peter Bruegel the Elder, c. 1570

tradition (which, of course, Marxists identify as part of the dominant ideology of capitalist Britain).

For historians in the neo-Malthusian neo-Ricardian tradition, and here we include the pioneer Wilhelm Abel writing in 1935 as well as members of the more recently created *Annales* School in France, the explanation for long-term rural social change or its absence lies in fluctuations in the levels of human population and staple foodstuffs such as wheat, rye and barley. Arguing that agricultural technology altered but little during the early modern period (admittedly there were no motorized tractors or threshing machines until well after 1720), these historians hold that the amount of food available for consumption on a per capita basis varied inversely with population size; wage levels and land rents were also affected. Anticipating what we will say later, according to this theory whenever conditions were most favourable for peasants – an abundance of good arable land, low food prices, low rents, high wages for their landless sons – peasant numbers began to climb. In time, with the fragmentation of family farms, land again became scarce with the result that living standards and social expectations fell. Wherever this two-phase cycle of growth and decay dominated the rural scene peasants remained peasants; the basic structure of social relationships did not change.

Rivalling this pessimistic neo-Malthusian scenario is the neo-Marxist interpretation recently put forward by Robert Brenner and others. This sees the differing property systems upheld by landlords and the territorial prince or state as the determining force in encouraging or hindering social change among cultivators. The difficulty with this interpretation is that it ignores the role played by the cultivators themselves. This deficiency is born of ideological commitment and reflects the fact that Marx's own opinion of peasants was not much different from that of Sebastian Franck, the mid sixteenth-century social satirist quoted earlier. Like Franck, Marx saw peasants as disorganized groupings of untamed, wild people. But the empirical facts point in quite another direction. Rather than simply being the brutish passive recipients of whatever the forces of Nature, the landlords and the territorial princes dealt out, cultivators who still fit the construct of the ideal-type were fully sentient beings who were quite capable of taking advantage of whatever opportunities came their way even if this meant gradually breaking with customary practices and attitudes.

The peasants who most comfortably fit the ideal-type were the sort of people found in tightly-knit nucleated settlements numbering between 200 and 600 men, women and children. Such settlements were usually found in lowland regions. In the more southerly lowlands which stretched from the island of Sicily to southern Spain and to Picardy in northern France, wheat was the principal crop supplemented by cattle and sheep. Further to the north, in the lowlands of north Germany or Scotland, rye or oats were the staple. In all of these lowland regions peasants lived near the manor house in rude structures clustered around the stone-built parish church. Here they were under the watchful eye of resident gentleman landowners or in their absence – as was the case in most of the great aristocratic estates in Castile – the surveillence of estate agents, priests and of each other.

As Sebastian Franck reminded us, the lowlands consisted of hundreds of different cultural regions, and it is, therefore, useful to distinguish between two different 'structures' in the *Annales'* sense of the word. The first set of structures provided the best setting for the ideal-type peasant and a little changing or immobile village. Such villages were usually far from any major road or navigable river or from any expanding commercial or industrial centre. Yet the actual distance measured in kilometres mattered less than the peasants' own perceptions of space and what they took to be the limits of the known world. The second sort of lowland region had all the structural advantages which the other lacked; good roads, easy access to a city, etc. Yet whether it was the landlords or the peasants who gained most from these advantages depended entirely upon local social relationships and perceptions. For example, in the second half of the sixteenth century the Sabine region in the Campagna south of Rome was ideally suited to provide a wide range of foodstuffs over and beyond wheat to the rapidly growing urban centre; between 1530 and 1600 Rome's population increased from around 30,000 to 100,000. Yet the property system and the absentee landlords' own perception of Roman dietary needs ensured that wheat alone was grown. Rural people's own needs for a more balanced agrarian régime which might encourage peasant initiative and wealth accumulation were ignored. Not until the end of the eighteenth century did estate management policies allow the extensive cultivation of rice and American maize. Here then in a potentially privileged lowland region, the landlords' policies ensured a backward and impoverished rural population.

In most, but certainly not all, upland regions or areas of heavy forest or in swampy regions such as those found along the coasts of fifteenth-century Holland, seigneurial and ecclesiastical controls were weak. Thus, in much of southern France and northern Spain sixteenth-century upland peasants held allodial rights to their land, having no seigneur but their distant Valois or Habsburg king. In barren upland regions where sheep herding was the mainstay of life, supplemented by a little arable, settlement was widely dispersed. Here the scattered neighbouring families only rarely came into contact with each other in the ordinary course of their work. Yet here too there were exceptions. In southern Italy, near Naples, and in Northumberland in the sixteenth century where transhumance was practised, all the menfolk sharing communal rights to pastures in the hills 30 to 60 kilometres from their scattered homesteads left in a body early each summer in company with their sheep and only rejoined their womenfolk at home in the late autumn. Courtroom testimony suggests that mutual surveillance was one motive for this group activity. In all pastoral areas, whether transhumance was practised or not, the theft of a herd of sheep or cattle could wipe out the assets of a rich man overnight. Here, where fortune was so mutable, the inequalities of wealth and status between neighbours were much less marked than they were among the closely settled, less mobile lowlanders.

In the sixteenth century the generous commons and open spaces of the uplands attracted settlers from the lowlands who were willing to forgo the greater security of their own areas. For in the uplands life was precarious at best. With poor soils and wet summers, upland regions were rarely self-sufficient in food and except in years of bumper harvests peasants had to exchange their sheep, cattle and dairy products for essential foodstuffs from the lowlands. In years of scarcity, such as the 1620s, the uplands were especially vulnerable to famine. In southern Italy and in much of southern and central France, in years of dearth uplanders migrated to lowland towns and cities while retaining their communal rights to pasture in the hope of eventually returning.

For uplanders an alternative technique for survival much used in sixteenth- and seventeenth-century England and Switzerland was to take up some sort of industrial by-employment, weaving rough cloth, woodworking or working in metals. In forest areas where the abundance of wood provided fuel for charcoal furnaces, metalworking and mining might well become the economic mainstay of small communities of forest dwellers. Most rural by-employments or full-time rural artisan tasks required only a little capital from outside but a considerable amount of individual initiative. The individualism displayed by uplanders went together with their reputation among lowland people for being lawless troublemakers. Speaking for many of his fellow lowlanders in the early seventeenth century the London-based surveyor, John Norden, found forest dwellers:

given to little or no kind of labour [of the usual agrarian sort] living very hardly with oaten bread, sour whey, and goat's milk, dwelling far from any church or chapel, and are as ignorant of God or any civil course of life as the very savages amongst the infidels.[2]

The great demographic cycle

Personal eccentricities, the presence or absence of communal constraints on initiative, the property system upheld by landlords, and the structure of the region in which a peasant lived all came into play when determining the sort of response local people made to changes in population density. As we saw earlier, by 1450 population levels in most parts of Europe were only half or two-thirds what they had been before the Continent was struck by the Black Death in 1347–9. In the period of reconstruction, which in France lasted from 1450–80 to 1500–20, landlords sought to attract new tenants to their semi-derelict villages by offering lands at low rents and by ceding to village communities rights to forest and pasture. Thus favoured by landlords and the goddess of peace, most peasants were content to go back to using the agricultural techniques devised by their ancestors between 1000 and 1300; there was little incentive to cultivate the land more intensively. As in the past even the better sort of villager continued to live in a thatched and mud-walled hut which they shared with their livestock. But unlike their fourteenth-century forbears who had lived on black bread, gruel and water, in the era of reconstruction peasants could expect to find meat regularly on their table. Yet aside from food, drink and rough clothing there was little else on the market for the peasant to buy. As far as consumer products were concerned no qualitative changes marked this period off from the high Middle Ages; the changes that occurred were only quantitative.

In this era of reconstruction young able-bodied landless men who were wage-earners also had an opportunity to live in a modicum of rude comfort and to enjoy the occasional services of a prostitute. Because labour was in short supply for work on the large farms and in the craftshops in the towns, wages were high in relation to the cost of foodstuffs. In short, even in the lowlands the extremes of wealth and poverty were less marked than they had been a century earlier.

All of this began to change with the inexorable growth of population between 1520 and 1550 and 1620 and 1630, a phenomenon which marked the beginning of the second phase of the great demographic cycle. Once again there was an increasing pressure on the supply of land which culturally-derived perceptions saw as limited (in fact a large portion of northern Europe remained covered with forests which might have been cleared for use as arable land). Already by 1520 in many of the villages of western Germany there were double the number of inhabitants there had been only two or three generations before. In particularly favoured regions near a cluster of rapidly growing cities – as, for example, in Flanders and Brabant – farmers confronted this challenge by aligning their agrarian and household régimes even more closely than before with the needs of the growing urban market. With some justification then one can speak of a rural renaissance (i.e. a rebirth of the spirit of innovation and adventure last seen in rural Europe around 1250). Yet this renaissance was far from universal. In Languedoc and the Hurpoix, south of Paris, after 1550–60 smallholders subdivided their farms into units which were too small to support the subsistence needs of heirs who inherited them. For example, on the death in 1612 of Noël Dangente, a wine grower in Boissy-sous-Saint-Yon, his smallholding was divided equally among his six children. Though one son, Robert, was able to secure leases to three of these fragments from his brothers and sisters the acreage of vineyard finally under his control was little more than half that of his father. In the sheep/corn areas in the Lincolnshire Wolds, described by Sir William Pelham of Brocklesbury, in the years 1618–24 small tenants were giving up their farms entirely and eating their horses and dogs; some were reduced to selling their bedstraw for food. Also badly hit were wage-earners in town-based industries who had to buy their food on the market. Largely because of population increases, but also because of the sudden influx of gold and silver brought in from Spanish America, the price of foodstuffs tripled or quadrupled in the three-quarters of a century after 1580–90. Since the price increases for food were greater than those for manufactured goods, many craftworkers who had no back garden from which to supply their table fell upon hard times.

In a period when the destinies of the various social groupings were changing in relation to each other, two sorts of people were best able to hold their own or even to better themselves. In one group were the holders of middle-sized farms who had effective control over most of what they produced (they had a favourable form of lease or tenure) and who were able to sell their farm surpluses in the local market towns on good terms. Surviving wills, inventories and houses reflect the new wealth and new consumer demands of these middle-sized farmers. In northern Holland peasant inventories from the late sixteenth and early seventeenth centuries show them collecting linen sheets, napkins, shirts, clocks, mirrors, fancy tables, gold and silver buckles and oil paintings. In Bergischland north of Cologne peasants were collecting solid oak furniture and gold and silver jewellery. Everywhere on the Continent peasants began to develop the richly embroidered costumes which distinguished the people of each district on festive occasions. In England, where there was never a distinctive peasant costume, this period saw the rise to full prominence of the yeomen as the acknowledged leaders of their communities. A few yeomen who were certain that favourable conditions would continue during their life-time built new-style houses before 1620. However, most were more cautious and waited until the last decade of the seventeenth century before building the solid oak-framed, five to ten roomed houses which still exist in great numbers.

The other social grouping which, except on the political level, was able to hold its own in the troubled conditions of the late sixteenth and early seventeenth centuries were the great landlords. Confronted by the need to maintain their status at a time when traditional revenues were falling and when status demands were themselves in flux (new style horse-drawn coaches cost a great deal of money) the more competent landlords began to use more efficient estate management techniques. Some consolidated their holdings and managed them with professional estate agents. Others let out their demesnes on short-term leases for monetary returns which could be adjusted to keep up with inflation. Thus in one way or another, by 1600 the seigneurial element was coming to reassert its claims to be the dominant partner in the landlord–tenant relationship. This trend would continue into the eighteenth century and beyond.

In the 1620s or 1630s the rate of population growth began to level off until by the 1660s it had become almost static. Typically in the Hurpoix, just south of Paris, the population in 1700 (80,000 hearths) was at much the same level as it had been in 1640. In Europe overall growth would not again resume until the middle years of the eighteenth century when it appeared – wrongly as it turned out – that a new demographic cycle had begun.

A static or only slowly growing population was part of what used to be called the general crisis of the seventeenth century but which is now recognized to be simply a period of rapid readjustment. In part, because of adverse climatic conditions (the little ice-age), harvest yields in wheat and in other traditional cereals declined; so too did the demand for these staple crops. Moreover, traditional industrial centres in the Mediterranean world such as Florence, Milan and Venice saw the level of their profits melt away in the face of new competition from north of the Alps. In northern Europe, too, there was widespread dislocation. Much of this can be credited to the attempts of rulers to create large nation states with dependent empires and the dynastic wars which these sometimes successful and sometimes abortive attempts brought about.

The toll of war

A useful barometer of peasant well-being was the size of herds of oxen and other plough animals; without these beasts normal agriculture was impossible. If a region was ravaged by soldiers who requisitioned plough animals for carriage or for food, it might easily take ten or fifteen years before herds again approached their former size. Meanwhile, the local human population was short of food and the mortality rates among the very young, the elderly and the poor were unusually high. The cumulative effects of war were even worse if the region was ravaged anew in twenty or thirty years' time; here the peasants had scarcely built up a surplus before the basis of their livelihood was again swept away.

Regions which fit this grim pattern were common enough in northern and central France where four wars were fought; the Hundred Years' War with England ending in 1453, the Wars of Religion which claimed three million rural lives between 1562 and the mid 1590s, the wars of the Fronde in the 1640s and 1650s followed by the frontier wars of Louis XIV beginning in the 1670s. Some inkling of the effects of conflict upon a local population can be found in reports written about conditions in the Vivarais in the Rhône Valley during the Wars of Religion. According to one statement

The inhabitants are reduced to such an extremity that they can no longer survive the exactions and expenses they endure, having nothing to live on for the rest of this year as a result of the ravaging, pillages, ransomings and other hostile acts daily committed on the said province even to the point where their lands remain untilled because of the violence of the war, lack of livestock and dearth of seed.[3]

A series of wars might also cripple a small city which was the focus of marketing and credit for the countryside round about. One such city was Nördlingen in south-central Germany. In 1634 its immediate hinterland was the scene of the battle in the Thirty Years' War at which the forces of the Catholic Habsburg Emperor, Ferdinand II, decisively defeated the forces of Protestant Sweden. In later years, after Cardinal Richelieu brought France into the war on the Protestant side, professional soldiers and blood-thirsty mercenaries on both sides repeatedly harassed Nördlingen. Then in the years before 1714 the city was again besieged by French soldiers, this time under the direction of Louis XIV's commanders. In 1721, seven years after the conclusion of a peace treaty between the Habsburg Emperor and the French (at Rastatt, 1714) the city fathers of Nördlingen reported that because of the ruinous wars:

with their consequent marches and counter-marches, camp provisioning and winter-quartering, extortion from and plundering of the city's rural subjects, not to mention garrison costs, bombings, encampments and conquests, the city has gradually and unfortunately declined from its former sound position and has fallen into the uttermost ruin, so that ... the citizenry – which formerly numbered 2,000 men and included various nobles and other prosperous families [has] now been reduced to less than half its original size ....[4]

One reason why England's cultivators were able to forge ahead with their agricultural revolution in the years between 1540 and 1720 was that they had only to contend with one major conflict fought on English soil, the Civil War of 1642–53. Although no mercenary soldiers who bashed in peasants' skulls to amuse themselves in the lulls between battles were found in England (admittedly, the behaviour of Cromwell's soldiers in Ireland was not much different from that of the mercenaries in the Germanies), even in England small cultivators feared that their livestock and, more important, the social order to which they were accustomed, would be destroyed. Organizing themselves into bands, clubmen fought off marauding soldiers from both sides. These hearty souls can be compared with the wretched peasantry of France in the 1680s when Louis XIV was at war with the coalition known as the League of Augsburg and was busy increasing levels of peasant taxation. In the words of the contemporary social commentator, Jean de La Brùyere:

One sees certain fierce animals, male and female, spread over the fields, black, livid, and burnt by the sun, fixed to the earth which they dig and turn with an unconquerable obstinacy. They seem to be able to speak, and when they rise themselves to their feet, they reveal a human face; and in effect, they are men. At night they withdraw to their dens, where they live on black bread, water and roots.[5]

But even the peasants about whom La Brùyere wrote (he was a relatively sympathetic élite observer) were more complex beings than he was prepared to admit. This can be seen by considering the several characteristics of that useful construct, the ideal-type peasant.

Self-sufficiency

For the ideal-type peasant the patriarchal family, dominated by the husband and father, and beyond that the village community, formed the basic social structures of day-to-day existence. The family grew or found most of the food and other materials needed for subsistence on its own farm and on the lands which were administered by the village community in partnership with the local seigneur. In this almost self-sufficient family economy most of the necessary labour was provided by family members. Over and above its own immediate needs and those of the next planting season the peasant family only produced a little surplus for sale at the market. With the money obtained from selling this surplus the family purchased salt, iron-edged tools and plough-shares and other essential goods not available locally. This money was also used to pay the taxes to the State as well as the rents and dues owing the seigneur and the church which could not be paid in kind. Archaeological digs in many parts of Europe have uncovered thousands of small coins used for these purposes. But within a village community itself most transactions were by barter, either in kind or in labour. For example, among village people in Wigston Magna in Leicestershire, little money changed hands before the end of the seventeenth century. During that century in Sweden, a backward peasant society, even the taxes owing the State were often paid in kind rather than in coin.

Subordination

The ideal-type peasant was necessarily an underdog, a member of a subculture (the Little Tradition) which was subordinate to outside élites. Before the marriage of chivalry and humanism in northern Europe in the sixteenth century (this had occurred in the fifteenth century in northern Italy) these élites consisted first, of the clerics and professional lay people who were educated in the classics – the Great Tradition – and second, of the knights and nobles who possessed a monopoly of the ultimate coercive force – military power. A peasant owed his seigneur or seigneurs (he might have several) rents and fines for his land or tenancy. He might also be required to grind his corn at the lord's mill and use the lord's press for pressing his grapes into wine. The profits the seigneur gained from such uses were known as *banalities*. Other *banalities* included the lord's exclusive right to hunt over the land, his monopoly over fishing, and his right to keep the dove-cote whose feathery occupants ate a peasant's standing crops.

Wherever serfdom existed a lord had the right to claim death duties from the serf's survivors. Often this *heriot* consisted only of the family's best cow, but sometimes it involved much more. In 1524, for example, tenants in Upper Swabia in the German Empire complained to the Abbot of Kempton about the case of Konrad Fraydinng, one of the abbot's local bondsmen. According to the tenants:

Konrad Fraydinng, serf, had a wife who died; he then had to share her inheritance with the abbot and paid him 50 fl. Then he took another wife, who was a free *Zinser*. She died on him also. But my lord again wanted half of the inheritance. He had to give him 30 fl. Then he took a third wife, who died on him also. The abbot then took the half-share again, and he had to pay him 20 fl. In the end he died himself. The half share was taken again. His children therefore found these monies paid out in advance. Nothing was left except 18 pounds *Heller*. The abbot wanted to have that sum as well. He took everything and some of the children had to go begging. They would have been spared this fate, had their father's property not been taken away in this manner.[6]

The weight of seigneurial exactions also rested particularly heavily upon the peasantry in Brittany, Franche-Comté and Burgundy.

Because of the military power which they had always had in reserve and of their privileged position in relation to the Crown, the great landlords were far better equipped than peasants to dictate how landed resources should be used. Thus, around the village of Orret in Burgundy in the late 1660s large landholders consolidated their hold over woodlands and forests so that they could enjoy a complete monopoly over the sale of forest products. This movement was furthered by the Water and Forest Ordinances of 1669 which empowered armed guards to prevent new settlements by squatters. The Royal Ordinances also greatly curtailed the valuable wood-rights which were enjoyed by the existing forest dwellers. Another example of legislation intended to benefit only one stratum of society was the English Game Law of 1671. This Act forbade anyone other than a landed squire and his guests to hunt wild ducks, deer or rabbits, all animals which were probably commonly found in the stew-pots of the poor. According to the Act, illegal hunting could lead to imprisonment or deportation to the wilds of Virginia.

When dealing with sitting tenants on arable land, however, landlords everywhere had to take into account the constraints of custom. In the Hurpoix, for example, custom set the levels of the *cens* (ground rent) in 1500, and despite inflation, which eventually reduced the real value of this *cens* to less than a quarter of its original value, the level of rental payment remained virtually unchanged until 1789. But despite this, the collection of a rent so apparently favourable to the tenants, provided wily landlords with a way to dispossess unwanted tenants. In Wissou, also in the Hurpoix, between 1654 and 1658 estate agents collected arrears on *cens* of thirty years standing and took legal action to turn out defaulters. The hapless peasants had supposed that these long outstanding dues had been forgotten and had used the money for other purposes.

The surpluses which a peasant family produced might also be expropriated by the State in the form of *tailles*, taxes on salt (the *gabelle*) and the like. In time of war the State might also demand a quota of able-bodied young men to serve as soldiers. For example, the Spanish king demanded 200 men from the town of Cáceres in Castile, a community of 1500 people, in each of the years 1552, 1556, 1569, 1580 and 1588; 100 men had been drafted in 1542 to fight against Valois France.

Material, as opposed to human, surpluses were also expropriated by the Church in the form of tithes. Depending upon local customary usage, the tithes amounted to between 8 and 12 per cent of all the produce from the land. In most of the territories which became Protestant at the time of the Reformation tithes continued to be collected, either by the Church or by the laymen who owned this privileged form of property (expropriated tithes). Thus, in total, the exactions demanded by seigneur, the Church and the State (either in cash or in kind) might amount to anything from 20 to 40 per cent (or more) of the peasant family's produce. Their inferior role in the social order, despite their overwhelming numerical superiority, was justified by the theory that peasants received services in return: prayers from the priests and monks, military protection from the lord against thieves and bandits, and the upholding of an abstract concept of justice by the distant monarch or local territorial prince.

Jurisdictional controls

In addition to the economic subordination, pure and simple, all members of a community of ideal-type peasants were subordinate to the judicial authority of members of the outside élite. One aspect of this was centred on the court which the local seigneur or his steward held in the great hall of the manor house. Attached to this court, with its powers to enforce tenurial regulations, were many other powers which had accrued to it during the long centuries when the authority of the central government had been weak. These included the right to do justice in criminal cases and in various civil suites. In France by the mid sixteenth century criminal suites had reverted to the Crown, but in less centralized parts of Europe such as Poland or north-eastern Germany they still remained in the control of the owners of private courts. Some owners retained their courts because they were a convenient way of making money (fiscal feudalism); others saw them primarily as a way of keeping their tenantry in order and of advertising their owner's status. An empty gibbet outside a Castilian grandee's country house left nobody in any doubt that he was a person of consequence. In France by the early eighteenth century many seigneurial courts (there were 70,000 jurisdictions covering 40,000 villages) were run at a loss and only continued because they bolstered the owners' prestige by serving the needs of local peasant proprietors. Properly run, a seigneurial court could provide a peasant with quick, cheap justice in cases involving gleaning rights, illegal pasturing of neighbouring cattle, trespass and many other cases of vital concern to him. In England some manorial courts, such as that at Boughton Monchelsea, still served this function in the sixteenth and even in the seventeenth century, but the tendency was for all private jurisdiction to give way to the overwhelming authority of local Justices of the Peace or to the royal courts. Wherever leasehold or other non-customary forms of landholding such as sharecropping had come into existence, manorial courts also lost their rationale.

It was within the context of his private court that a lord or squire could show himself to be a true paternalist, and an impartial arbitrator of the disputes of 'his people'. These noble attributes harked back to the tribal times of the early Middle Ages, but were given new prominence by the literary men of the Renaissance. In real life these ideas were best expressed by the behaviour of a modest-sized Norman landholder like the Sieur de Gouberville. According to the journal which he kept between 1549 and 1562, Gouberville lived in a ramshackle house, ate much the same food as his more prosperous peasants and enjoyed many of the same pastimes, story-telling, drinking and wenching (he never married). He usually reconciled disputes among 'his people' by using a few well chosen words or a kick in the pants rather than by convening the seigneurial court and protected them from troublesome outside officials. Gouberville was content with the dues and services allotted to him by custom and made no attempt to alter the agrarian régime he had inherited from his uncle.

Half a century after Gouberville's time, in 1600, Oliver de Serres wrote his *The Theatre of Agriculture*. In this book the paternalism becomes more calculating, and the peasants are regarded as an inferior species. Half a century after de Serres had written this book the economic and social responsibilities of landlord and tenant were calculated with even more finesse by Thomas Fuller. According to this spokesman for what would later come to be known as the Protestant work ethic, a sensible landlord:

lets his land on a reasonable rate so that the Tenant by employing his stock and using his industry may make an honest livelihood thereby ... when Landlords are very easy, the Tenants (... out of their own laziness) seldom thrive ... our Landlord puts some metall into his Tenants' industry, yet not grating him too much, lest the Tenant revenge the Landlord's cruelty to him upon his land ... he raiseth his rents (or fines equivalent) in some proportion to the present price of other commodities.[7]

When Fuller was writing in the mid seventeenth century a quite different breed of seigneurial landlords was still to be found in southern France, the noble brigand thief. One of the best known of these genteel brutes was the Seigneur de Montvalat. According to testimony presented against him in 1665 at the Grand Days of Clermont, a special royal court, de Montvalat was not above murdering an opponent to end a quarrel; he kept his tenantry in fear, multiplied their services and *corvées* (compulsory work on roads), increased fines and confiscated beasts and lands at will. Behaviour such as this would not have excited any comment in the early fifteenth century – one of Joan of Arc's companions regularly murdered the ganymedes he recruited in his villages – but by the 1660s, with the reformation in manners, it was no longer socially acceptable.

A fixed life-world

The ideal-type peasant with whom landlords had to deal was by nature a conservative. His participation in the daily world of social activities was largely governed by the interpretative patterns stored up from preceding generations. In this 'life-world' of daily experience, as Jürgen Habermas terms it, consensus and custom rather than 'rationality' were the basis of thought and of considered action. The ideal-type peasant was thus the antithesis of another ideal-type: the 'economic man', but quite unlike the economic man, the peasant aimed only at simple self-sufficiency and a bit more. He was not interested in profits in the capitalistic sense or in setting himself in economic competition with his neighbours. A peasant held that the acquisition of too much visible wealth would arouse the cupidity of fellow villagers, state tax-collectors, landlords and casual thieves, and so he had no interest in working towards that goal. Short-term reserves of wealth were used to acquire land on which to set up a younger son or to marry off a daughter and were not intended to improve the social status of the family in the long term.

In the peasants' life-world risk avoidance was an important element. Shaped by the experiences of harvest gluts followed by harvest failures, peasants were unwilling to venture further than they thought they could reach under minimum harvest conditions. They were slow to adopt new crops brought over from America in the sixteenth century, such as maize and potatoes, or to use new techniques. If a peasant's ancestors had been content to use spades and shovels to dig up the earth rather than employ a plough drawn by a horse or mule, he was content to do the same.

The traditional peasant might persevere in his resistance to change even when alternative life-styles were clearly before his eyes. A case in point is the situation in French villages where customary tenants (*censives*) coexisted with sharecroppers (*métayers*). Through the terms of their leases the sharecroppers were closely tied to the local market economy, but since they seldom prospered (landlords took half their produce) there was little in their more economically rational life-style to encourage emulation. Here *censives* tended to remain fixed to their old life-world.

The space of the village

Each village had its own perceived 'space' and did not readily welcome strangers. Thus the northern French *censives* we have just encountered made it clear that the sharecroppers whom landlords brought in did not share in the 'space of the village'. Perhaps nowhere was the feeling of village space more intense than in the thousands of peasant villages, *pueblos*, found in the Spanish kingdoms. Rather than identifying themselves with their province or kingdom or with the kingdom of Spain, which had been formed by the union of the Crowns of Aragon and Castile in 1479, Spanish villagers gained their sense of identity and their ascription of honour through their *pueblo* alone.

In France until at least the end of the seventeenth century about half of the peasants perceived a known world or *pays* in terms which would have been recognizable to the Spanish peasants. For them the 'space of the village' was limited to the church, houses, fields and forests in use every day by the network of neighbours, and to the scattered hamlets lying just out of sight of the village proper. Yet within most French villages there were some people whose *pays* extended further afield to include the hinterlands around one or more market towns. Such people regularly travelled to these small commercial centres to exchange goods with people from other villages and with traders and hucksters who lived in the market towns. Most of the parties to these transactions spoke the same dialect and thought of each other as belonging to the same culture and *pays*. The perceived *pays* of even more adventurous people, such as the *laboureurs-receivers*, who were trusted with the management of the lord's local estate, might well extend to the whole of the province or county.

The village assembly

The 'space of the village' concept found its best institutional expression in the village assembly or its local equivalent (we will look at its spiritual dimensions in Chapter 5). Central to the working of a village assembly was the notion that in a pluralistic society the village, and the lands which local people worked, was a self-governing semi-autonomous community (or, as the Germans call it, *Gemeine*) and that village members had the ancient customary right to make and enforce decisions concerning all aspects of their communal life.

Although their precise origins are obscure, there is no reason to suppose that village assemblies were particularly ancient. In the German-speaking lands west of the Elbe, the semi-autonomous rural *Gemeines* which worked in co-operation with the lords seem to have been a creation of the peasants themselves in the fourteenth or early fifteenth centuries. Here, where lordship over the village was often divided among several lords, the assembly of peasants provided the village with a single coherent governing body. Speaking of western Germany, Blinkle argues that with their sense of peasant co-responsibility for the maintenance of the political order, assemblies reflected the peasants' growing political awareness. The same sort of process may also have been at work in France, although it has recently been argued that here it was the seigneurs rather than the peasants who first called the village assemblies into existence. Certainly, in France before 1679 no meeting of a village assembly could take place without the prior permission of the local seigneur.

The 'space of the village' concept was clearly reflected in the villagers' insistence that the village assembly meet in a public place which was open to all villagers. In France, a common meeting-place until the mid sixteenth century was in the nave of the parish church. This part of the building had been paid for by the villagers' ancestors and continued to be maintained by an assessment levied by the elected churchwardens who maintained the lands and monies (the *fabrique*) set aside for the support of the services of the church. After 1563 and the Council of Trent, when parish churches were closed to secular activities, some French village assemblies convened outdoors under the cover of the great porch of their church. Others met in a cemetery near the church, in symbolic recognition of the unity of the living and the dead. Another favoured place, particularly in the German-speaking lands, was under the sheltering branches of an aged oak or chestnut tree in the centre of the village. Some humanist scholars well read in the pagan classics of Greece and Rome saw this as a link with the pre-Christian past when certain trees were held to have magical properties; practical minded peasants, however, probably only saw the tree as a convenient shelter in case of rain.

The type of villagers who attended these assemblies and who had full voting rights varied greatly from one region to another. In Lower Saxony in the late sixteenth century only the tenure of certain houses gave the holders voting rights; people who built new hovels on wasteland were not enfranchised. In France during this period all the local *laboureurs* were qualified to attend and vote. *Manouvriers*, landless wage-earners and women who were household heads, might also attend but little that they said in debate was taken seriously by the better part of the village. In Villejuif in Lorraine, widowed household heads were made to sit near the public slit-trench toilet; here they were literally out on the sidelines. Between 1660 and 1702 only five of them attended village assemblies. During the same years the Villejuif asembly was attended by 1269 men. In Boissy-sous-Saint-Yon in the Hurpoix, of the forty-one assemblies held in the early seventeenth century, women were only recorded as being present at two. Levels of participation among male heads of households also varied, depending upon status and the gravity of the matters to be discussed. Of the 120 households at Boissy-sous-Saint-Yon, anywhere between five and sixty-four male household heads attended the meeting of the village assembly.

In Spain, in France and in the German-speaking lands during the golden age of the traditional peasantry, which lasted until about 1550, the members of the assembly met each year to elect a headman; the *syndics* of northern France and the *consuls* of the south. It was the headman's responsibility to bring his fellow villagers into line whenever they acted against the wishes of the seigneurs or other higher authorities. In the German-speaking lands the post of headman or *schulz* was usually hereditary. This was not the case in France until around 1702 when the Crown concluded that a headman of this sort was a useful form of social control and made an effort to replace elected *syndics* with an officer who purchased his office, a venal *syndic-perpétuel*. Yet no matter how the headman gained his office, at the very least village assemblies were able to elect a number of under-officers. These included the village constable or beadle, the village shepherds and harvest watchers, the village midwife, and in northern France by the seventeenth century, when literacy was coming into esteem, the village schoolmaster. In the German Empire in the 1480s and 1490s, at a time when secular and ecclesiastical authorities had not yet reasserted their control, some villages elected their own priests.

Once officials were elected the village assembly set about managing that part of the agrarian régime which required communal supervision. They passed by-laws and enforced them with social sanctions and/or a system of fines. In Castile and in the Basque country, village assemblies periodically redistributed arable land by lot among heads of households who held recognized homesteads (the people known as *etxekojaun*). In sixteenth-century Valencia and in Westmorland in the 1620s, town meetings raised funds to pay for lawyers to defend the interests of the community before royal or seigneurial courts.

In most parts of Europe the golden age of village assemblies was over by the late seventeenth century. In France this institution had fallen under the control of a handful of exceptionally rich local men, the *coqs de village*. Decisions which before had been made following rough principles of participatory democracy were now reserved for the king's chosen official in the locality, the *intendant*. Similarly, in the German-speaking lands west of the Elbe, following the Peasants' War of 1524–6 and accelerating after the Thirty Years' War (1618–48), village assemblies lost their initiative to seigneurial or territorial courts. Through these agencies the territorial princes enforced their *Bauernshutz* programme of protecting peasants from themselves and from their immediate overlords. Peasants were now forbidden to subdivide their holdings among their heirs or in any way to weaken the economic unity of each family farm. Under these conditions of enforced paternalism, the decisions remaining in the hands of village assemblies were only of minimal importance. Yet so long as a village assembly existed it continued to express what purported to be the consensus of the community, which is to say the consensus of the better sort.

Village inequality

Even during the golden age of the peasants, roughly 1480–1550, inequality within the village was a basic fact of peasant life. The richer peasants had access to greater knowledge and power than did lesser people. They were better fed (they had barns in which to store their produce and wider market contacts), lived longer and were less subject to debilitating diseases than were their poorer neighbours. Poor villagers had more children than the rich and were less able to give their growing sons and daughters a helping hand when they were preparing to leave home. Yet it is probable that during this golden age social cleavages within a village were less marked than they would be two centuries later. Temporarily favoured though they were, the richer farmers of the fifteenth century knew that a flick of the wheel of fortune – a run of bad harvests, a farmyard accident, the falling-in of a lease – might cause them to plummet to the ranks of the village poor. This realization kept them within the bounds of the moral community of the village. The same sort of misfortunes, of course, might occur some two centuries later, but by then most of the wealthier peasants had developed links with others of their kind in a larger region which tended to cushion them against sudden mutabilities of fortune. Supported by loans from friends, they could live out their lives in

reduced circumstances and still regard themselves as socially superior to the
life-long poor of their village.

Within a village a man's status (a woman's status hinged on that of her
husband) depended upon how other villagers perceived him. In the lowlands,
status was closely tied to how much arable land a man had under his working
control. In German-speaking villages by the end of the sixteenth century the
highest status peasants were serfs living in the heart of the old village. They
had a hereditary right to family-sized farms which consisted of the best land
and they could generally count on the good offices of their landlords. As farm
managers these wealthy serfs gave employment and short-term credit to many
lesser village people including the free cottagers who lived on the village
wastes. In Electoral Saxony in 1550 nearly half of the peasants in a typical
village were serfs of this sort. During this period in Normandy and in the Ile
de France it was the *laboureurs* who formed what Guy Bois termed the
cellular tissue of rural society. At the very least each *laboureur* owned his own
plough and team; in regions of good soil they held perhaps 10 acres or in
regions of poorer soil 25 or more. Most *laboureurs* employed part-time or
full-time field hands who were either smallholding *manouvriers* who had no
plough of their own or nearly landless cottagers. In a socially well-balanced
village, such as Avrainville or Trappes in the Hurpoix in the 1550s, nearly 60
per cent of the village families were *laboureurs*; in villages around Strassburg,
then in the German Empire, nearly three out of four villagers were *laboureurs*,
the rest *manouvriers* or cottagers. But in Castile, the principal Spanish
kingdom, by the seventeenth century, the number of productive full-holding
families was far less, only one in five. Most of the other customary tenures
were held by paupers or were deliberately left vacant and converted to sheep
pastures. Sometimes this was done without the knowledge of the owner. On
lands of the Count of Oropesa, for example, in the 1630s, crooked estate
agents kept large numbers of tenancies vacant so that they could pasture their
own flocks on the land. Similar processes of converting arable to pasture –
sheep dispossessing men – were at work in the Spanish dependency, the
Kingdom of Naples.

In the Soissonnais, in the Cambrésis, and many other parts of northern
France the old ordered hierarchy of the village began to fall apart in the second
half of the sixteenth century following the disasters of the Wars of Religion. In
each village one or two farmers who were already more prosperous than the
rest secured leases to the absentee lord's demesne and gobbled up tenures lost
by smaller farmers. Among these *gros laboureurs* by the late seventeenth
century farms of 300 to 500 acres had become common. These new *coqs de
village* were seldom fully individualistic or capitalistic in their outlook and
were yet to be fully integrated into the urban-centred world of the Great
Tradition, the world of the men educated in the classics of Greece and Rome.

Nevertheless, they cut themselves off from the moral community of the village and married solely among themselves. As the principal local employers and wielders of power (though their own mental world was in a confused state of transition) these *coqs de village* were in a position to accelerate the social decline of their more traditionally-minded fellow villagers. For example, in the parish of Choisel in Hurpoix in the 1670s only two sizeable farmers remained. The remaining *laboureurs* who as recently as 1662 had possessed farms of their own were now forced to hire themselves out as ploughmen; many poor men and widows were beggars. Similarly, in the formerly well-balanced village of Trappes, by 1665 only seven men held tenures or leases to farms of their own. The remaining ninety-three household heads were *manouvriers*, small merchants, artisans or tavern keepers who lived in small shacks on the edge of the settlement. They were utterly dependent on the custom and good will of the seven great farmers.

In the Beauce, Cambrésis and several other parts of northern France, the *gros laboureurs* also had considerable success in forcing the landlords to deal with them on their own terms. According to the custom of *mauvais gré* (bad will), a landlord could not re-let a tenancy without the permission of the sitting tenant which, local power relationships being what they were, meant the *gros laboureurs*. A new tenant coming in would find that the villagers refused to have anything to do with him. If social and economic ostracism did not have effect, strange fires would break out in the newcomer's house and barns. In the Soissonnais, such was the corporate strength of the *gros laboureurs* by the late seventeenth century that landlords were scarcely able to bring in any new tenants at all.

Neighbourliness

Lying at the core of the ideals which gave coherence to a community of ideal-type peasants was the concept of neighbourliness. Among other things, neighbourliness involved submission to community-established rules and by-laws governing the practice of husbandry, the pasturing of cattle, the maintenance of ditches, fences, hedges, roads and the like. At this level of practice, in northern common-field régimes at least, the concept of neighbourliness was as binding on a landlord who lived up to the peasants' expectations of a proper lord as it was upon the tenantry. This was because the strips of land which the lord held for his own use – the demesne – were generally intermingled with those of the tenants. Here, common-sensical co-operation between the two parties served as a constraint on arbitrary seigneurial authority.

As it affected relationships among the peasants themselves, neighbourliness meant voluntary submission to the unwritten community consensus. This common understanding usually had little direct connection with the laws of the land established by the prince and the local Estates or with the official teachings of the Church. Instead it was based on ancient concepts of natural rights and obligations as modified by local customary usages. Among other things, a good neighbour was obliged to assist the people living nearest him who were in distress with the same generosity that he would show to a kinsman. In order to carry them over a short-term emergency a good neighbour was obliged to give fellow villagers food, clothing and shelter. And even though it might be personally inconvenient, a good neighbour was obliged to attend his neighbours' weddings and join the relatives in accompanying a corpse to the grave. At Seaton Delaval and Hartley in Northumberland in 1592 womenfolk were expected to wait upon a neighbouring woman who was in the throes of childbirth 'within half ane howre after warning'. Similarly, all able-bodied neighbours were expected to take up the arms they had readily at hand – in France and Spain most self-respecting peasants had guns – to join the hue and cry after a suspected thief, a murderer or a suspicious wandering stranger.

Yet in some villages neighbourliness was conspicuously absent. In Sennely-en-Sologne in the early eighteenth century, an archetypal immobile village, local people ignored the pressing needs of their own families and near neighbours and instead preferred to give lavish charity to wandering strangers who had no ties at all with the village.

To be meaningful, neighbourliness required constant surveillance, not only of strangers but of each and every member of the community by all fully-accredited village members. Falling within the purview of the neighbours' concern were the relationships between young unmarried men and women, between able-bodied people at work in the fields and at play, between husbands and wives, between parents and children and between the impotent aged and other village people. The purpose of this surveillance and the informal attempts of village elders to reconcile disputes which followed from it, was not to eliminate interpersonal violence or behaviour which the Church regarded as immoral, but simply to keep violence within manageable bounds so that it would not permanently unsettle the peace of the community. If a man continued to trouble his neighbours by moving their boundary stones, or if a woman continued to abuse people with her tongue, the neighbours might decide that some form of direct action was required. When sexual offences were committed or the proper ordering of relationships between men and women was upset, direct action, as we saw earlier, might take the form of a charivari.

Quite different from their rural counterparts were the urban ideals of neighbourliness as scholars have found them expressed in Lyon, Nörd-lingen, Nuremberg, Florence and Coventry. The urban ideals were the creation of people at the top of society and reflected late medieval and Renaissance ideas about civic humanism. In most cities, many of the inhabitants were recent immigrants who had come in from widely scattered regions to find work and to become – they hoped – upwardly socially mobile. Among such a heterogeneous population no common consensus about civic responsibility and order would be found unless it was the corpus of social policies deliberately created by the controlling oligarchy in the town council and guilds.

Intermediaries

Living within the ideal-peasant village, though not necessarily attaching themselves fully to the moral community of good neighbours, were the intermediaries between the community and the world outside. In his classic formulation, Robert Redfield suggested that intermediaries served to filter out cultural influences likely to strike at the vital core of community routine. However, intermediaries might also serve as the self-conscious agents of change. Most of them were literate in the local written vernacular (i.e. Castilian, Tuscan, Midland English, etc.) though not necessarily in Latin, the language of the Great Tradition.

Intermediaries included priests, estate stewards, small traders and merchants and, except in England, notaries. Unlike most of the unlettered members of the community, they regularly travelled to local market towns and provincial centres of government and (except for the celibate Catholic priests) chose their wives from a wider catchment area than that of the ordinary, less mobile village people. Because of their wider knowledge of worldly ways, these brokers often served as spokesmen in voicing local grievances to landlords and princes.

More closely integrated into the local moral community, yet standing in a special position, were the specialists in something other than agriculture, whose professional activities made their premises a frequent meeting place for villagers. Such people included blacksmiths and millers; even though the miller took his one cup in ten, few people found it worth their while to grind their corn at home. In prosperous regions in the West, such as England, where most people could afford to buy shoes by the seventeenth century, the premises of the shoemakers were also focal points for community discussion. As one would expect alehouses and taverns were also important meeting places. Yet, because they were often operated by poor men and women who had recently immigrated into the village and were beholden to those in authority, they were suspect places. It was a wise peasant who chose not to trust the local publican with his secrets when under the influence of drink.

Common-field villages

Peculiar to the peasant communities of northern lowland Europe was the common-field or open-field village. Here the principal activity was the cultivation of wheat, rye or oats to produce the bread which was still, as in biblical times, the staff of life. From the point of view of jurisdictional controls, the common-field village was divided into three kinds of land. The demesne was the land held directly in the hands of the lord or leased out to a large farmer. Customary tenures, as the name implies, were governed by the customs of the manor or lordship and were let out, using a wide variety of tenures, to peasant cultivators. The third category comprised the lands which landlords could let out to tenants-at-will. Such cottars or squatters could be moved off after they had harvested their standing crops and were not normally protected by the customs of the manor.

From the point of view of the *uses* to which they were put, the lands of the village, and here we include the demesne, were divided into three types. One was permanent pasture and meadow, another the wastes and the forests, and the third the arable land. In northern lowland Europe, the way in which each of these three types of land was utilized was linked to the existence of ploughs. First developed in the ninth or tenth century, the northern wheeled plough enabled farmers to cultivate rich soils along the lower slopes of hills and in river valleys which in earlier times had been covered with heavy forest and densely tangled shrubs. With its iron-tipped ploughshare (blade), coulter, mould board and wooden frame mounted on wheels, the northern plough was too heavy to move by hand and had to be drawn by a team of two, four or six oxen or horses; to feed these beasts some land always had to be left in pasture. In Mediterranean lands where the top soil was more shallow, lighter swing ploughs were used but they too had to be drawn by a horse or, less satisfactorily, by a mule (mules are highly strung temperamental beasts). Farmers who could not afford a plough of their own and could not borrow one from neighbours had to cultivate their lands using hoes or shovels. Hand cultivation was well suited to some of the market garden crops introduced into Europe in the sixteenth and seventeenth centuries, but it was obviously impractical to use in the cultivation of great fields of wheat and other cereal crops.

In large measure then, the standard of living of each village family, and of the village itself, depended on the number of plough teams which could be maintained on village pastures. Without an adequate number of beasts it would be impossible to plough, replough and harrow the land properly. A shortage of cattle also led to a shortage of manure and a fall in the yields on arable land; to say nothing of a shortage of fresh meat and milk.

One technique used when pastures were limited was to introduce stints. Here the number of cattle which a man was able to put out to graze on the common pasture depended on how much arable land he held. In Lower Saxony in the late seventeenth century, cottagers or *Brinksitzers* were allowed to build rough houses on the village wastes and even to pass them on to their heirs; however they were explicitly denied the right to use the village pasture. Yet, if they were lucky they could find a stint or two to rent from a semi-retired farmer who no longer needed all of his for his much-diminished herds.

In addition to the common pastures, another category of land was the waste and forests. Here, according to ideal-type peasant custom, all the people of the village had the right to collect firewood, to cut down the trees and reeds needed to build their rude houses, to pasture a hog or two, to hunt wild animals, to collect wild berries and nuts, and to fish. By using the bounty of nature found in the wastes a poor peasant might even acquire a small surplus to pass on to his heirs. Landless though he was by law, the waterman William Pardye, who lived in the wastes of the fen country of Willingham in Cambridgeshire, was able in 1593 to bequeath his son two cows, a boat, wading boots and other gear. Thirty years later, after Dutch engineers employed by Charles I had drained this land and converted it to rich arable, this level of peasant achievement would have been impossible.

In a common-field village the third category of land was the arable; this of course was where the principal wheat and cereal crops required by market-conscious élites were grown. The arable land itself was divided into great fields some of which were under crops and some of which were fallow, serving as a temporary pasture. Just how many fields were producing cereals and how many were temporary pasture depended on the system of crop rotation in use locally. A two-course scheme was much used in the Mediterranean world, but further north, in climatically and geologically well-favoured regions such as the Paris Basin, it was possible to use a three course rotation. This provided for a spring harvest of winter wheat which had been planted in September or October and a second harvest of rye or barley in the late autumn. Alternatively, landlords might demand that farmers sow wheat as their second crop as well; this was still the common practice on the great plains around Chartres in the eighteenth century. Monoculture provided greater profits for the landlords but left the peasant cultivators much more exposed to the hazards of bad harvest. If they had a choice in the matter, most peasants preferred to cultivate a diversity of crops; then, if the wheat crop failed there was always beans or rye to put into the cooking pot or make into bread.

In a northern common-field régime, each field under crops was divided into long narrow strips moulded by centuries of ploughing. According to tradition, one strip was ploughed by a man and his team of plough animals in the morning beginning at dawn until they came to the headland about midday. After a break for dinner and a short nap, the peasant turned his plough and team round and headed back on the next strip in the opposite direction; the two strips together measured about an acre. But rather than lying consecutively in a row, a family's farm consisted of a number of strips scattered about in the great fields, some under crops and some fallow. This system required farmers to spend much time moving themselves and their equipment from one field to the next and allowed them time to talk among themselves; for them farming was a convivial activity. Moreover, the scattering of strips gave each tenant some land which was relatively fertile in years of normal rainfall and some which was less good. This was yet another example of the peasant practice of sharing risks.

In a common-field régime there was no ownership of land in the modern sense. Instead, over each and every bit of land several people from different stratas of society had use rights. After a harvest had been gathered in from the arable land, all of the less fortunate people in the village had the right, guaranteed by custom, to collect the gleanings and stubble, the grain which had not earlier been collected by the harvesters. After the poor had taken their share, and the gleaning days were over, the entire arable field was thrown open for grazing by the cattle owned by the lord and the villagers. In addition to these communal use rights, the lord might also have the private rights – sanctioned by custom – to hunt over this land.

Despite their ageless appearance, common-field villages were conscious creations probably dating from sometime between the ninth and the eleventh centuries. But if their origins remain shrouded in mystery, rather more is known about how they came to an end. This process was most clearly marked in England. Beginning in the 1440s when population was still low following the Black Death, in several parts of the lowlands enterprising farmers agreed among themselves to allow some land to slip clear of communal regulations and be permanently separated from communal land by ditches and hedges. Depending upon the individual farmer's perceptions of market conditions, this enclosed land or ley might be used either for the pasturing of sheep – wool was England's major export in the fifteenth century – or for crops in great demand on the local market. By the early sixteenth century 20 per cent of the arable land in the common-field village of Wigston Magna had been set apart by farmers in this way.

The initiative for enclosure might come from landlords, particularly when the village was semi-derelict already. In France, western Germany and the English Midlands during the period before 1480 when human population was still small, some landlords dismissed all of their remaining tenants and converted the land on which the village had stood into sheep pastures. On the site of these deserted villages all that remains in the late twentieth century are the slight rises in the fields which mark the old ridges and furrows and the foundations of peasant houses and village churches. Of course, this process was not unique to the common-field north; in the two centuries before 1500, nearly one village in four in the Roman Campagna disappeared.

In England after 1500, dramatic enclosure accompanied by depopulation was far less common than enclosure of a gradual piecemeal sort. In the course of such a process smallholders would usually be compensated by a token payment for the loss of their use rights in woods and pastures. If the newly created landless peasants lived in a parish which was not dominated by a small group of landlords who wanted to control the size of the labour force, they might be permitted to stay on as casual wage-earners; otherwise they might be encouraged to find work somewhere else. Either way, for smallholders the experience was traumatic. For the two other sorts of people most directly affected, farmers and landlords, enclosure was also an emotive issue which might set them in opposition to each other. Both parties fully recognized that life-styles and social relationships in a village occupied by landless wage-labourers and by farmers who held exclusive property rights over contiguous blocks of land which were fenced off and enclosed from other farmers' land and pastures were quite different from what they were in a common-field village occupied by people who held strips in the arable and who regulated their own behaviour in a village assembly.

Divided villages in the Mediterranean world

When a common-field régime in the northern world was fully operative it was worked by a community of neighbours who, despite gradations in status, formed an organic social whole. Such unity was not to be found in many of the villages south of the Alps where common-field régimes had never been used. One such village was Altopascio, 55 kilometres north-west of Florence, on the coastal road to France. With a population of between 600 and 700 in the late sixteenth and seventeenth centuries, the only common understanding which the *mezzadri* (sharecroppers), the leaseholders and other elements of local society shared was that they were all subject to the overwhelming political and moral authority of the great landowning family, the Medici Dukes of Tuscany, the rulers of post-republican Florence. In his recent study, Frank McArdle found that the weight of ducal authority rested particularly heavily on the 20 per cent of the families who were *mezzadri* and the 5 per cent who were landless. The *mezzadri* held their farms by an unwritten contract which could be terminated by the estate agent at a few days notice and owed the estate a straight half of the crop whatever it happened to be. Though each *mezzadri* family was expected to provide its own seed, mules and other plough animals, housing and the inspiration behind agrarian improvements were provided by the estate. Each *mezzadri* farm was enclosed and set apart from neighbouring farms and was maintained as an indivisible farm unit. The physical separation of the farms, together with the fact that Altopascio was divided into five separate jurisdictions were among the reasons why the concept of neighbourliness was almost completely absent. Then too, there was almost no need for inter-peasant surveillance by villagers themselves. Because it was to the best interest of the estate to see that each farm unit was run efficiently using the labour of co-resident extended family members, ducal agents had full authority to intervene in any family quarrel which threatened to immobilize the labour force. Ducal agents searching for stolen goods entered *mezzadri* houses with impunity, and now and again dispossessed a troublesome family to give an example to the rest.

Mezzadri farmers were forbidden by the estate to hold any land which fell outside the control of the duke or take up carpentry, carting or any other by-employments of the sort commonly practised by Altopascio leaseholders. When an occupational survey was made in the 1760s, two decades after prosperity had begun to return to the region after the seventeenth-century slump, it was found that none of the *mezzadri* womenfolk were engaged in weaving cloth, though this occupation was common among women in leaseholding families. Similarly, the task of spinning flax into thread seems to have been preserved entirely for women from landless families. Estate policy also discouraged the *mezzadri* from engaging in any venturesome market transactions. They were forbidden to sell their half of the crop until the estate had first sold its share; in a glutted market the price for *mezzadri* grain would be low. Moreover, sharecroppers were forbidden to borrow money, food or seed from anybody other than estate agents. By law all the members of the extended family were responsible for repayment; though the family farm could not be inherited the family debt was.

Yet built into the life-world of the *mezzadri* was the realization that ducal paternalism protected them from some of the vagaries of life. Ducal agents kept away the roving tricksters and money-lenders of the sort which plagued gullible peasants in many other parts of Europe. Then too, sharecroppers were not called upon to provide family members for military service. Just as was the case in fifteenth-century Pistoia a few miles to the north-east, they did not have to pay taxes. Moreover, the estate instituted several important land reclamation schemes and encouraged crop diversification so that some sort of food would always be available. And if they were in want of bare necessities docile sharecroppers always knew that they would be given a fair hearing if they went begging cap in hand to the Deputies of the Royal Possessions in Florence. For such people abject humility and grovelling subservience were a necessary way of life.

Far more rational in the Habermasian sense were the world views of Altopascio leaseholders. Permitted by estate policy to divide their farms among their heirs, those leaseholders who strove to be upwardly socially mobile limited themselves to small nuclear families and persuaded all but their eldest sons to be celibate. A similar range of choice prevailed in leaseholders' economic activities. Secure in their leases for a term of three lives (i.e. the names of the three living people written into the lease) and as long as they paid their rents, leaseholders could hold non-estate lands, sublease land to sub-tenants (often sharecroppers), grow whatever crops they wished and take up industrial by-employments.

Those leaseholders who made the most of these opportunities could expect that they or one of their sons would become a merchant or a village notable who would be closely integrated with the culture of the élite world which lay outside the village and live in a fine stone house in the centre of Altopascio. But leaseholders who were improvident and fell into debt could expect to become impoverished. Thus, in their freedom of choice and ability to make rational decisions, the leaseholders lived in a mental world which was quite different from that of the harried *mezzadri*. Only the accident of co-residence in Altopascio brought these two quite different groups together.

Peasant indebtedness

Chronic indebtedness was another characteristic of peasants. In Castile, in the Kingdom of Naples, in Burgundy, the Massif Central and the Paris Basin control of credit rested largely with urban merchants, town dwelling churchmen and minor state officials who lived in small provincial centres and market towns. Since these lenders were on the look-out for rural lands to enhance their social status and used credit as the instrument by which they could achieve this end, in these regions we are justified in seeing credit as a tool of 'urban imperialism'. In France this sort of development or perhaps more accurately, underdevelopment, took place around Rouen, Dijon, Bordeaux and all the great provincial capitals in which local Parlements with their hives of bureaucrats were located. It also occurred around many mean local administrative centres, the walled *bourgs* whose leading inhabitants had special corporate privileges, and of course around the greatest French city of all, Paris.

The move to acquire rural estates involved great, middling and small bureaucrats as well as the occasional prosperous artisan who wanted a country place with a few acres on which to spend his holidays. The new owners were usually not unwilling to invest some money in the land. A small bureaucrat holding a venal office who was struggling up the ladder of social promotion and who had foreclosed on rural debtors, first set about consolidating his new holding. He then set about building himself a fine stone farmhouse or perhaps even a château; hundreds of such sixteenth- and seventeenth-century buildings still exist. The new owner then set aside part of his land as his reserve. From this land he provided his town house with his own good wine, his own butter and cheese, his own bread and other foodstuffs and thus demonstrated to his betters and peers that he was a gentleman with solid roots in the countryside. But since nouveau-riche owners regarded all peasants with contempt, the basis of old-style paternalism no longer existed.

Wherever a village community represented by its village assembly had corporate responsibility and legal control of part of the village common land, rural indebtedness might be of two sorts, individual or corporate. Let us look at corporate indebtedness. Whenever marauding soldiers were on the prowl threatening to hold whole villages to ransom, as in the German Empire during the Thirty Years' War, village assemblies borrowed large sums of money from urban money-lenders and local seigneurs to pay for their own defence. With the coming of peace, the village assemblies seldom found it possible to pay off their debts. In France, many villagers made a last ditch effort to save the community lands on which the mortagages were based by raising a common purse, hiring lawyers and presenting their case in a court of law. But since the judges were themselves members of the urban groupings which were building up rural estates in order to enhance their social standing, they seldom found it possible to interpret the evidence in a way favourable to the peasant defendants.

With the confiscation of the common woodlands and pastures and the establishment of urban-owned deer parks and home farms, the traditional economy and social structure of the village disintegrated. A case in point was the village of Noiron-les-Cîteaux in Burgundy. Inhabited on the eve of the Thirty Years' War by prosperous peasants, it was ravaged repeatedly by French and Swedish soldiers and by Imperial forces during that conflict and fell hopelessly in debt to Dijon money-lenders. By the 1650s the legal formalities were complete and the money-lenders were safely in possession of the village lands. They invested heavily in agricultural improvements (a phenomenon which was perhaps less atypical than was once thought) and forced the inhabitants into a condition not far short of serfdom. By 1666 Noiron-les-Cîteaux was yielding the new owners handsome returns. In this instance there was a clear link between rural indebtedness and the rise of a nasty form of rural capitalism. Further west in Avrainville, in the Hurpoix, Paris élites were also intent on buying up tenancies from impoverished peasants who had fallen into debt. Here, between 1562 – the beginning of the Religious Wars – and 1670, the amount of peasant-held property dropped from 47 to 20 per cent.

Such developments did not escape the attention of the French Crown. In an effort to stabilize relations between seigneurs and tenants, in the 1660s Louis XIV gave seigneurs clear control of one-third of all village common land. And to ensure that peasant cultivators would continue to have the capacity to pay their *taille* and other taxes, in 1679 the Crown decreed that village communities should in effect become wards of the state. Under the new régime village assemblies might freely convene without their lord's consent to discuss tax assessments; however, they could no longer alienate land or transact any business of consequence without the permission of the local *intendant*. Once thriving centres of participatory democracy, after 1679 village assemblies became little more than instruments of state control.

Most *individuals* who fell into debt were less well protected against self-inflicted ruin. Individual indebtedness might arise when a cultivator borrowed money to pay for seed, for a family celebration or, as was the case of Jehan Crespeau living in Sunay in the Gâtine, to pay arrears in rent and taxes. In the early modern period it was a rare cultivator who borrowed money to pay for capital improvements which would have enabled him to farm his land more intensively. Creditors often chose to establish an arrangement, known as a *rente* in France or a *censos* in Castile, whereby the borrower paid a modest sum of interest each year and then had to pay off the capital sum borrowed at the end of the agreement. Failure to pay led to confiscation, the fate which befell poor Jehan Crespeau of Sunay in 1576.

In most such transactions the flow of wealth in the short term was from the rural areas to the towns. For example, among the 110 debtors found in Boissy-sous-Saint-Yon in the Île de France between 1632 and 1638 were forty-two wine growers, two *manouvriers* (men whose landholdings were too small to support their families and who had to work part-time for other larger farmers), and a sizeable number of widows. Their creditors were generally well-off bourgeoisie from Paris or Étampes; only twelve of the creditors were themselves men of small means. Yet, in the long term, some of the new wealth might return to the countryside. In the Hurpois and the Gâtine new owners replaced customary tenants (*censives*) with sharecroppers (*métayers*) whom they provided with seed and herds of cattle under the system known as *baux à chaptel*. Equipped with three or four plough oxen, each *métayer* family was able to cultivate lands which before had provided subsistence for ten or twelve *censive* families. As used after the 1560s, this system proved particularly advantageous to landlords; *métayers* owed them half of what they produced. Earlier, when land had been more plentiful and there was greater competition for reliable tenants, *métayers* had only had to give their landlords a third of the crop.

As we have seen, in France and Burgundy rural indebtedness sometimes cleared the way for more intensive agriculture. But in southern Italy and Spain (excluding Catalonia) this seldom appears to have been the case. Here bonds of indebtedness contracted between urban élites and ecclesiastical corporations on the one hand and rural people on the other simply led to large-scale depopulation. A case in point is the village of La Yesa in Valencia. Burdened by a debt of 24,800 *lliures*, by 1681 the community had shrunk to only eighty households, less than 40 per cent of the number only thirty years earlier.

The effects of rural underdevelopment by urban élites were even more severe around Naples, the administrative capital of that Spanish dependent kingdom. With a population of 280,000 in 1598, more than double that of any other city in the West, Naples had provided commercially-minded farmers with a good market for grain during the boom years of the sixteenth century. But when grain sales began to fall off in the seventeenth century – by then most Neapolitans were too poor to be good consumers of the luxury staples – commercial farmers failed to heed the warnings and continued to borrow heavily from urban money-lenders. After the brutally unscrupulous urban élites foreclosed and took control of the land they converted it from arable to sheep pasture. Many of them used their ill-gotten profits to build fantastic baroque palaces, and to commission oil paintings from Caravaggio and his school which today are the connoisseur's delight. But the cost of all this magnificence in the Kingdom of Naples was peasant destitution. Burdened by debt and taxes, traditional cultivators in the upland regions followed the lead of commercial farmers in the lowlands and gave up their holdings. Cut off from the land, they fled to the metropolis to work in textile and woollen industries or – as was more usual – simply to beg for a living. Even after plague wiped out two-thirds of Naples' population in 1656, the city was still dependent upon grain imported from northern Italy.

In marked contrast to the rural misery and underdevelopment brought about by the confiscation of peasant lands by urban parasites was the situation in countries such as England where a second type of rural credit was found. Here nothing like the institution of *rentes* or *censos* existed; instead people in the village or in the next village but one lent money to their neighbours on reasonable terms. The extent of the rural wealth which could be used for loans is clearly shown in probate wills and inventories. In East Anglia and the east Midlands the lenders came from a wide range of social groupings; enterprising graziers who fattened cattle for the market on leased lands, artisans, shopkeepers, small merchants, lesser gentry and small farmers. In one study widows and other single people contributed a surprisingly large percentage of rural credit – 45 per cent – although they only numbered 6 per cent of the creditors. Such men and women apparently preferred to put their money to work in a secure place (bonds of indebtedness were enforcible in the courts) rather than keeping it idle under their beds as French peasants were wont to do.

Typical of the many English wage-earners who lent money to neighbours was Robert Cole of Duxford in Cambridgeshire. At the time of his death in 1662, Cole held bonds of indebtedness worth 12s.10d, though his personal estate was worth only £12.18s.6d. In addition to these bonds and the 5s. in his purse, Cole's estate consisted only of his clothes, his poor hut, 'one shouell and one Iron Rake, and an old bedstead'.[8] Although his household furnishings were little less meagre than those of Cole, a more prosperous labourer who lent out money was Thomas Doggett of Over in Cambridgeshire. At the time of his death in 1666 he held bonds of indebtedness worth £76.

These two generic models of peasant indebtedness and rural credit, the English Midland and the Neapolitan, are probably closely related to two quite different peasant perceptions of the role played by towns and cities. For the English small cultivator, market and county towns were a natural and essential part of the known world; few peasants felt overtly hostile to them. But for peasants in the Kingdom of Naples, in the Massif Central or perhaps even in Switzerland, the towns were alien cancerous growths. It was not only that these walled, privileged places contained the houses and businesses of their creditors and the prisons into which debtors were thrown; they were also the headquarters of the hated tax collectors and the soldiers so often employed to enforce payment.

The burden of taxation

By the standards of a modern western European mixed economy, relative to conjectural gross regional or national product and total population, taxation levels in the early modern period were low. For example, in mid seventeenth-century Castile, only about 11 per cent of the gross national product was taken up in taxes which ended in the hands of the State. However, because of the Spanish Crown's weak hold over its agents in the localities and the corruption of tax agents, much more than this was actually collected from the peasants. Similarly in France, a far more effectively centralized state than Spain, on taking up office in 1661 Louis XIV's finance minister Colbert found that only about a quarter of the money paid over by peasants in taxes ever reached the royal treasury, though admittedly some of the balance went in servicing the state's debts. Colbert tightened his hold over the tax farmers and by 1683 was able to bring nearly 80 per cent of the tax yield into the treasury. This move went along with a dramatic rise in the level of direct taxation.

From the point of view of peasants the difficulty was that this burden fell very unequally on different sectors of the population. In France, where direct taxes such as the *taille* were the main source of revenue after 1439, the lands of the Church were exempt. So too until 1695 were the nobles in the northern two-thirds of the country. In the rising new state of Prussia in 1653, the great landowners in the east, the Junkers, were given complete immunity from taxation. Here the per capita rate of assessment on the remainder of the population was twice the French rate. This situation did not however prevail everywhere in the Holy Roman Empire. In Electoral Saxony, in Hesse and in heavily governed Catholic Bavaria, after the holocaust of the Thirty Years' War, local rulers realized that state solvency was closely linked to the existence of a flourishing tax-paying peasantry. In all of these regions the towns paid proportionately far more in taxes, especially the indirect excise tax, than did rural areas.

In France before about 1550, when participatory democracy was still functioning in the village communities, the urban tax farmers who purchased their office from the state, with a view to making as much personal profit as they could (venal officers), usually struck a bargain with the elected members of the village assembly. The agreed amount was then made up from assessments levied on individual villagers by the village elders. These men felt themselves bound by the constraints of community to assess their fellow villagers roughly in accordance with their wealth.

But the casual old order based on neighbourliness crumbled during the Wars of Religion which began in the summer of 1562. The decay of neighbourliness in matters of tax assessments became even more marked in the next century especially in the central French regions where there was no Estate (the consultative body consisting of churchmen, nobles and bourgeoisie) to mediate between the Crown and local taxpayers. According to a commissioner's report from 1648, when the returns from the *taille* were four times what they had been in 1632, people no longer came to church for fear of falling into the hands of the collectors of the *taille* 'who arrest them even at the altars and take them off to prison'.[9] By the 1660s, when finding money to fight aggressive foreign wars to round off France's 'natural frontiers' had become a major determinant of Louis XIV's policies, the decision about how much each person in the village had to pay in taxes had come to rest with the new *coqs de village*. In the Hurpoix, for example, there were countless instances of well-connected *gros laboureurs* who were able to have their share of the *taille* set ridiculously low and who made up for the short-fall by assessing their poor neighbours heavily. Thus in 1677, Jacques Charlot, a *gros laboureur* in Courances who held land in several other villages as well, was held liable for a *taille* of only 30 livres, while a mere *manouvrier* in Auverneux was taxed 60 livres. Further south in the Gâtine west of Poitiers a rich *laboureur* who had won the ear of the tax farmer in 1661 was assessed only 80 livres; subsequent litigation suggests that he should have been assessed 200 livres. In Languedoc (despite the fact that here there was a local Estate), in the Beauvaisis and many other parts of France there seems to be little question that it was the burden of taxation which finally tipped many small men into the abyss of destitution. Yet all developments were not for the worse. After 1670 a small fraction of the money wrested from peasants in taxation was used to provide permanent garrisons for soldiers so that villagers would no longer be required to provide hospitality in their homes for these barbarians. Similarly in Prussia, a new bureaucratic institution, the *General-kriegskommissariat*, supervised all aspects of army life and provided regular barracks for soldiers.

In France in the 1760s the followers of François Quesnay known as Physiocrats were greatly impressed by the progress of agriculture across the Channel in England. They assumed that the best way to force backward village people to give up the life-world of self-sufficiency and to become more closely tied to the market economy was to compel them to pay taxes. However, the actual English experience in the two previous centuries was quite different. Although English peasants were heavily taxed in the 1520s and again in the 1540s, tax strikes and parliamentary protests prevented the brutish Henry VIII from establishing any permanent direct tax on the model of the French *taille*. By the time of Queen Elizabeth I the principle was well established that the heaviest burden of taxation should fall on the broad shoulders of men of middling means and above who were represented in Parliament. Typically, in Elizabethan Wigston Magna only about one household in twelve had to pay any direct taxes. Although few people were immune from paying *indirect* taxes on consumer goods, either in the form of jacked-up prices for goods which were protected by a monopoly or, after the 1640s, in the form of a Dutch-style excise tax, this still left the better sort of countrymen with the money needed for enhanced rents whenever landlords got around to asking for them. In the meantime they could calculate how best to use the coins in their pocket for the purchase of food and drink, plough animals and consumer durables. Relatively untouched by tax agents (especially if they had access to smuggled goods), small and middling sized farmers in late Tudor and Stuart England were far better off materially and psychologically than were most of their contemporaries on the Continent. This advantage was one of the factors which gave them the opportunity to break out of the fixed life-world of a peasantry, and in many cases to cease being peasants at all.

Notes and references

1 G. Benecke, 'Labour relations and peasant society in northwest Germany *c.* 1600', *History*, **58** (1973), p. 350.

2 J. Thirsk (ed.), *The Agrarian History of England and Wales*, vol. 4, *1500–1640* (Cambridge 1967), p. 411.

3 J. H. M. Salmon, 'Peasant revolt in Vivarais, 1575–1580', *French Historical Studies*, **11** no. 1 (1979), p. 9.

4 C. Friedrichs, *Urban society in an age of war: Nördlingen 1580–1720* (Princeton 1979), p. 168.
5 Quoted by P. Zagorin, *Rebels and Rulers, 1500–1600*, vol. 1 (Cambridge 1982), p. 176.
6 H. Cohn, 'Peasants of Swabia, 1525', *Journal of Peasant Studies*, 3 (1975), p. 21.
7 J. P. Cooper, 'In search of agrarian capitalism', *Past and Present*, no. 80 (1978), p. 53.
8 M. Spufford, *Contrasting Communities: English villagers in the sixteenth and seventeenth centuries* (Cambridge 1974), p. 212.
9 C. S. D. Davies, 'Peasant revolts in France and England', *The Agricultural History Review*, 21 (1973), p. 125.

4 Contrasts in rural Europe

The second serfdom

Historians who are not closely tied to the gloomy historical traditions of central Europe and the lands to the east of the Elbe see the events of the sixteenth century as marking a clear break between two generic types of social systems; in the East serfdom unmitigated by any outside cushioning force; in the West a free tenantry, or at worst serfs who were protected from the worst excesses of arbitrary power by territorial princes and the enlightened self-interest of landlords.

Serfdom of the sort which required heavy labour services on a lord's demesne or on the demesne of an abbey had been common enough in France as late as the twelfth century and in England as late as the fourteenth. But in the wake of the demographic collapses brought about by the Black Death, and in some cases long before, most lords leased out their demesnes in exchange for money, keeping only a small portion of it under their direct control so that they could provide foodstuffs for their own household. The labour services they had formerly demanded of their serfs were either relaxed entirely or exchanged for a sum of money (commutation) or converted into a nominal annual recognition payment.

In western Germany, a key area in these discussions because of its proximity to the East, many lords retained jurisdictional controls over their serfs in a form of serfdom known as *Leibeigenschaft*. Yet over the decades the rights over these controls became fragmented among several lords as peasant sons and daughters moved about in search of spouses, lands and well-tempered lords. In a petty west German principality in upper Swabia by 1450, one lord might have the legal right to control the free movement and marriages of a bondsman and his family, another the right to do justice upon the serf

Detail from 'Country Concerns' by Peter Bruegel the Elder

in his court, while a third had ultimate control over the land the serf worked. If the size of the payments owing to all of these lords was kept within reasonable bounds, which was what the enforcement of the customs of the village *Gemeine* was all about, they need not prove ruinous to the peasant. Though they reduced the amount of cash and surplus goods the peasant had for his own use, they were less exploitative than the requirement that the serf spend two or three precious working days each week on the lord's demesne.

East of the Elbe in 1450 the social institutions governing relations between lords and tenants and between full holders and sub-tenants did not differ in any qualitative way from those known further west; Europe was still recognizably one. East of the Elbe where the *Leibeigenschaft* form of serfdom existed the demands made on serfs were only casually enforced. In part this laxness was a consequence of earlier migration patterns. Beginning in the ninth century with the Frankish Emperor Charlemagne and the establishment of the East March (military zone) against the pagan Slavs in what is now Austria, and then again in the twelfth century under the influence of Christian military organizations such as the Teutonic knights of Prussia, German-speaking settlers from western Europe were invited to take up sparsely populated lands confiscated from indigenous Slavs. Because the German landholding knights urgently needed settlers to work the land, pay rents and serve as footsoldiers, they were prepared to give them land on generous terms. By the mid fifteenth century the descendants of these first settlers were equipped with village charters or declarations of custom and with well-organized village assemblies headed by a *Schulz* whom other villagers regarded as a full member of the moral community. These villagers were thus in a fairly strong position to resist the knightly landlords or the squeezing churchmen who tried to encroach on their grazing lands or raise the level of their rents and labour services. In coastal East Prussia, where landlords regarded all of their tenants in much the same way whatever their ethnic grouping, the indigenous Slavic peasants were also able to keep much of what they produced for themselves.

However, further inland, in Poland, chronic poverty was a way of life for thousands of people who belonged to the *chalupniki* class. Housed in wretched huts with only a little land on which to grow food, they lived from hand to mouth and during the long harsh winters suffered excruciating misery. Not much better off were the very small farmers who belonged to the *zagrodniki* class. Similarly poor were a sizeable proportion of the *szlachta* class, the landed gentry, who constituted perhaps 10 per cent of the total Polish population.

Relative to their landlords in the fifteenth century, the comparative strength of the East Elbian peasantry was buttressed by the chronic shortage of labour and the primitive state of the market. Although the coastal strip facing the Baltic was as heavily populated as northern France – thirty to forty-five people per square kilometre – elsewhere population was seldom more than ten to fifteen per square kilometre. This paucity of population was reflected in the near absence of any towns of more than 1000 people, again with the exception of the Baltic coast and the cities which had flourished in the fourteenth century when the old Hanseatic League had been strong, and of Kraków in the south.

This scarcity of towns had several implications. Peasant sons who perceived that they had no future at home found it difficult to find urban employment. The scarcity of towns also meant that the territorial rulers who followed the precedent of their contemporaries in the West and claimed superior jurisdiction over landlords had no powerful urban merchant class from whom they could borrow money to enforce their claims of jurisdiction over greater and lesser nobles. In turn, the near absence of indigenous enterprising merchants meant that there was no core of educated laymen on whom the territorial prince could draw when attempting to establish a state bureaucracy on the model of those coming into existence in France, Bavaria and England. A consequence of this, at least in part, was that East Elbian territorial rulers were at the beck and call of their nobles and greater gentry and felt unable to intervene in any matter which concerned landlords and tenants. In Poland as early as 1518 the king decreed that his courts would no longer hear peasant complaints against landlords. Of course, another reason why the Polish king came out with a decision such as this was that in that country the king was essentially a figurehead, often a foreigner, who was elected to the office by the greater gentry.

The rulers' enforced indifference to the ways in which their rude warrior knights, gentry and nobles treated their German-speaking and Slavic tenants was not of great moment before the mid fifteenth century. Then with the quickening of population growth through natural increase and the growing demand for food, the price of the foodstuffs needed in large knightly, noble and clerical households began to rise. Perceptive landlords noted that the profits which accrued from market transactions fell into the hands of small-scale peasant producers and they set about redressing this imbalance. As early as 1440 the monastic Chapter at Ermsland in East Prussia attempted to extend its rights in the woodlands and wastes by forcing tenants to spend more time in labour services felling and dressing trees for sale to building merchants and shipwrights. Tenants who lived near coastal streams were forced to spend their precious time catching fish for the Chapter. In the negotiations which followed work-stoppages and protests by the Ermsland peasants, the Chapter won out. However, by maintaining a unified front the peasants with full holdings greatly strengthened their own sense of solidarity.

West of the Elbe in upper Swabia, on the lands of the Abbot of Kempton and the Cloister of Weingarten, and in several other parts of western Germany where market forces favoured the full peasants at the expense of the landlords and the landless in the same way as they were doing in the East Elbian lands, several Ermsland-type disputes occurred in the two decades after 1490. What really began to distinguish the course of social developments in the two regions was the opening of the great international market for wheat and rye in Amsterdam around 1550.

At this time this great Dutch city was overtaking all its northern rivals and was well on the way to becoming the greatest capitalist entrepôt in north-west Europe. A city of between 100,000 and 150,000 inhabitants (about the same size as Venice), in 1581 Amsterdam took the lead in the Calvinists' struggle against the rule of the Catholic Duke of Burgundy, King Philip II of Spain. Five years earlier, in 1576, its chief commercial rival, Antwerp, then a Calvinist stronghold, had been sacked by mutinous unpaid Spanish soldiers with the loss of 8000 citizens and the flight northwards of many of its most enterprising Calvinist merchants and bankers. Within the seven northern provinces, which were later to become the Dutch Republic, Amsterdam was located close to Leiden, Delft and several other cities with populations of between 30,000 and 50,000 souls. Also accessible to Amsterdam merchants, by way of the splendidly sea-worthy ships Dutch shipwrights built, were scores of other cities in the northern world and in the Mediterranean. Though the Dutch were productive farmers themselves – they grew more than 80 per cent of the food needed for the Amsterdam market – country people found it worth while to specialize in dairy products and non-staple crops (including tulips) rather than concentrating solely on the production of grain. Thus the creation of a market for grain in Amsterdam and its effective hinterland – the port cities of the whole of Europe – meant that any East Elbian landlord who established contacts with Dutch agents in Danzig, Königsberg or Hamburg was well on the way to making a fortune. All that the magnate or petty landlord needed was greatly enlarged demesne and an unlimited supply of cheap labour to work it.

Pomerania was one of the first regions in East Elbia where landlords began to consolidate their jurisdiction over cultivators by exchanging jurisdictional rights among themselves and to require heavy labour services either in person or by deputy. Writing in 1614, Bethasar Prutz described recent events just west of the now famous city of Gdansk (formerly Danzig):

In our territory serfdom did not exist fifty or a hundred years ago, nor was it known even before then, but latterly it has been brought in ... with the help of the authorities [the territorial prince]. To sanction this, steps were taken for some of the jurists to draw up regulations whereby a peasant cannot sue his landlord without special permission, or make any claim, much less a criminal suit against him; cannot will away his property, cannot marry without his lord's permission, cannot send his children to the town to learn a trade without permission, nor give them a marriage portion nor marry them off, nor leave them an inheritance .... But he must follow the lord as a vassal, give him aid and support against his enemies, contribute to the marriage portion of his daughter, accept him as judge even in cases that concern him ..., plough, harrow, sow, harvest and thresh in the lord's field with all his capacity even to the neglect of his own, perform other services, carry timber and tend, without payment; feed and lodge himself, put up with beatings, lend his horse and hands, and perform other services required by the lord, or in default of service give money, or for money give corn.[1]

Yet the rapid spread of the systems of serfdom, known as *Gutsherrschaft* and *Gutswirtschaft*, in the more southerly parts of East Elbia which did not have access by river barge to the Baltic coasts cannot be linked to the massive new demand for grains in the capitalistic West. Instead it was a consequence of the staggering population losses caused by the Thirty Years' War and the permissive social climate. In Bohemia the population at the end of the war in 1648 was only about 60 per cent of the level it had been in 1618 when the agents of Frederick, the Protestant Winter King, threw the Catholic Emperor's representatives out of the window in Prague. In the immediate post-war period, landlords from Bohemia to the Baltic (where population losses of 50 per cent were common) could choose either to work their demesnes using wage-labour entirely – obviously an unpalatable alternative – or to hire only a few skilled workers and make up the shortfall by enserfing whole populations. Choosing the second alternative, landlords set to work creating demesnes which were larger than anything known in the West by confiscating vacant holdings and incorporating them into their own lands. Lands in the hands of resident tenants were engrossed. In a not untypical case near Straland in Pomerania, fourteen peasant holdings were replaced by a single large estate. Even where peasants did not lose their lands they were enserfed and made to use their own plough and equipment for several days a week on the lord's demesne. If the land was later sold, they were sold with it; no longer regarded as fully human, they had become mere chattels.

Ironically, by the 1650s the motor force behind the first hesitant moves towards serfdom in the northern East Elbian lands – capitalist Amsterdam – found new sources of grain in the Spanish Netherlands, France and England and was less willing than in the past to buy unlimited amounts of serf-grown East Elbian wheat; between 1600 and 1700 sales dropped by half. Yet so long as there was *some* demand for eastern grain in Amsterdam, and with a recovery of population a growing demand for foodstuffs in eastern Europe itself, East Elbian landlords in the north continued the process of enserfing the peasantry. Further south, in Bohemia, the market pull behind this move was exercised by Prague, Nuremberg and Augsburg (with populations of between 40,000 and 60,000) and by the 'great village' which was the Imperial Habsburg capital, Vienna. And because the system gave the landlords such psychological satisfaction – some people always liked to be surrounded by abject subordinates – it was rapidly extended further east into the heartland of Russia and further south to the borders of the Ottoman Empire where, of course, serfdom and slavery already existed.

In Poland, the consequences of landlords' policies were especially apparent. After reaching peak production levels around 1569, the gross yields of peasant farms began to drop because their menfolk were required to spend so much time on their lords' demesnes. While performing labour services there under hated bailiffs Polish peasants became expert at pretending to work without actually accomplishing anything. Long days were spent drawing peasant-owned ploughs and teams through the fields and stirring up the top soil without actually cutting deeply into the ground as good husbandry required. As a result, by 1660 much demesne land was left to return to waste; that which was still being used for arable could only be expected to yield 2.5 bushels of grain for every bushel of seed sown. But on plots which serf tenants who were highly placed in the hierarchy of serfdom cultivated for themselves yields of up to 4.7 bushels per bushel sown were common – however, this discrepancy was not much commented on by thoughtful men for another hundred years. In part because of the growing inefficiency of agriculture, the amount of grain available for licit sale dropped significantly (peasants disposed of their own surplus in other ways). On the huge estate at Rebkov, for instance, 1000 bushels of grain had been marketed in 1559, but only sixty-six in 1660. Here, as elsewhere in the East Elbian lands, nearly 95 per cent of the wheat and 88 per cent of the rye produced was required to feed the growing number of underemployed serfs on the estate. Even this was not always enough to prevent starvation – the Malthusian positive population check. As late as 1708–11, 250,000 of the 600,000 people in East Prussia died of hunger or of diseases associated with malnutrition. In Bohemia, where the landlords had a monopoly over the production of beer, large quantities of grain were converted into alcoholic beverages to serve as an opiate for the hapless peasants.

Thus between 1550 and 1650 or 1660, the rural social structure east of the Elbe came to be qualitatively different from that further west. In a typical English village in the sixteenth century anywhere between a third and a half of the householders were making cloth, tools, stockings, pins, nails, leather goods or other products for sale in the market towns. But in Poland only one or two craftsmen were found in each miserable village. During the second serfdom the material needs of most peasants were simple – a few crude wooden tools, a shirt, trousers or dress and rough food – and could easily be produced on the estate. Such people had no need of towns.

Village level crafts, market towns and even cities (in Poland these already contained special quarters for Jews) might have been better supported had the landlords been willing to buy local products. However, apart from a few simple items, most landlords who had a disposable income greater than that of a rich peasant serf on a better-managed neighbouring great estate (in Poland many small landlords didn't fit into this category), purchased all they needed to support themselves in a life of material ease from the intermediaries between Amsterdam, Venice and other emporia in the West. Living in great country houses based on out-of-date western models and completely ignorant of rural capitalism and improvement, to say nothing of the Great Tradition, most East Elbian magnates and nearly all the squires adhered to a fixed life-world. In Poland and in formerly Protestant Bohemia this fixed outlook was firmly supported by the teachings of the Jesuit-dominated Catholic Church. In the West, the only groupings of landlords who resembled them were those found in Spanish southern Italy and in Spain itself.

Spain

Early modern Spain remains an enigma. Usually regarded as a vibrant part of the core of western Europe in the early sixteenth century, at a time when it had more large cities and thriving urban industries than France, by the end of the century it had slipped on to the sidelines and became what is known today as an underdeveloped country. As James Casey has recently pointed out (1982), compared with what we know about stress points in peasant societies on both sides of the Elbe and in France and England, relatively little is known about peasant societies in lowland or mountainous Spain (less than a fifth of the country was suitable for arable cultivation) except that they were being increasingly exploited to support the upper strata of society.

In theory the Spanish Crown collected a fifth of the wealth of gold and silver taken from America, where it was mined and processed by Indian and black African slaves. Yet, in a way similar to what goes on in oil-rich Third World countries today, in practice much of this American wealth made its way into the pockets of Genoese and Netherlandisth capitalists resident in Spain. This huge slippage meant that the Crown was poor unless it could raise money from loans on future income or from taxes. In fact nearly three-quarters of all royal expenditure came from these last named sources.

Beginning in the time of Charles V (the Habsburg Emperor who in Spain was known as King Charles I and ruled until 1556), and until the early eighteenth century, the Spanish kings saw themselves as the champions of Catholic and Habsburg dynastic interests everywhere; in western Europe, in

Asia (the Philippines), in America and in south-eastern Europe where they confronted the Ottoman Empire. In consequence, in most decades there was nearly always a war going on somewhere, either with another dynastic power outside the boundaries of Spain or with a rebel grouping somewhere in the Iberian peninsula. In 1571 Philip II (1556–98), far and away the most competent of the sovereigns who regarded Spain as their homeland (something which Charles V had never done), joined with the Republic of Venice and the Papacy to smash the Ottoman fleet at the Battle of Lepanto. Four years later he decided that whatever the cost he would crush the Protestant rebels who had been in rebellion in the southern Netherlands since 1568. This war with the northern Calvinists finally brought him into conflict with Elizabeth I's England and led to the debacle of the Spanish Armada in 1588, and finally to the permanent loss of the northern Netherlands, the United Provinces led by Holland, a region which had already become the most advanced enclave of commercial capitalism and banking in Europe. After he annexed Portugal in 1580, rebellions there and in Catalonia, together with renewed wars with Valois and later Bourbon France in the 1590s and late 1630s further weakened the Crown's shaky finances.

Harassed by foreign powers, rebellious subjects and a small army of greedy aristocratic parasites at Court, the Crown was forced to sell to speculators, bureaucrats and nobles its ancient rights and privileges over peasant lands in Castile and elsewhere. During the reign of Philip IV (1621–65) alone, some 40,000 families were transferred to the overlordship of private individuals or ecclesiastical corporations. Through this process the Crown withdrew from its traditional position as the largely passive protector of peasant populations.

Until the 1560s and the beginning of Philip II's all-out effort against the rebellious Calvinists in the Netherlands, there had been numerous symptoms of healthy enterprise in the still economically underdeveloped countryside. Particularly in the central provinces of Castile – Cuenca, Toledo and Madrid – ambitious cultivators were busy growing the cereals, vines and cattle needed to feed and quench the thirst of the expanding population of the industrial and port cities. For example, in the Castilian village of Santa Cruz de la Zarre peasants took over land from the communal wastes and forests and refused to accept the constraints of traditional village controls. Contrary to custom, they sold, leased and purchased land which they had engrossed from the wastes as if it were theirs by right.

Yet beyond the village were constraints which were less easily overcome. For centuries it had been government policy, particularly in Castile, to set a maximum price on cereal crops in order to favour consumers over producers. In time these controls were extended to cover the sugar and rice grown in irrigated fields in the lowlands as well as the maize and other new crops brought in from America. Moreover, because Spain was a principal point of entry, by way of Seville, for American silver and gold, it was hit earlier and with more devastating effect by inflation than were the lands to the north. Although the cause and effect relationships of inflation are not easily worked out – in an inflationary period *some* people always manage to make tidy fortunes – in the case of late sixteenth-century Spain many small farmers suffered acutely. For example, in Valencia by 1600, cultivators who tried to specialize in olives, wine, wheat or mulberries for the production of silk found that foreign products imported into Barcelona were cheaper than their own. Dependent on selling their products on the market in order to buy essential foodstuffs, many Valencia farmers found they could not make ends meet and had to return to subsistence cultivation. At one time a net exporter of wheat to great cities like Naples, by 1600 Valencia had become a net importer of grains. Even worse hit was the long-suffering peasantry of Castile.

In a period when the near-universal distress in Spanish Europe suggested that the Christian God was putting his Spaniards to the same sort of test which Job had been made to endure in Old Testament times, the Spanish government decided to drive out anyone who was not a believer and of 'pure blood'. Building on earlier precedents when Jews and Christians with Jewish ancestry were banished, in 1609 some 300,000 Moriscos, converts or descendants of converts from Islam, were harried out of Spain. 117,000 were expelled from Valencia alone, between a quarter and a third of that kingdom's total population. For the Christian survivors the effects of the expulsion were beneficial in the short term, but in the long-term simply accelerated the processes of rural decay which were similar to those which afflicted much of rural Spain. For this reason the expulsions deserve closer examination.

With the expulsion of the Valencian Moriscos, their lands, usually only marginal at best, were given to local old Christians. Initially the new settlers were treated fairly. The *senyors* (seigneurs) who had jurisdiction over, but did not own, their lands did not compel the settlers to stand surety for seigneurial debts as their Morisco predecessors had done. Then in 1614 the Crown, under pressure from the seigneurial interests, decreed that the *senyors* could repudiate these old debts. The *senyors* took this as a signal that the Crown would allow them to use the peasants under their jurisdiction as they wished. Too lazy to build up vast new demesnes on the East Elbian model, the Valencian *senyors* used the system of land obligations (*arrandamiento*) to raise the level of feudal exactions demanded of new and old settlers alike. Rather than accepting a level of dues which was set for a term of years and thus provided the peasants with some idea of what would be expected, they began to demand a percentage of each peasant's crop, often a half.

Confronted with these demands the first thing a peasant might do was to sell off his livestock and take to cultivating his land with a hoe. As late as 1724, when much of Spain was finally beginning to recover from the disasters of the seventeenth century, 118 of the 339 families in the comparatively rich village of Gandia in Valencia had no mules or other plough animals of their own. After selling off the livestock the peasants might then mortgage their common lands to urban-based notaries or lawyers or to a cathedral, church or monastery. The inevitable consequences of such actions were indebtedness, confiscation and flight from the land to the towns. In the twenty-five villages around Trujillo in western Castile, where around a quarter of all peasant property was mortgaged in the decades before 1690, the population declined from 25,000 to 15,000. A similar situation prevailed in the far south in Granada. In 1621 a representative from Granada told the Cortes that:

Numerous places have become depopulated and disappeared from the map, in some provinces as many as fifty or sixty, their churches decayed, houses in ruins, property wasted, and fields uncultivated. The vassals who formerly cultivated them now wander the roads with their wives and children, searching from district to district for a living, and eating herbs and roots to keep alive. Others go to distant provinces which are not so burdened with taxation, with the *millones*, the *alcabalas* and other impositions; for it is the weight of taxation and the oppression of tax collectors which are the principal causes of this depopulation.[2]

Denied the opportunity to carry on subsistence cultivation in the time-honoured manner of a peasant bound to his *pueblo* or the opportunity to break free of cultural constraints to become farmers specializing in the production of goods for the market, thousands of ambitious Spanish countrymen adopted the ethic of banditry. This world-view held that anyone who made his living by honest manual labour was a half-wit. Court room testimony at the trials of Pere Cortés of Benisanó, Vincent Ferrer of Torrent, Joseph Vicent of Paterna and countless other artisans and cultivators who put aside the tools of their trade to become bandits in the 1680s and 1690s shows how pervasive the ethic of banditry had become (see Chapter 6).

By the early eighteenth century, under the new Bourbon king, Philip V (1700–46), something resembling peace had descended on an exhausted Spain. In those parts of the country not torn by banditry or rebellion, yields of maize, wheat and rye increased. Allied with increasing yields was a renewed move to break free of traditional village constraints. For example, in Saint-Étienne de Baigorry, in a valley in the rugged Basque country just south of the Pyrenees, younger sons who under the co-resident extended family system would not inherit their parents' properties, began to cut themselves off from the authority of the village assembly. Bitten by the bug of individualism they carved up village common lands for their own use and privately marketed the timber and firewood they collected from the wastes. Even more suggestive of the ways the winds of change were blowing, several village people with landed inheritances of their own began to follow the lead of dissident sons. In a last ditch effort to prevent the sale of stolen timber, in 1704 the peasant court of the valley of Baigorry, which had jurisdiction over Saint-Étienne, initiated a scheme which gave anyone who denounced a private profiteer a quarter of the fine assessed against the guilty party. By introducing a profit motive in the fight against profiteers, the peasant court itself helped to kill willing acceptance of voluntary unpaid collective discipline. The Basques, at least, had rejoined the mainstream of European development. Another group who benefited from the new prosperity of the eighteenth century were the owner-occupiers of sizeable farms in Catalonia who were willing to invest capital in irrigation schemes and to work their farms with the labour of sharecroppers.

Peasant movements

In the fifteenth century Catalonia provided the setting for one of the most successful of the many peasant movements found in early modern Europe. Though the province was closely linked with the flourishing economy of the Mediterranean world through the great port of Barcelona, until 1486 the sort of people who profited most from this prosperity were the urban merchants and the rude undisciplined local nobility. Nearly a quarter of the people in the province owed landlords an especially onerous feudal due known as the *remensa*. These peasants of *remensa* could not move away from their farms without paying their lords the *remensa* fine and were subject to frequent beatings and other abuses. In the decades before 1486 the lords increased their exactions and imposed new ones including the hated *malos usos* (the evil uses). But unlike the situation in the East Elbian lands, the Crown of Aragon to which Catalonia was subordinate (Spain was not united until 1479), intervened on behalf of the peasants of *remensa*. This was part of its policy of undercutting the power of the untamed feudal nobility and of local landholding churchmen. Thus encouraged, by 1448 leading peasant cultivators had organized themselves into a secret inter-regional league. Working through this organization they secured the Crown's formal permission to establish a communal organization headed by elected *syndics*. These peasant advances, together with the royal interference, were strongly opposed by the territorial magnates, churchmen and merchants who together formed the Cortes (Estates) of Catalonia.

In 1462 the Cortes broke into open revolt against the Crown. Military clashes and negotiations dragged on until 1472 and left both sides exhausted. For their part the elected peasant *syndics* decided that the time was ripe to negotiate with the lords for an end to the *malos usos* and other innovations. But when it became clear that these negotiations were achieving nothing a split occurred in the peasant movement. A radical wing under leaders such as Pedro Sala demanded the abolition of all rents and services, old and new alike. In the bitter anti-seigneurial struggles which followed after 1481, peasant troops attacked the strongholds of aristocratic power and destroyed the written records of feudal dues.

As usual in most such peasant movements, in the end the greater military skills and resources of the nobles enabled them to defeat the radical peasant rebels. This still left a large number of moderate peasant cultivators who were prepared to negotiate. For its part the Crown recognized that further bungled negotiations might lead to another long war of attrition and perhaps to the permanent collapse of the rural social order. In 1486 in the Sentence of Guadalupe, King Fernando I accepted the demands of the defeated radicals and abolished all feudal dues and payments. This was done in exchange for a huge sum of money which was to be paid to the Crown over the next twenty years. Through skilful organization, but at a cost to small cultivators and marginal holders which will never be known, the peasant association managed to pay off this debt.

This brief narration of events in fifteenth-century Catalonia has introduced several of the themes which are important in the study of any of the hundreds of peasant movements in early modern Europe. Although they all differed in detail, most peasant movements began when either the local landholders or the State, or perhaps the two in combination, began to increase the level of exactions demanded of the peasant community. The peasants saw these innovations as threats to the accustomed social balance between lords and tenants and as an unnatural infringement of customary communal peasant rights. An innovation such as the introduction of the salt tax (*gabelle*) in Guyenne on the French Atlantic coast in the 1540s or the sudden increase in seigneurial dues as in Brittany in the 1590s, encouraged peasants in each village to organize themselves into small bands and to find spokesmen. Still working only at the village level or at the level of the lordship which shared the same customs, these spokesmen entered into negotiations with the lords and their agents. If negotiations failed there was the option of driving out the new more compliant tenants whom the lords tried to bring in, or of withholding services or rents. Thus in 1522 in Palaiseau near Paris, where lords customarily received a *champart*, a quarter of the total grain crop, peasants refused to render up this due. At this stage most peasant movements petered out ingloriously because the peasants realized that with their powers of extra-economic compulsion the lords had the upper hand.

Only in exceptional circumstances did peasants from widely scattered villages having different lords and different customs establish a large regional organization numbering several thousand members, as did the Croquants of Aquitaine in 1593. At this point radicals frequently came forward and demanded the use of force. Often these leaders were either outsiders from the towns or resident intermediaries between the peasant communities and the culture of the cities. In France a village priest, such as the green-hatted Vicar of Cressac found in the vanguard of the Pétault rebels in 1548, was often instrumental in organizing the revolt.

Among their other tasks the leaders had somehow to legitimize the peasant movement. Often they did this by compelling compliant minor noblemen or gentlemen to join the rebel band and to stand as leaders, a process known as 'forcing out'. Almost without exception, at the early stages of a revolt, peasants respected the need to maintain the hierarchical order of lords and peasants; in this they differed from the *jacqueries* which had swept over large portions of northern France and the Low Countries in the fourteenth century. Indeed several of the great so-called peasant uprisings, for example the Lincolnshire phase of the Pilgrimage of Grace (1536) and the peasant rising in the Friuli north of Venice in 1511, turn out, on closer inspection, to have been brought about almost entirely by dissident members of the local élite. To further legitimize their revolt in their own eyes and in the eyes of local seigneurs, leading rebels might also call upon a village cleric or literate layman to draw up a written programme. In the era of religious reformations, peasant programmes sometimes demanded the acceptance or rejection of new religious doctrines. More often rebel programmes took the form of a demand that the distant king should dismiss his evil councillors (often assumed to be low-born men) and take the advice of ministers who were more in tune with accustomed ways than parvenus could be. For most peasants most of the time the theory was that the king was the natural head of the social hierarchy, the true father of his people, and that he personally could do no wrong. Thus in France, before the practice of rising in armed revolt to protest about new taxes or new sorts of tax officials faded away around 1675, the rebel cry was often 'Death to the tax collectors, long live the king'.

Their preparations complete at last, the peasant bands moved off slowly towards a stronghold or town where they hoped to find arms, money and munitions and to win control of the local communications network. Yet, apart from Switzerland, that strange confederation of autonomous peasant cantons laced with urban centres which effectively won its independence from the Holy Roman Emperor centuries before the fact was finally recognized in 1648, the armed phase of peasant movements nearly always ended in defeat. This was largely because peasant armies consisted of cultivators whose livelihood depended on working the land and getting in the harvests; they could ill afford to be away from home for long. Although they might win over or capture a nearby town, peasants were usually not prepared to travel further afield into unknown country. Drawn up against them were the well-trained troops of the lords with their household retainers and mercenary soldiers, armed with cannon and muskets. Confronted with the ordered armies of the élite, the peasants deserted their ragged army hoping against hope that their presence in the rebel force had not been noticed and that they would escape the retribution which the nobles' armies were sure to mete out. Kings commonly pardoned noble rebels while wreaking harsh vengeance on their peasant followers.

No general explanation has yet been found why some peasant societies rose in revolt against seigneurs or the centralized state while most did not; actual peasant rebellions, as opposed to the ever-present threat of rebellion, were rare. Confining our attention for the moment to late sixteenth- and seventeenth-century France, where there was remarkably little armed resistance to seigneurs, it has been noticed that all of the major anti-government rebellions – among them the Pétaults of 1548, the Croquants of 1593–5 and the Nu-Pieds of 1639 – took place in peripheral areas. These regions still retained strong provincial *parlements* or Estates and a sense of provincial autonomy which peasants no less than seigneurs perceived as being threatened by the encroachments of the central state. Then too the rebel regions were usually in a *bocage*, with small enclosed farms scattered in deep forests and large wastes. Here notions of family and village autonomy were far more strongly held than they were in the open lowlands nearer Paris.

In the sixteenth and seventeenth centuries there were no revolts in the French lowlands even though conditions in some areas were dire. In the Beauvaisis during the crisis of subsistence of 1693 men were kept so busy scrounging for 'measures of rye to mix with oats, peas and beans to make bread to half fill their bellies' that they had no time to seek vengeance on the human and impersonal forces which had brought them to ruin.[3] Later, with the return of normal harvests, traditional habits of deference together with seigneurial controls and the increasingly visible power of the State prevented the formation of any rebel movement among French lowland peasants. But as the French say *l'Europe est multiple*. Thus entirely different from France was the situation in early sixteenth-century Germany where the effective power of central authority in the localities was weak and where paternalism and deference were stone dead.

The German Peasants' War

The German Peasants' War was the greatest of all the rural movements which occurred in early modern Europe. From the point of view of historians it is also the most controversial and the least susceptible to convincing generalizations. In 1524–5 rebels – some of whom belonged to the life-world of peasants and some who did not – created vast regional associations, like the Christian Union of the Allgau, and the Baltringen and Lake Constance Bands, which blanketed almost the whole of southern and western Germany. Though the thinly-populated East Elbian lands (except for Samland in East Prussia) remained untouched by rebellion, in the urbanized regions in the west only Bavaria remained quiet. This was probably because the Bavarian territorial ruler had brought the landlord class firmly under his control and by 1500 had granted the peasantry secure rights of inheritance to their tenures. Elsewhere in central and southern Germany, stress points within each village community and between the rural *Gemeines* and the landlords produced an explosive situation.

In Franconia, Thuringia and Tyrol, all important centres of revolt, serfdom had all but disappeared by 1524. But in other parts of south-western Germany the issue of serfdom was a leading source of conflict between the peasant cultivators and artisans who were specializing in the production of cattle, foodstuffs or industrial goods for the market and the landlords who were doing the same. Here, in contrast to the East Elbian lands, the lords were not attempting to reimpose labour services or to create vast demesnes. Instead, they were in the process of consolidating their administrative and jurisdictional controls over their serfs in order to convert the fragmented bonds of personal lordship – where one serf might be subject to three or four different lords – into the more coherent and financially rewarding bonds of *land*lordship and territorial rule. To this end the lords sought to intervene in every aspect of village life and to undercut the *Gemeines'* pretensions to local autonomy. Because rent levels were securely fixed by custom, one of the easiest ways through which lords could bolster their landed income was to increase the number of cattle which they pastured on village common lands. For example, according to a complaint which villagers from Oepfingen and Griesingen in Swabia presented to their landlord Junker Ludwig von Freiberg early in 1525:

when it happens that a poor man has one meadow or more on which he pays an annual rent, our Junker has as large a stud farm as he wants, who daily pasture on such meadows as are prescribed [by custom]; the village is harmed and overburdened so we claim that we should be relieved from this grievance ...[4]

Elsewhere in Swabia, in return for a fee, landlords granted squatters the right to settle on village wastes. According to Peter Blickle's interpretation of the evidence (1981), as early as 1502 the leading peasants of the monastic estate at Ochsenhausen had complained to their abbot landlord and ruler about his practice of granting their non-inheriting sons and brothers bits of land on the common wastes which inheriting tenants claimed they needed for themselves. Although an accord was worked out between the tenants and the abbot in 1502, the issue still rankled in 1525 when Ochsenhausen joined in the general revolt. This example highlights an important point; in the tense months before the aspirations of competing groups of peasants were all subsumed in the general rebellion the interests of all the people who happened to coexist in a village were far from identical. Artisans, craftsmen and others who had been deprived of land of their own because of local customs of impartible inheritance or the whim of cranky parents, used in their crafts valuable resources which the landholding members of the community regarded as theirs by customary right. In central Germany another group who upset customary land use patterns were the peripatetic miners who came into a village in search of copper and silver. Although miners often had small holdings which they farmed when they were unemployed, they had an individualistic ethic of their own and regarded ordinary full-time cultivators as hidebound traditionalists. With some important regional exceptions miners failed to support peasants in what is sometimes called the Revolution of the Common Man.

This raises the important question about the role which cities and market towns played in the revolt. Cities such as Nördlingen and Rothenburg did come over to the rebels' side and provided them with arms and a focus for communications. But none of the great Imperial Free Cities of Alsace or upper Swabia voluntarily sided with the rebels. At Memmingen, where the famous rebel programme, the Twelve Articles, was drawn up early in March 1525, by month's end the city fathers had regained control of the situation and brought in the noble Swabian League – just back from crushing Francis I of France at the battle of Pavia in northern Italy – to force the rebels back to the countryside.

In most cities it was the middling to low status people in the suburbs who had direct dealings with the peasantry as they went about their marketing – butchers, carters, wine merchants, food sellers and the like – who came out in support of the peasants. Artisans in the same cities were, however, often reluctant to do so. Instead of seeing rebellious rural craftsmen as allies in a common cause they still thought of them as economic competitors who were drawing much-needed business away from the towns. In those cases where urban artisans did in the end co-operate in the great uprising it was only to further their own particular goals.

According to studies of the German Peasants' War which are rooted in Gunter Franz's interpretation of 1933 (which was intended to refute Engels's earlier study) what gave coherence to the hundreds of localized discontents was not economic grievances but the ideology of the Lutheran and Zwinglian reformations. These new religious teachings seemed to suggest to peasants and artisans that the old customs which had been created while the rural life-world was still fixed should give way, not to some rational forward-looking scheme but instead to the Divine Law found in the Holy Scriptures. The two men who drew up the most famous Divine Law programme, the Twelve Articles, were Sebastian Lotzer, a journeyman furrier and Lutheran lay preacher in Memmingen, and Christoph Schappler, a Protestant clergyman from that city. The Twelve Articles demanded that each community be permitted to elect priests who would preach the pure scriptural word of God and that the community be allowed to use the greater tithe (on grain) to pay for their services. The lesser tithe, a recently introduced levy on cattle, was to be abolished. Unwilling to break with the institution of lordship entirely, the Twelve Articles demanded the abolition of serfdom and the payment of *heriots*, and required that labour services be regulated; rents and fines were to be firmly fixed. Further it demanded that all accredited members of a village should have free use of woodlands and the freedom to hunt and fish. In its concluding words the programme stated that:

if one or more of the articles set forth here were not in agreement with the Word of God ... we would abandon them .... Likewise if more articles shall be truthfully found in Scripture ... we reserve these also and wish to have them included in our resolution....[5]

This programme was truly revolutionary. Though it drew on the writings of Middle Eastern Iron Age peoples that had been collected into a single corpus by AD 200 as well as upon the folk memory of a more recent, semi-mythical Germanic past, it clearly aimed at preventing the institutions of landlordship and lordship from encroaching further on peasant surpluses. In place of a system in which the lords had the upper hand, it sought to establish the peasant *Gemeines* as full working partners with a much regulated landholding class. The revolutionary intent of the Twelve Articles is also shown in their attack on the prerogatives of the Church. The pre-war Catholic Church had been so intent on wringing every last penny of profit from the people committed to its charge as parishioners and tenants that it no longer furnished the good-lordship and fatherly care peasants expected. Though German peasants were not actively anti-Christian, they were certainly anti-clerical and during the disturbances occasioned by the Reformation after 1517 large numbers of them refused to pay their tithes. During the German Peasants' War monasteries and religious houses were the first targets to be plundered.

The importance of the Twelve Articles lies perhaps less in its appeal to waverers in the poorer sections of each village than on its effect on the landlord class. Confronted with a peasantry who were apparently united behind a common programme (though some districts created programmes of their own), the greater and lesser landlords and territorial rulers forgot their own internal differences (which had surfaced in the Knights' War of

1522–3) and organized armies like those of the Swabian League which defeated the peasant armies at the battles of Frankenhausen (12 May 1525) and at Bablingen, Zebern and elsewhere.

The ways in which the rebel troops first formed provide us with a valuable insight into the rural social system in revolt. As was to be the case with the Pétaults of Bordeaux and Poitou in 1548 and the Croquants of 1593–5, in the rising of the German peasants in 1524 the first stage was the mutual recognition by the leading men of several villages that they all had grievances which urgently needed redress. In a large, relatively centralized region such as Saxony under its ruling duke, the institutional framework within which these grievances were set was quite different from that of a region where there was no centralized administration and where power lay scattered in the hands of individual landholding knights and abbots whose only overlord was the distant Emperor Charles V.

Peasants were able to gain information about their mutual grievances while waiting for their horses to be shod at a blacksmith's, while waiting for their flour to be ground at a mill, or while talking together after church. Logic then suggested the need to organize a mass protest movement which would force the landlords to come to terms through peaceable negotiations. We can see this process underway in the villages around Baltringen in upper Swabia just before 16 February 1525. According to a chronicler at the Monastery of St Gallen:

When the hour was at hand, at which the fire of this revolt was to be lit, it happened in Shrovetide (as it is called) when people are accustomed to visit one another that about six or seven peasants in a village near Ulm, called Baltringen, came together and discussed many of the current troubles. As was the custom among peasants at that time, they travelled from one village to another as if calling on neighbours, and ate and drank together in convivial fashion; the peasants in the village then also journeyed onwards with them. If anyone asked where they were going or what they were doing, they replied 'We are fetching Shrovetide cakes from one another', and in such company, they travelled about every Thursday and grew every time in numbers until they were four hundred men.

This ever growing company then met at Baltringen and decided to appoint a spokesman to present their grievances to their landlords but, according to the chronicler, 'When they looked around they found no one in their midst who had ever been accustomed to speak before lords or who knew how to broach the matter properly.' Accordingly, they cast around for a suitable intermediary and finally decided on Ulrich Schmid, a blacksmith in the village of Sulmingen. When they approched Schmid he hesitated for a time, saying that he and his family had no quarrel with their own landlord. Then recognizing that his friends' grievances were well founded, he consented to serve as spokesman. Here then was the mediator who had had the role forced upon him.[6]

Yet in other cases men who had contacts both with the literate world of the city and with unlettered rural people seem to have taken it upon themselves to organize the protest movement almost from the beginning. In Saxony there was Thomas Müntzer, a millenarian fanatic. In Samland in East Prussia, where there was a brief rising in 1526, the initiative was apparently taken by Caspar von Kaymen, a miller who had many contacts among the recently-formed Lutheran community in the port city of Königsberg. It is likely that he had joined the Lutherans in their houses at their private Bible reading sessions and looked on himself as God's agent. Early in September 1525, when most of the great peasant armies further west had already been defeated, von Kaymen called a midnight meeting which was attended by leading German peasants and, coming from their separate villages, leading non-German speaking peasant Prussian freemen and peasants. The charismatic self-appointed leader made a speech in which he condemned the oppression of landlords and claimed that they were enemies of the laws of God, of justice and of property. He also gave his listeners to understand that the territorial prince, a recent convert to Lutheranism, would support them against their landlords. For the benefit of his non-German speaking audience he circulated documents bearing the territorial ruler's coat of arms. Thus, through words and symbols, von Kaymen forged an inter-ethnic coalition of men of small property. In Samland destitute and landless men took no part in the rising.

Once the leading men of several villages had grown weary of the double-dealing and prevarications of the landlords and had decided to resort to armed force, it was necessary to bring all the neighbouring villages into the confederation. In Franconia early in May 1525 the leaders of peasant troops warned non-complying villagers that: 'if you do not join us we shall visit you in a way that will not please you at all, and we shall attack your persons'. Within a village uncooperative villagers could find themselves placed under a secular ban. In the Black Forest, for example, leaders of the several thousand strong Christian Alliance warned that its members

shall keep no company at all with those who oppose and resist entering the brotherly alliance, there shall be no community of eating, drinking, bathing, milling, baking, ploughing or mowing with them, nor shall food, corn, drink, timber, meat, salt and other provisions be delivered to them ... nor shall anyone buy anything from them or sell to them ... but let them remain cut off in those respects as dead members .... All markets, woods, commons, pastures and waters which do not lie within their boundaries shall be barred to them.[7]

The landless peasants who numbered perhaps half of the rural population and who formed the bulk of the rebel peasant forces in southern Germany probably did not need the threat of the secular ban to persuade them to join. For unlettered men with limited mental horizons, the sight of a printed woodcut on the cover of a rebel programme (which generally contained words less fearsome than the woodcut suggested) may have been enough to convince them that peasants everywhere had decided to play the part of true men. No longer would they meekly submit themselves to their masters like dumb dogs. There were other types of symbols as well; one was a raw-hide peasant boot which in its roughness contrasted with the fine leather boots of the nobles. Whether placed on a pole or incorporated into the design of the banner carried aloft before the rebel host as it marched through the villages, the sight of the peasant boot was a clarion call to action. And as sociologists of rebellion point out, the very sight of other armed peasants may well have been all that was necessary to win the support of the landless. For these simple unlettered men, the agency of rebellion itself had become the persuasive force; to them the high flown ideologies adopted by the upper strata of peasant society were meaningless rhetoric.

Surviving sources give us some inkling of how the German peasant bands prepared for military action. Meeting in a great circle on a hill-top overlooking several villages the troop elected a commander, lieutenant, supply sergeants and the rest, giving each man his vote in true democratic fashion. In almost all these cases these military commanders were not themselves peasants. In upper Swabia a few of the newly-elected military commanders were mercenary soldiers home on leave. Yet even there efforts to recruit knights as commanders usually came to nothing; knights were gentlemen, peasants and artisans were not. Once officers were elected, the first priority was a regular food supply. Rather than living off the land as professional soldiers would have done, the peasants divided their armies into three or four units and kept only one in the field at a time. The others were sent home in rotation to tend the crops. These arrangements pinpoint the essential weakness of the great peasant interregional leagues which were smashed at the battle of Frankenhausen and elsewhere in the summer of 1525.

What then were the consequences of this great rising besides the loss of between 50,000 and 130,000 peasants killed in battle or slaughtered in their villages? The old orthodox view held that the German peasantry were left completely disarmed and disconsolate; they were removed entirely from the political scene and became 'mere objects of history'. However, more recent studies suggest that after the landlords had had their fill of hanging peasants and had levied crippling fines on rebel villages so that they could replace the draughty old castles ruined in the conflict with comfortable modern quarters, they set to work coming to terms with peasant demands. In 1526 the Imperial Diet at Speyer examined the Twelve Articles of Memmingen in some detail and recommended ways in which landlords could regularize landlord–peasant relationships in the interests of both parties. Although the Diet could no more enforce compliance upon landlords than the General Assembly of the United Nations can on its member states today, in many cases its recommendations were respected and were reflected in new territorial constitutions and ordinances. In many of the small territories along the Rhine in upper Swabia and in German-speaking Switzerland, serfdom was abolished. And although the majority of German peasants continued to be denied political rights in any institution higher than a village assembly, there were important exceptions. In the Tyrol, the Voralberg, in Salzburg and in the Black Forest peasant representatives continued to form one of the units in the provincial Estates. In other parts of Germany, where peasants were excluded from territorial assemblies, the dynasts who were seeking to establish absolute control over landlords and peasants alike now recognized that it was essential to treat the peasants as responsible partners. Especially in the smaller polities, information channels between the very highest and the lowest were left open so that grievances could be aired. Thus in Lippe in 1593, a young serf named Knickencken felt able to appeal directly to the local count when he felt that he had been wrongly assessed for taxes. More than anything else in the years after the holocaust of 1524–6, it was the memory of what a rebellious peasantry could do which guided the thinking of landlords and territorial rulers.

The end of the peasantry in favoured regions

Just as was still true of the peasants in the Loire valley in France in the nineteenth century (recently studied by Gregor Dallas), in the late seventeenth century many of western Europe's peasants still clung to their traditional life-world for all intents and purposes. Though they were willing to use the facilities of the market-place when it suited them, they were still far from thinking in economically rational terms. For them, true security rested with the family farm and with traditional subsistence crops. It never seems to have crossed their minds that the intensive use of family labour part of the year alternating with long annual periods when there was nothing much around the farm for family members to do was wasteful of labour resources and uneconomic. Inured to the life of a peasant, such people would remain peasants.

Yet even before 1450 an important minority of rural western Europeans were well integrated into the economy of the market-place. No longer subsistence farmers, their perceptions were in part tempered by urban values. In the sixteenth century the challenges presented by the growth of human population, inflation and wage/price adjustments encouraged even more people to participate actively in commercial relationships and to slip clear of a fixed life-world. This movement was in no way lessened in the years of crisis in the seventeenth century when the diminished rate of population growth and dislocations caused by war brought about a falling demand for old-style foodstuffs and traditional cloth. In the privileged parts of the northern world and to a somewhat lesser extent in the Mediterranean world rural people – the mentally flexible minority – redoubled their efforts to find new ways of making a living. Closely linked to their changing attitudes, though not explaining this phenomenon fully, was their desire to satisfy recently acquired tastes for an increasingly wide range of foodstuffs and consumer goods produced in Europe or brought in from the non-European world. From tropical and semi-tropical lands came coffee, tea and sugar, manufactured goods such as Indian cottons and Chinese and Japanese ceramics (soon to be imitated at Delft in Holland), and industrial raw materials such as cotton, dyes and timber (the first English chair made of mahogany from Brazil dates from 1617). And from the American lands further north came the potatoes and Indian maize which in time would become the new dietary staples of ordinary Europeans.

Though new consumer demands were most marked in the cities, they also touched many rural areas. This movement was assisted by slow, little-noted improvements in transport; the building of new roads and, in the United Provinces, canals, and of more efficient square-rigged ships on the Dutch model. And even in remote hamlets consumers were within range of peripatetic pedlars and chapmen. By the late sixteenth century, much to the consternation of shopkeepers in the market towns, these convivial gossips were driving pack-horses to settlements which were far from navigable rivers or roads suitable for heavy carts.

For their part the great landlords in the West shared in this new demand for an increasing range of consumer products. Even a cursory comparison of lists of household effects in a noble household in 1450 with those of two hundred years later shows the extent of the new demand for comfortable bedsteads and mattresses, finely carved chairs, chests and drawers and tables, for draperies, hangings, kitchen equipment and clothes for every occasion. One of the most costly items needed by a mid seventeenth-century gentleman and his lady was an elaborately furnished coach complete with springs and spoked wheels. Yet the greater nobility and the great urban merchants who were seeking to accumulate enough wealth to become landed gentry or aristocrats themselves were too few in number to effect a quantitative change in demand patterns.

Before the 1690s, the social groupings which did most to extend commercialization in the privileged parts of rural Europe were farmers of middling or small means and the innovative craftsmen and artisans who had little or no land of their own. Turning first to the full-holding farmers, let us examine the precocious developments in Brabant and Flanders, where the farms were very small indeed. For reasons still unknown, these regions were only lightly touched by the bubonic plague of 1348–9 and subsequent years. This meant that there was still an abundance of cheap labour and a ready market for foodstuffs at a time when most of Europe was suffering from the effects of depopulation. Because most of the new techniques developed by local farming entrepreneurs were labour intensive (there were no tractors in those days) the abundance of day-labourers in Brabant and Flanders enabled small farmers to forge ahead in making innovations at a time when there was little incentive to do so elsewhere. Before they were battered by mercenary soldiers in the employ of Philip II of Spain in the 1560s and 1570s, the farmers of Brabant and Flanders were almost uniquely well favoured. To begin with, nearly two-thirds of the population of the two provinces lived in sizeable cities located near rivers that were tributaries of the Rhine, the principal north–south waterway in western Europe. These cities, particularly the greatest, Bruges, provided ready markets for anything the rural population chose to produce. Then too, most rural people were fortunate in their landlords; rents were low and lease arrangements generally favoured the tenant. Moreover, constraints at the village level were weak. Because most holdings were small, eighteen acres or less, farmers had never seen fit to bind themselves closely to a three field system. This left each enterprising farmer at liberty to plant whatever crops he felt would best fit his work schedule and yield him the best returns on the market. Although the world-view of people in Brabant and Flanders was not recognizably modern, they were, at the very least, well on the way to becoming commercial farmers rather than mere peasants.

Beginning in the late fourteenth century, Brabant and Flemish farmers started to plant a wide variety of crops. In addition to the old standard cereals, there was hemp and flax (for the making of cloth), hops for beer, madder, woad and pastal for dyes for the local urban cloth industry, turnips, beans and peas and a wide range of legumes which local people found helped to restore the fertility of the soil. In their innovative scheme, no less important was their use of every bit of organic material which could be transformed into fertilizer in a compost heap. In addition to their own household wastes, they brought in nightsoil from Lille, Bruges and other nearby cities. At a time when the Archbishop of Rouen's Norman tenants were dumping animal manure into the river Seine, thinking it of no value, Flemish and Brabant farmers were carefully husbanding it. When Sir Richard Weston, an experienced farm manager, visited Flanders in 1643–5, when recovery from the earlier Spanish holocaust was well underway, he was particularly impressed by the way in which local people placed straw in compost heaps to produce a fertilizer which not only restored the fields to good heart but increased their yields to new high levels which were nearly double those found on good lands elsewhere in Europe. Not until the discovery of chemical fertilizers in the late nineteenth century would such yields be exceeded. Not content with increasing yields on arable lands, enterprising Flemish and Brabant farmers also developed important new techniques to provide fodder for their cattle. No longer willing simply to graze their beasts on common pastures or wastes, they established permanent meadows which were planted with rich clovers and other nutritious fodder crops. As a result, there was a great increase both in the quantity and in the quality of meat and milk.

In Flanders and Brabant the secret of success in breaking free from Malthusian constraints and converting cultivators into commercial farmers lay in labour-intensive cultivation and the diversification of crops. But only a hundred miles further north, in the northern provinces of the Netherlands, another pattern developed; farm specialization. Before 1500 this region had been as impoverished as any in Europe; covered with bogs and swamps it seemed to have no natural advantages. Just about the time when the Renaissance was beginning to be felt in artistic circles (it was Netherlandish painters, not Italians, who first developed the technique of painting in oils), northern Netherlandish peasant cultivators with full-sized family farms began to organize themselves into district committees to reclaim swampy malarial lowlands from the sea. Realizing that they could not perform the tasks of pumping and diking themselves, they pooled their resources and hired experts. Thanks to windmills, watermills, sluices and dikes, lands which before had been covered by the sea or salty tidal marshes were transformed into lush pasture and arable fields. The peasant committees also bought out the residual jurisdictional rights of feudal and urban landlords. Fortunately for the course of specialization these regions were close to Amsterdam and to several other cities which provided ready markets for rural products. These conditions favoured specialization in cattle and dairy products on some farms, wheat and rye on others and, later in the seventeenth century, of tulip bulbs on others. The prosperous commercial farmer class which developed was assisted by a class of landless field-hands who, like the artisans and craftsmen, were made to live in separate well-regulated villages. In Friesland, for example, inventories for the period after 1600 show rural artisans and craftsmen to be almost divorced from agriculture; they owned no farm equipment or livestock other than a single pig or cow. Labourers who could not fit into either the agricultural or the rural–industrial sphere were encouraged to go off to Amsterdam or other cities to find work in food processing, shipping or craft industries.

These two patterns, diversification in Brabant and Flanders and specialization and social segregation in north Holland, provided models which were modified and adopted by farmers in many parts of northern Europe. In the

Mediterranean world the models most readily at hand were found in the north Italian plains where there was intensive cultivation of rice, madder, woad, mulberries and vines and where wheat was relegated to a subsidiary position. But whether they originated in Italy or north-western Europe, these models were often first brought to the attention of place-bound peasants by well-travelled gentlemen such as Sir Richard Weston or Michel de Montaigne, or by agricultural publicists such as Oliver de Serres and William Lawson. Beginning in the early seventeenth century, publicists began to publish accounts of contemporary agricultural practices rather than simply relying on what the experts in the late Roman Empire had written. In progressive areas local farmers themselves began to compare notes about the yields of seed and new techniques which might profitably be used. Perhaps even more than the new printed manuals on agriculture, it was the informal chatter of farmers gathered in an inn after a day of marketing which did most to spread the spirit of innovation.

The effects of all this were noticeable in France. In 1600 the authors of *La Maison Rustique* observed that:

a good farmer will make a profit from everything, and there is not (as we say) so much as the garlic and onion which he will not raise gain of by selling them at fairs most fitting for their time and season, and so help himself thereof and fill his purse with money.[8]

By 1620 it was possible for visitors to France to ignore the countless immobile villages where the peasant way of life had changed little since the late stone age – one recalls La Bruyère's 'certain fierce animals, male and female, spread over the fields, black, livid and burnt by the sun' – and instead to see a nation blessed with an abundance of fruit orchards, mulberry trees, olive groves, fine fat cattle and, of course, vines; it was during this period that quality French *vintage* wines, as opposed to wines which were barely drinkable, began to be produced.

In England the new ideas about how best to use the soil and water resources have justly been called an agricultural revolution. In the years after 1550, this revolution involved the extensive use of nitrate-fixing crops, such as clover, and of fertilizers on light sandy soils which had earlier produced only indifferent harvests. These innovations could be applied by small farmers at a modest cost. Thus in 1688, one could find clover seeds for sale in the shops in Exeter in Devonshire for only two or three pence a pound. This level of pricing – and this type of distribution system – explains why, between 1675 and 1720, yields increased by more than 11 per cent, an increase which was far greater than the rate of population growth.

Paralleling these developments in southern England was the conversion of arable fields in the heavy clay soils of the Midlands into properly managed pastures which after a period of years could be converted back into well-managed arable. Although, of course, it was easier for a large holder than a small farmer to try his hand at convertible husbandry, the process was not utterly beyond the financial capabilities of an innovative, calculating middle-sized farmer. In Herefordshire, Wiltshire and other parts of southern and western England, middling and large farmers who had access to capital created water meadows (pastures lightly flooded in the winter months) to provide cattle with rich fodder all the year round. At a time when agriculture in most parts of France was developing at a slower pace than in England, the greater material well-being of the English was undoubtedly due to the greater abundance of cattle, not only for ploughing, but also as the source of the Roast Beef of Old England. The average Frenchman had difficulty even in finding pork for his stew-pot.

In England the burst of improvements which began in the 1550s particularly favoured yeomen freeholders, who, as a class, held between 25 and 33 per cent of the land. It was not until the period of 1670–1710 that they were finally overshadowed as agricultural pacesetters by the great landlords and the gentry who between them had come to hold 55 to 70 per cent of the land. Even in the latter period, however, middle-sized farmers continued to thrive; some remained independent owner-occupiers closely tied to the market, others became prosperous tenant-farmers who invested capital in their enterprises and who held leases from capitalistic landlords. Besides the capitalistic landlords and the capitalistic tenant-farmers, the classic triangle of eighteenth-century England also included the hundreds of thousands of wage-earning field-hands who no longer held any land or use-rights of their own. Landless though they were, many of them retained the attitudes typical of the life-world of a peasant well into the nineteenth century.

For the small man who *did* have a little land under his control but who wanted to break free of the peasant mould while retaining his independence, one alternative was market gardening. Indeed, when confronted with this option, the question became not how much land was available but how the little there was could best be used and how new dietary tastes could be instilled into the minds of consumers. Fortunately for market gardeners, as the sixteenth century wore on there was a weakening of culturally-derived taste taboos for strange new foods among the rich, the middling sort and, to a lesser degree, the poor. Provided with the incentive of ready sales, market gardeners could grow lettuce, cauliflowers, artichokes and a whole range of other plants which required intensive cultivation and the use of new techniques. Many of these innovations began in France and the Low Countries and included such things as planting the seeds in rows (rather than sowing them broadcast), frequent weeding and the use of glass bell-jars which increased the temperature in the immediate environment of the plant. Since it required full-time work by the whole family and daily or twice-weekly trips to the produce market in Amsterdam, Paris, London or other large cities, market gardening was obviously not an option open to every poor man.

For people who lived further from urban centres and who were seasonally employed in other tasks there were some new crops which they could grow to supplement their incomes. In Veluwe, east of Utrecht, in the Hainault in the Spanish Netherlands and in the Vale of Tewkesbury in western England one of the most important of these new labour-intensive crops was tobacco. Selling at between £25 and £100 an acre the profits from tobacco sales were far in excess of a comparable acreage of wheat or rye. More important cultivation could be made to dovetail nicely into the work schedule required of labourers who were seasonally employed in the cultivation of staple crops. Tobacco was planted in April and May, after the cereals had been sown, and harvested in August and September, after the wheat and rye had been brought in. Curing and processing took place in November at a time when most labourers would otherwise be idle. As practised in western England around 1619, tobacco growing required the active participation of three strata of society. Intermediaries, such as the London-based merchant entrepreneur John Stratford, provided labourers with the necessary contacts with landlords. When the profit was split three ways the labourers found themselves with a welcome new source of disposable income which they could use to buy new textiles, reasonably well-made furniture and the new range of foodstuffs which had been introduced into Europe by European explorers. Theirs was no longer the life-world of the peasant.

In addition to new crops there were also the options offered by the development of domestic industries, for example, rural cloth-making, knitting, metalworking, woodworking, leather-working. None of these industries demanded heavy concentrations of capital but were labour-intensive and nicely fitted the capabilities of underemployed people who were innocent of capital but willing to use their time profitably. In England the regions where proto-industries were most likely to develop were the uplands where the practice of pastoralism left many people with time to spare. By way of contrast, in France, the area in which domestic industry flourished was the corn-growing lowland regions where farmers held plots of land which were too small to occupy all their attention during the daylight hours. Yet even in the uplands of the Massif Central, people who were loath to make ends meet by begging or migrating elsewhere found it worth their while to rear silkworms, harvest chestnuts or make up a bit of cloth at home.

More than anything else, it was the availability of raw materials which determined which sort of by-employment local people would take up. In the sheep-rearing moorland regions of the German Empire local people spent their spare time making woollen cloth. In Rhineland areas, where local farmers grew flax, the production of linen cloth was carried out. In the Techenburg area, where smallholders grew both hemp and flax and where there was a market for strong sails, poor people spent their otherwise idle hours making canvas.

In the most favourable circumstances the rise of rural industry permitted a poor family to begin to govern its productive activities with the objective of accumulating a profit which could be used to purchase new foods and consumer durables made by other poor people like themselves. This objective was quite alien to the ethic of the true peasant. Yet the size of the profit depended entirely on how the rural industry was organized. Best suited to reap a sizeable disposable surplus were those who were able to grow their own hemp, flax or wool or who had use-rights to forest products, and those who were able to market their products themselves. But in many parts of Europe another system developed, the putting-out system or, as the Germans called it, the *Verlagssystem*. Here the initiative and most of the profits accrued to urban or rural entrepreneurs who provided weavers, for example, with the raw materials and credit and came back at the end of the week to pick up the finished cloth for sale in the market towns which were out of range of the producer. When markets were buoyant both parties benefited, but when markets collapsed it was the village worker who was left with outstanding debts and dashed hopes. At best the *Verlagssystem* was exploitative.

The development of rural industry and the expansion of commercial relationships which went with it were thus among the factors which produced a new complex of tensions in the countryside. No longer was every person tied down to a nicely ordered agrarian régime where lords, priests, greater and lesser tenants and wage-labourers knew what was expected of them. Little wonder that in nearly all of the religious institutions which were in the control of the élites in the sixteenth century and later ordinary people were enjoined to submit meekly to duly constituted authority. This then brings us to the world of the supernatural.

Notes and references

1 H. Kamen, *The Iron Century: Social Change in Europe 1550–1660* (London 1971), pp. 219–20.
2 J. Lynch, *Spain under the Hapsburgs*, vol. 2 (London 1969), p. 144.
3 P. Goubert, 'The French peasantry of the seventeenth century: a regional example', *Past and Present*, no. 10 (1956).
4 Quoted by H. Cohn, 'Peasants of Swabia, 1525', *Journal of Peasant Studies*, 3 (1975), p. 19.

5 ibid., p. 18.
6 ibid., p. 25.
7 ibid., p. 27.
8 Quoted by J. Thirsk, 'Policies for retrenchment in seventeenth century Europe', *Comparative Studies in Society and History*, **22** no. 4 (1980), p. 633.

5 *The supernatural and the rural world*

In the long era of unrest, anticipation and reformation which lasted from 1450 to 1648 and beyond, shared religious beliefs and practices – using the word religious in its broadest sense – served in some corners of Europe as a cement which bound families, villages and whole regional societies together. Yet in others, particularly after late medieval heresies began to re-emerge and in Protestant forms to triumph, religious ideals and practices were corrosives which dissolved old unities into factions and left contenders in a state of mutual incomprehension.

In marked contrast to late twentieth-century post-Christian Europe, at the beginning of the early modern period one thing which all Europeans had in common – with the possible exception of fatalistic beggars and other people at the limits of misery – was their belief in the existence of supernatural powers. Whether of pre-Christian pagan or of Christian provenance (here a Christian is defined as one who believes that the Jesus of Nazareth who was crucified around AD 30 was the Son of God and that together with the Holy Ghost, Christ and God the Father form the Holy Trinity), these supernatural powers were thought to intervene constantly in the petty daily affairs of men and women. These powers could be placated by corporate ritual or by individual practices which were based on the community's common expectations; at that time religion was not an individual's own private affair. Then with the coming of the Protestant and Catholic reformations after 1517, an increasingly sizeable minority of townspeople – privileged bourgeoisie, artisans and craftsmen – and in socially differentiated villages, the better sort of countrymen, came to reassess the role of the sacred in their daily lives. Although traces of older thought patterns based on community solidarity rather than on the niceties of theology continued in the hidden recesses of

Detail from 'The Witch of Mallaghem' by Peter Bruegel the Elder

their minds, like tea leaves at the bottom of a pot, in public such people came to confine their belief in the supernatural not to a host of nameless powers but to the single transcendental Christian God. They also held that the salvation of their immortal souls depended upon each individual's personal acceptance of the Christian God either through the mediation of the Church (the Catholic tenet) or through faith alone (the Protestant). This acceptance by the better sort and their imitators of a more individualized and less communal form of Christianity in time led them to try to convert all rural people to their new ways of thought. Europeans who had only recently discarded older forms of thought for a new 'truth' were not notably tolerant of those who had yet to do so. In some regions acculturation with the new essentially urban-based ideals proceeded smartly and left few casualties. In others the process was much more bloody (the French Wars of Religion, the Spanish *auto de fe*, the coercive policies of Duke Albert V in Bavaria before 1579) and remained incomplete at the beginning of the eighteenth century.

A world of anxiety

For the late twentieth-century European who is part of the despiritualized post-Christian world in which death by starvation need not occur (though it sometimes does) and in which people can expect to live out their allotted three-score and ten in dignity, it requires a very considerable effort to visualize a world in which fear and chronic insecurity played dominant roles in shaping people's life-world. Despite the presence of medical doctors and village healers, in early modern Europe there was almost no known way to overcome even the trivial diseases which left unattended resulted in debilitation and death. Moreover, despite pragmatic, unsystematic improvements in agriculture in a few favoured regions (see Chapter 4) adequate famine relief measures and scientific harvest controls were unknown. And at a time when banks and insurance policies did not for all practical purposes exist most people kept their wealth in flimsy barns and houses which could easily be destroyed by fire or flash floods.

Yet confronted with the wreckages strewn about by the Four Horsemen of the Apocalypse either in their own time or in the recent past, ordinary unregenerate Europeans refused to give way to total despair. Instead, they convinced themselves that through corporate and individual ritual acts sanctioned by local custom and picked from the incoherent rag-bag of pagan Teutonic, Celtic, late Classical and Christian ideas which rattled around in the life-world of a traditional peasant, it was possible to compel the forces which controlled the world to act on their behalf. In this they differed markedly from the ever growing minority of fully authentic Christians who believed in the doctrine of original sin and in accepting meekly with prayer and resignation the punishments which the just God hurled down upon them.

Ordinary unregenerate early modern Europeans demanded several things from whatever form of belief in supernatural forces they consciously or unconsciously considered to be their religion. This religion had to provide them with ways to restore good health (most of them were suffering from at least one chronic disease); it had to provide for the protection or the restoration of human fertility so that the human stock of the village could be perpetuated; it had to provide ways of securing a good harvest, healthy herds and adequate food; it had to provide enough rain for the crops and protection from floods and hailstorms; it had to provide protection from fire and from outside spiritual or human interference; and finally religion had to provide ways to ensure sociability among the living and between the living and the dead.

Something of the flavour of the old rural beliefs, together with the horror with which they were regarded by Christian clerics who thought in terms of a dichotomy between religion and superstition (superstition was anything not authorized by the Christian Church to which the cleric belonged) is contained in a visitation report written by a German cleric in 1594, some seventy-seven years after Martin Luther had nailed his famous ninety-five theses to the door of the Castle Church in Wittenberg. Writing of the behaviour of the people in the county of Nassau-Wiesbaden, the cleric found that

the use of spells is so widespread ... that not a man or woman begins, undertakes, does or refrains from doing anything ... without employing some particular blessing, incantation, spell, or other such heathenish means. To wit: in pangs of childbirth ... when cattle are driven into the fields or are lost etc., when windows are shut against the night .... All the people hereabouts engage in superstitious practices with familiar and unfamiliar words, names, and rhymes, especially with the name of God, the Holy Trinity ... numerous saints, the wounds of Christ ... verses from the New Testament ... They also make strange signs ... they do things with herbs, roots, branches of special trees; they have their particular days, hours and places for everything .... And all this is done to work harm on others or to do good, to make things better or worse, to bring good or bad luck to their fellow men.[1]

Similar reports about rural people who used a mixture of pre-Christian and Christian phrases and practices in their incantations and group rituals could have been written about peasant populations in almost every part of Europe which remained cut off from the intellectual stimulus provided by urban life. Thus according to a Catholic missionary who was in lower Brittany in 1610 local people customarily scattered some of the buckwheat they had harvested into the ditches surrounding the fields as a thank-offering to the natural forces which had granted them a harvest. Strange rituals were also reported in the eastern regions of France, in Lorraine.

An animistic world

For the traditional unacculturated peasant whose life-world only included a few fragments of the teachings brought in by Christian missionaries in the early Middle Ages, the dominant idea was that death and misfortune were caused by forces which came from *outside* the sacred space of the village. Only later when the leading peasants in the village were in the process of assimilating urban-style ideas such as the Christian notion of sin into their mental outlook did the idea rise that evil forces lay *within* the confines of the village itself. Yet even then the *coqs de village* resisted the idea that the only evil which counted in the sight of the Great Judge who sent souls to heaven or hell was that which lay within their own hearts.

As examples of villages in which the transference of the 'other' had yet to occur let us turn to the forested regions of Luxembourg and the Cambrésis in the century before 1570 as recently described by Robert Muchembled and Marie-Sylvia Dupont-Bouchat. Here peasant life remained firmly grounded in the annual cycle of sowing and harvest and the longer human cycle of birth, copulation and death. Outside the ring which encompassed the homelots, pastures, fields and forests which the network of neighbours used every day, lay the world which was occasionally visited by villagers in the course of recovering stray cattle, hunting for game, searching for a potential spouse and marketing. Beyond this known landscape lay the vast expanse of space which was almost entirely unexplored by village folk. It was here that the most potent forces and demons were thought to have their abode.

Fundamental to the life-world of these traditional peasants in Luxembourg and the Cambrésis was the conviction that nothing happened by chance or through mechanistic causal means (i.e. if one used a ladder with rotten rungs, one might fall to the ground and be killed). Instead, for them every event was ultimately caused by animistic spirits, demons, witches, werewolves or the dead. If the rituals used to control these forces had not proved effective and misfortune occurred it was not that the rituals were useless, but simply that they had been improperly performed. In this seemingly irrefutable logic lay the secret of the duration of this ancient explanatory system.

In the world of the immobile villages such as those found in Luxembourg and the Cambrésis, it was held that vitalistic forces were to be found everywhere and in everything; in stones, trees and streams, in the winds and in the birds and beasts which were the cousins of man. Not entirely unlike Giovanni Pico della Mirandola, Theophrastus Paracelsus and other learned fifteenth- and early sixteenth-century Neoplatonists who revived the late classical concept of the universe as an organic unity, the village animists believed that there was a connection or correspondence (these are Neoplatonist terms) between what happened in the macrocosm of the universe and the microcosm of ordinary human affairs. Each happening in nature had a meaning. In Luxembourg, for example, the eerie howling of wolves announced the coming of pestilence. This belief in signs and portents lingered on long after most people in a village had become acculturated. Thus in Brailes in Warwickshire in England, a village with many urban contacts, it was noted in the parish register, presumably by the vicar, that: 'The grat plag 1603 in it 50 died and 50 ravens flw about the stepell till all the 50 was ded. A grat wonder to see it.'[2] Similarly, there was a correspondence between the actions of ill-disposed persons and other people's misfortune. Thus in late seventeenth-century rural Normandy male impotence or sterility was associated with the idea of a cord drawn tightly over the base of a man's genitals. According to local thinking, a husband's inability to perform the sexual act was caused by an ill-doer who knotted shoelaces and muttered incantations in the secrecy of her own room.

Cunning folk

In a village not yet acculturated it was held that no single force worked entirely for good or for ill. This moral ambivalence was also reflected in the activities of specialists in magic. Take the case of Perrée, the wife of Gilles Pingret of St-Martin-en-la-Rivière in Cambrésis. In 1446 magistrates from outside any of the villages concerned learned that Perrée1 had often been asked by the inhabitants of Valenciennes and of the villages in the Cateau to remove the evil spells which witches had laid on their near relations. Perrée was also reputed to have the power to compel husbands who had abandoned their wives to return home to their spouses and to be able to detect the woman with whom an unfaithful husband was having an affair. What brought Perrée to the attention of the magistrates was not that she could help estranged wives but that she had caused the death of several people in the villages of Vaux-en-Arrousise and Saint-Souplet. A similar ambivalence hung over the reputation of Margaret Jeger of Lucerne in Switzerland. In the 1440s Margaret was credited with the ability to devise charms which could keep lovers true to each other and to be able to bring rain to fields suffering from drought. But in 1450 she was hauled before magistrates and accused of using a hail storm to destroy her neighbour's crops.

In both these examples the causal agent of misfortune and death was seen as an identifiable human being. But in some other rural societies such as the villages in the Friuli north of Venice, the identity of the cause was deliberately left vague. Until the 1570s when the Venetian Inquisition upset their semi-pagan explanatory system, the Friuli villagers held that unknown malevolent witches from beyond the sacred space of the village marshalled during the Ember Days four times a year to destroy crops and murder children. To counter this threat the spirits of the good men of each village, the *Benandanti*, left the bodies of their sleeping owners at home in bed and went to do battle with the witches in the fields. Evil-working witches were also thought of in impersonal terms in the Spanish villages of Zügarramurdi and Urdan in the Pyrenees in the 1580s. One incident involved a child, the niece of a shepherd named Miguel de Goiburu, who had awoken one morning covered with black marks. After the child's death a few days later, villagers credited the tragedy to nameless blood-sucking vampire witches.

The idea that the cause of misfortune lay with persons or nameless forces *outside* the village was strengthened by some of the pre-early modern legal systems. For example, in the German Empire before the sixteenth century the old customary law of retribution, the *lex talionis*, was commonly used. This ensured that anybody who wrongly accused another person of causing death by magic or of other serious offences would be subject to the same punishment as the accused would have received if the latter were found not guilty. It is likely that this cut down the number of malicious prosecutions between near neighbours. The malicious prosecution of resident witches was also difficult to sustain in any court of law which still used accusatory procedures which invoked magical forces. Here the accused was able to confront his or her accuser in person to refute the charges. Depending on their respective reputations in the community, the judge then compelled one of the parties to submit to a judicial ordeal. The person was tied up with ropes and thrown into a pond to see if he would sink or float. If he floated it was a sign that the water had rejected him and that his testimony was false. The feud was another institution which, though its use was limited to parties of roughly equal status, helped to preserve the notion that the cause of misfortune lay outside the network of neighbours. In Luxembourg and Cambrésis the fact that many village priests were outsiders unsupported by a nearby kinsgroup which would begin a vendetta on their behalf may partially explain the high level of violence directed against clerics before 1570.

In villages which had pretty well come to accept the Christian moral distinction between good and evil, witches might be of two sorts. As John Gaule, an English witchcraft expert, put it in the 1640s:

According to the vulgar conceit, distinction is usually made betwixt the White and the Blacke Witch: the Good and the Bad Witch. The Bad Witch, they are wont to call him or her, that works Malefice or Mischiefe to the Bodies of Men or Beasts: the Good Witch they count him or her that helps to reveale, prevent or remove the same.[3]

In Lorraine, Essex, Nassau-Wiesbaden and probably in most other parts of western Europe one of these cunning men or women was likely to be found within 30 kilometres of every village or hamlet.

Serving as diviners, healers and contact people with the supernatural, cunning people provided answers to questions about the cause of misfortune, which from the point of view of village people were far more satisfactory than those provided by Christian clerics who worked only in their official capacity. Of course some clerics such as John Vaux, curate of St Helens in Auckland, County Durham, dabbled in magic on the side to supplement their meagre incomes. But priests who were true to their vows taught the hard lesson that personal misfortune was God's punishment for sin. Cunning people, on the other hand, gave the comforting impression that misfortune was the consequence of action taken by a known human agent other than the victim. For them the question of sin was not at issue.

Because priests and cunning folk were in a manner of speaking competing for the same clientele, very considerable risks were taken by wise men and women who sought to earn some money by assisting their neighbours. For example, according to a report written by an official of the Florentine Inquisition, around 1472 a man who had lost some money went to a wise woman living near Lucca for advice. The client hid himself away and spied on the wise woman while she peered at the stars and then called on a demon. In due time the demon appeared and told her that the money had been swallowed by a pig. The demon also pointed out that the money had first been given to the client's wife by a priest with whom she had fornicated. Informed of all this, the Inquisitors caught the pig, slaughtered it and discovered the money in its entrails. But because the wise woman had used the services of demons, a capital offence, the Inquisitor had her burnt at the stake.

On the Continent cunning people who were trying to cure an illness or combat the effects of a farmyard accident often enlisted the assistance of a variety of potent forces. Thus in Lorraine, in the village of St-Die a cunning person offered to help a man who had broken his hip by filling the breeches the sufferer had been wearing at the time of the accident with manure begged from nine different neighbours (community solidarity; animal–human solidarity) and hanging them up in St Benedict's Church in Brecklange (solidarity with saintly intercessors and with the world of the dead).

In England curers appear to have used more standardized procedures. After a paying client arrived, he or she was told that the illness of the child, brother or sister was already far advanced and that it might be too late to do anything about it; the forces of evil had a head start. These cautionary words provided the cunning person with an airtight excuse if the cure failed. The healer then asked the client which ill-wisher had caused the patient's illness by using the evil eye or other means, and then set about searching for remedies which would counteract the witch's powers. Some cunning people used curious mixtures of herbs and urine (anything expelled from the body was held to have magical properties). Others devised written charms to be attached to the stricken person; some muttered prayers of the sort which, as we saw on page 165, were overheard by the German cleric near Wiesbaden in 1594. If the cure failed and the victim grew worse, the cunning person might suggest that the client use the services of a more powerful healer several villages away. In late sixteenth-century Essex, some people were sent up to London specialists – cunning people could be urban creatures as well as rural – and one was sent 450 kilometres to Newcastle-upon-Tyne. Here, just as was the case with pilgrimages to a Christian shrine, the assumption was that the greater the distance, trouble and expense to which the client went, the greater the likelihood of finding relief in the end.

In searching out stolen or mislaid property, the same care was taken first to learn which person the client most suspected and then to use the intimate knowledge of village life the cunning person had at his or her disposal to verify the truth of the client's accusation. After making initial inquiries of the client and of the villagers most likely to know the particulars of the case, the cunning person commonly used mirrors or a pair of shears to help focus suspicion on the suspect. If shears were used, as they were by the north-country English diviner Alice Swan in the 1560s, the cunning person laid them out and surrounded them with pebbles to each of which a suspect's name was assigned. Then she spun the shears so that they would stop pointing directly at the pebble bearing the suspect's name. If a mirror were used the client was asked to name the face he saw in it. Such were the powers of suggestion that the client inevitably named the person he or she had most suspected all along. When the suspect was confronted with this magical evidence, he or she was likely to confess lest magic later be used to do him or her greater harm.

In Luxembourg and the Cambrésis, where until the 1570s leading villagers were not yet accustomed to think of witches as either good or bad, resident village witches were regarded as a vital part of the defences against the malevolent forces which lurked outside. Yet because of their high magical potency, these same witches might inadvertently serve as lightning rods which attracted malevolent forces into the village. This threat, however, was neutralized by the corporate rituals undertaken by the villagers every six or eight weeks. In the course of these rituals village people expelled their own feelings of hostility and pent-up frustration against their neighbours, and once again might form an inviolate moral community. If death or misfortune later did occur, it was because this moral unity had been imperfectly restored and not because the reputed witch living in their midst had purposefully sought to work harm on his or her neighbours.

Village religious ritual

In traditional villages in northern latitudes, one of the most important of the festivals during which malevolent spirits were expelled took place between 24 and 29 June at the summer solstice. Here the triumph of light and life which marked the longest day of the year stood in contrast to the long winter months when darkness and night held sway for eighteen hours or more. Darkness was feared as the time when evil demons were most likely to penetrate the village defences and when lurking strangers might slip in undetected. Though English villagers customarily kept a candle burning by their bedside as early as the fourteenth century (a frequent cause of fires), before the coming of whale oil and cole seed oil lamps in the eighteenth century it was prohibitively expensive to use flares and torches to light up the inner spaces of the village during the hours of darkness. But on the eve of St John's Day (the day of the festival according to the Christian calendar) Nature and man co-operated to vanquish the darkness; man provided the great bonfires which lit up the four or five hours of darkness, and Nature the early rising sun. In Luxembourg and Cambrésis, in Norway and Sweden and in most other parts of the North, the lighting of the bonfires signalled the beginning of an orgy of dancing, leaping over the fire, nude swimming, love-making and loud revelry. Believing that the evil spirits preferred deep silence, villagers held that all of this commotion chased the demons from the hidden lairs into which they had crept during the last six weeks and sent them swirling around the inverted hemisphere which marked off the air-space of the village. The flight of the spirits gave these hours a special magic; it was then that the herbs and berries gathered by village healers had a greater potency than those collected at any other time. While the festival lasted the dancing, leaping, copulating villagers held themselves to be immune from all harmful forces and to be storing up the mystic energies needed to carry them through the next few weeks of hard labour in the fields. More than being a mere pagan fertility rite, the festivities of St John's Eve were a lively affirmation of common purpose and moral unity.

For ritual purposes, the psychic energies of traditional rural communities were held to be concentrated in special categories of people. Although few young unmarried men had mystic properties of their own, when organized into groups young men were held to have the power to cajole the demon forces which controlled the fertility of man, beasts and crops. On the physiological level, theirs were the loins from which all future generations of humankind would spring (the females' no less important contribution of seed was unknown). Theirs too were the strong hands, arms and backs which undertook most of the heavy work in the fields. Except for Spain and England

– and perhaps even there – all the young unmarried males who were accepted as being part of the moral community were organized into groups variously known as Youth Abbeys, Realms or Kingdoms of Youth. At the lower end, the age of members ranged from 16 to 18, and at the upper end from 24 to 26 or more depending on whether villagers had accepted the idea of late marriage.

For the years before the new teachings of the Counter-Reformation began to take hold – in Italy in the 1560s, in France in the 1620s – there is no record of how young men were recruited into a rural Youth Abbey or Realm or whether there was an initiation ceremony similar to those in an African society where an age-grade system was in force. However, it is known that each year new leaders were appointed bearing the name of king, prince or abbot in conscious imitation of the social hierarchy of the élites who were part of the Great Tradition based on the classics, a hierarchy which lay beyond the confines of the village. In northern France where the authority of the seigneur was strong, the choice lay with that personage. In the semi-Christian Auvergne, the office of leader went to the youth who had contributed most wax for the candles in the local convent or parish church.

Because there was little difference between the moral expectations and outlook of the older and younger generations of villagers, it was not thought incongruous to give the youth the responsibility for enforcing the moral taboos of the community. During the week before the annual festival which honoured the village saint – or the pagan deity which lay beneath the saintly forms – leaders of the Youth Realm formed themselves into a court and put on trial all those people who had broken community taboos. In some of the villages around Lyon in the sixteenth century, all of the men who had committed adultery between the feast days of St Symphorianus and St Bartholomew (22 and 24 August) were held to fall within the jurisdiction of the court and could be punished with a fine. During the rest of the year all newly married couples were required to recognize the authority of the Youth Realm by paying it a marriage fee. Couples who refused to pay were subjected to a charivari. So too were all ill-matched couples whose marriage broke community taboos. Illicit love, as defined by the unwritten code of the community rather than by the laws of the land, would, it was thought, stir up the wrath of supernatural forces and endanger the lives and crops of all the villagers.

Throughout the year it was the unmarried young men who took charge of organizing all of the other great festivals on which the prosperity and emotional unity of the village depended. It was they who usually rang the bells of the parish church on the night of All Souls, on 1–2 November; they who presided over the May Day mating rituals; and they who, in the Mediterranean world, presided over Carnival. Some of these great village festivals marked the transition from a period of intense hard work in the fields to a period of enforced idleness and short commons. 1–2 November, for example, heralded the coming of winter and the cessation of work in the fields. Carnival marked the approach of Lenten fasting and restraint. Other festivals, like the feast day of the Annunciation to the Virgins (25 March), May Day, and the Festival of St John's Eve, marked the beginning of a new agricultural year and the onset of a period of intense work in preparation for the harvest. All transitions in the pace of life, from slumber and death to life (the miracle of spring) or the reverse (the coming of winter frosts and snows) were held to be times of special danger when malevolent forces were most potent. Hence the perceived need in the rural world to counteract the danger with a show of ritual solidarity.

On the occasion of a festival the consciousness of danger from supernatural forces together with their own animal high spirits provided youth groups with an excuse to go on a rampage against outsiders. The violence often began during a ball game held between local village youths and those from a neighbouring village. Whichever way the game went it soon degenerated into a free-for-all with fist fights and the hurling of sticks, stones, dead or still screaming cats and other animals. The level of violence might escalate into a small war if the youths did service in the local militia and had firearms at their disposal. A particularly nasty brawl broke out in 1671 between youths from the village of St Jean-de-Lay in Aquitaine and those of nearby Cibours during the week of Carnival. The trouble began when the heroes of St Jean-de-Lay refused to allow the young men from Cibours to go through their town ringing handbells. But as far as the older generation of villagers were concerned, this youthful show of high spirits merely demonstrated anew the moral unity of their community and its determination to defend itself against any invader, human or supernatural. As the uncomprehending Puritan divine, Thomas Hall, put it in the mid seventeenth century when contemplating the violence of less formal village groups in England "tis no festival unless there be some fightings'.[4]

The urban contrast

In their symbolic importance and in the uses to which Youth Abbeys and youth-dominated festivals were put, a great gulf existed between rural customs and the pragmatic practices of urban centres. Though city workers occasionally laid down their tools and went out into the countryside to help with the harvest (pay was high during a harvest emergency), by and large they were cut off from the agrarian cycle and the unevenness of time which gave meaning to the rural rituals. In the city, masters and household heads with production quotas to fulfil (these were set by the guilds) were intent on instilling into the minds of youthful employees, who often had only recently come in from rural areas, the need to work regularly; for them all time was the same, except church sponsored holy days (holidays). As we saw earlier, in rural areas no such set of perceptual differences separated the older generation from the younger.

In the cities of southern France such as Dijon and Romans as well as in Switzerland and northern Italy one technique used to socialize raw youth into the values upheld by city oligarchs and married household heads was to open the membership of Youth Abbeys and Realms to married men under the age of 35 as well as to unmarried youths. Under the guidance of their mentors the youth were taught new ways. In a further effort to control the activities of the many Youth Abbeys found in populous cities – there were more than twenty in sixteenth-century Lyon – the council and aldermen themselves chose the young men who would head each neighbourhood Abbey or Realm. In practice this meant that the 'youth' in charge of each group was usually the son either of a privileged bourgeois family or of one which lay just outside the governing circle rather than an untutored young thug from the lower social orders. Symbolic of the full incorporation of the Realms and Abbeys into the social hierarchy of the city, the annual coronation of the new king or abbot was attended by the highest dignitaries in the region. Thus, in Vienne in 1548 the coronation was witnessed by the king's officer in charge of all local military affairs (the *vice-bailli*), two judges and six respected barristers.

The finances and activities of the Abbeys and Realms were also closely controlled by the urban élite. Working behind the scenes they appear to have authorized the violence inflicted on Protestant Huguenots in a Catholic city and the harm done to Jews and other aliens whose presence threatened civic unity. More commonly they authorized the charivari which, as we saw in Chapter 2, was inflicted by youth groups on married couples who had broken the moral code of the city. Thus the anti-social forces which might have been unleashed by the follies of youth were, in the words of a late fifteenth-century document from Dijon, harnessed into service by the urban élite: 'to conserve the happy tranquillity of the people'.[5]

In the cities of the Mediterranean world, again in marked contrast to the practices used in rural areas, the most important of the great popular festivals was the annual Carnival which took place just before Ash Wednesday and the enforced austerities and dietary taboos of Lent. In time of Carnival, men, women and, before the 1560s, even priests, donned masks which concealed their identity and gave them licence to do what they would when they cavorted around the town. The focal points of their activities were the great floats drawn in procession. These often featured a young giant such as Gargantua, mythical bears and dragons, and the cocks, bulls and other farmyard animals with whom human beings may have felt some affinity.

Hidden behind masks and costume disguises, players enacted pantomimes on street corners or floats which often suggested that the world was temporarily turned upside down. For example, a man playing the part of Noah's wife made it clear that it was she rather than Noah who had governed the ark during the great flood. Some plays took the rules of inversion even further and suggested that the rich and powerful were incompetent fools. In Rouen a magistrate who refused to take the customary hare from pleaders but instead insisted on receiving a large monetary bribe before he would consider the case, was held up for ridicule. In Clermont in 1666 the most feared of the king's officers, the local *intendant*, was portrayed as a pompous ass, much to the amusement of the members of the local *parlement* who were looking on. The apparent purpose behind all this was to remind people whose authority was unchallenged during the rest of the year that they had broken what the masqueraders took to be the proper customs of the community. It was intended that they should join in the laughter directed against them and to mend their ways in the future. Rather than effectively challenging the existing social order, Carnival simply gave it further legitimacy. For by being made the objects of ridicule, the authority of the temporary victims was openly acknowledged. When *mardi gras* was over everybody knew that the rigorous austerities of Lent and the privations of a world of social dependency and subordination would again be upon them.

The Christian presence

On the eve of the Reformations the great humanist scholar Erasmus of Rotterdam found that either out of ignorance or neglect the mass of the population were as superstitious as the pagans. By this he probably meant that even among the ordinary people who considered themselves to be Christians and regularly attended church, unorthodox beliefs and practices were rife. Certainly in the century before Martin Luther compelled the Catholic Church to reassess its religious practices, there was little qualitative difference between the religion of these people and the religion of the élite (excluding Nominalist scholars, mystics and a few others). Both sorts desperately wanted to believe that it was possible to win eternal salvation for their souls through using material and rituals provided by the Christian Church. Both sorts were willing to use new precision-built innovations (such as indulgences) and to drop earlier vague concepts. For example, in much of England already by 1500 people in search of intercessors before the throne of God the Father were turning to the Virgin rather than to local saints. The only way in which the religion of the wealthy differed from that of poorer Christians was that the former were able to have a greater quantity of whatever it was that was considered spiritually useful. They could build or endow beautiful late

Gothic or early Renaissance chapels and churches; poorer people had to make do with cheap tin images of saints.

In the long centuries before 1517 the Church owed its continued survival to its willingness to cater to popular tastes which did not run directly counter to Christian dogma, a policy known as accommodation. In the hands of a skilful manager of missionaries, such as Pope Gregory the Great (590–604) proved himself to be in directing St Augustine's mission to England in 594, the policy of accommodation in no way threatened core Christian truths. But under the guidance of later lesser men who were no longer filled with missionary zeal, the accretions of popular usage and belief which built up over the years became more important to simple people who thought of themselves as Christians than the core tenets of the faith. For example, in 1644 John Shaw reported that he had met an old man from Cartmel in Lancashire who claimed to have attended his parish church regularly for many years. Yet only once in his life, at a Corpus Christi Day play in Kendal, had he ever consciously heard of a man nailed to a tree – the Christ.

Purgatory

One of the most important of the several accretions which nearly smothered Christian dogma at the lay level was the doctrine of purgatory. First organized into a coherent scheme by Church theologians in the early twelfth century, the doctrine allowed ordinary tithe-paying believers as well as the élite to feel that they could control the destinies of dead loved ones and friends. Breaking with the earlier tradition of a single final last judgement of the sort portrayed over the west doors of northern French Gothic cathedrals such as Amiens, the doctrine of purgatory held that as soon as a person died he or she would either be hurled into hell or lodged in a temporary half-way house known as purgatory. The length of time which the souls of dead people spent in purgatory depended in part on the life they had lived on earth and in part on the number of masses and prayers said on their behalf by the living.

Yet it was not until the mid fifteenth century that the doctrine of purgatory finally caught hold on the imagination of urban people who were prosperous enough to know where their next meal was coming from, as well as the imagination of enlightened middling-wealthy country folk. Then, in a manner unprecedented in the past, western Europe was swept by a wave of lay religiosity which came close to fundamentally altering the character of the religious life of the Church itself. For in order to free their loved ones and confrères who were 'sleepless, restless, burning and broiling in the dark fire' of purgatory (the words are Sir Thomas More's) it was necessary for lay people to hire priests to say masses for the souls of the departed and for the Church to train thousands of new priests just for this purpose. And if one mass reduced the amount of time spent in torment, a full trental of thirty masses would reduce it even more quickly. Among the wealthy the practice was to establish a chantry, a special chapel attached to a parish church or cathedral where endowed masses could be said each day. In England, probably the largest of these chantries was the great building attached to Westminster Abbey where King Henry VII (d. 1509) gave directions that 10,000 masses be said for the repose of his soul.

Though the doctrine of purgatory gave wealthy people the impression that they could control their own destinies in the afterlife, many ordinary folk remained unconvinced. Even in economically progressive parts of Europe most people before the seventeenth century seem to have believed that the souls of the dead hovered around the space of the village rather than, as the Church taught, going to a place of confinement – purgatory. In Languedoc, in Catalonia and probably in other Mediterranean regions as well, some people held that the souls of the dead were carried around in the bodies of farmyard animals, especially pigs, asses and plough horses. Others held that the spirits wandered around on their own. But whatever their means of locomotion, these dead souls were held to have the power to intervene with supernatural forces; they would only intervene for good if they felt that they had not been forgotten. Here then the powers of the dead were seen as moral sanctions to guide the conduct of the living.

In order to remind the dead that their memory was still fresh in the minds of the living, the Church (in another example of accommodation) sanctioned the old pagan custom of ringing all the bells in the tower of the parish church on the night of All Souls (1–2 November). Many laymen, however, held that the ringing of the bells served to guide the wandering souls back to their tombs so that they would cease to threaten the village. In lower Normandy, as late as 1610, when the practice was noted by a disapproving missionary, responsibility for caring for the souls of the dead rested with each family rather than with the community at large. Here each family placed stones near the fire lit during the summer solstice so that the wandering souls could sit down and warm themselves and be made to feel welcome. In Haute Provence at the end of the seventeenth century the custom was to keep a supply of bread and wine by the tomb of the dead for at least a year.

In the popular mind not all of the souls who hovered around the space of the village were those of people who had once participated fully in the ritual life of the community of neighbours. The wandering spirits also included the malevolent souls of strangers who had been murdered while passing through the village or who had starved to death for want of simple charity. Probably one reason why a little Christianized population such as that of late seventeenth-century Sennely-en-Sologne was so eager to distribute alms to wandering strangers was to encourage them – after death – to intervene for good in the life of the village. The same rationale was at work in some of the public executions which took place at Caen in Normandy around 1661. Rather than allowing the souls of the condemned to join the malevolent forces which might later wreak vengeance on the community of the living, a kind of sacred theatre was performed at the place of execution to re-assimilate the criminal into civil society. First it was essential that the condemned freely confess his or her wrongs and ask the forgiveness of the crowd of attendant townspeople and priests. This done the crowd could demonstrate their compassion. At Caen it was the custom for a criminal being broken on the wheel – a particularly painful death – to chant the first stanza of the ancient Christian hymn, the 'Veni Creator', then for the crowd to chant the second, the criminal the third and so on until the sufferer was dead. Fully resocialized the dead criminal was now regarded as a human sacrifice whose execution served to propitiate the forces of the supernatural.

In the case of suicide the rituals were rather different. In most parts of Europe it was held that the soul of the suicide would return to the house where the action had occurred unless preventive measures were taken. For instance, in seventeenth-century Lille it was commonly thought that the soul of a suicide could be denied entrance to its own household if the corpse were removed from the house without allowing it to cross the threshold (just as in humans, entrances and exits to houses were held to be especially vulnerable to mysterious forces). This meant that the corpse had to be dragged face downwards through a tunnel dug under the threshold (not a great problem if the floor was of dirt) or hurled from a window as if it were a pot of human excrement. Once out of the house the corpse was denied burial in the sacred ground of the churchyard (a Church precept) and was commonly buried at a crossroads. This place of burial harked back to the ancient Teutonic custom of performing human sacrifices at the junction of roads. Once interred, a stake was driven through the heart of the suicide to prevent its spirit from haunting humankind. In England this was a legal requirement which was not removed from the Statute Books until 1831.

In one instance at least the enforcing agent was the local cunning man. At Widecombe-in-the-Moor in Devonshire in the late seventeenth century a sick man was convinced his illness was caused by the malevolent spirit of a neighbour who had recently committed suicide. Asked for his advice, the cunning man ordered two stout villagers to go to the place of burial in the night and to drive a sword through the middle of the grave. Whether or not the sick man was healed, the lesson was clear; suicides would be denied treatment thought appropriate to any other dead humans. This perpetual condemnation as anti-social beings perhaps explained why the suicide rate in sixteenth- and seventeenth-century England was comparatively low.

Not all of the wandering spirits who defied Catholic teaching that they should be confined to purgatory were invisible to humans; most western Europeans knew of somebody who had actually seen a ghost. Some ghosts were family members, some were strangers, some were mute while others spoke, but all fulfilled the cultural expectations of the people they had come to haunt; people who don't believe in the supernatural never see ghosts. Many ghosts became visible to terrified spectators to enforce a bequest that had been made during their life-time; for example, that property be distributed in closer accord with their written will or that more masses be said for their soul. Thus in the late seventeenth century a woman of Faubourg St-Marcel in Paris spoke to her husband after she had been dead for five years and commanded him to pray for her. But probably the most common kind of ghostly apparition was that of a person who had been murdered or grievously wronged by an undetected evil-doer. The ghost might either appear to the loved one and suggest the identity of the murderer, as did the ghost of Hamlet's father in Shakespeare's play, or appear before the murderer himself. Thus around 1624 the ghost of a Yorkshire man called Fletcher came to haunt his wife's lover until the latter confessed that he had killed his rival. In all of these cases the belief in ghosts provided other-worldly sanctions for the moral behaviour of the living.

In a traditional village or even in an urban neighbourhood where the immanence of one's own death and the death of brothers, sisters, sons, daughters and other kinsfolk who were still in the prime of life was part of everyday reality, the dead were not shut away and except on All Souls Day forgotten. Instead they were buried in the churchyard, a central location which served as a meeting-place for the community. Here in the burial grounds, where the living were in constant communion with the dead, all sorts of secular activity took place; buying and selling, soliciting by prostitutes, the staging of theatrical performances, ball games and dancing. As late as 1657 a visitor to the cemetery of the Innocents in Paris reported 'five hundred sorts of sports which can be seen within these galleries'.[6] Only in the 1660s did the Catholic Church and respectable laymen close off burial grounds with fences or hedges (a practice followed in Protestant lands as well) and set them apart as a quiet place for mournful meditation. With the closing of the burial grounds the dead were finally removed from easy converse with the living (and one might add so too was a likely source of disease and death). Yet even then the dead were not forgotten.

Confraternities

In Catholic lands until the late eighteenth century and in Protestant lands until the 1530s, special lay organizations existed to do service for the dead. A confraternity was a small extra-parochial lay solidarity which cut across differences of sex, profession, neighbourhood, kinship and, within limits, social status. Thus, in the Champagne no *manouvriers* are known to have belonged to confraternities. Flexible in organization, each confraternity established its own rules and decided how to use its own corporate funds. First recognized by the Church in the twelfth century (the time when the doctrine of purgatory was given ordered form), in Italy confraternities only became numerous in the late fourteenth century. A century later they had become common in the northern world as well. In Hamburg most of the confraternities in existence in 1517 had been founded since 1490. Thus they can be seen to be an essential part of the great pre-Reformation movement of lay piety.

Except for the confraternities which were given over to flagellation in imitation of Christ on the way to his crucifixion (a practice not much found outside northern Italy), the primary function of most of these lay solidarities was to ensure that members were given a proper funeral and remembered in the years after their death. Just as had been the case with their pre-Christian ancestors, the confraternity members regarded death as the appearance of contamination and disorder within the family. By taking charge of the funeral, the solidarity redefined the role of the dead and at the same time helped to wash away the contamination which had cut off the family from normal concourse with the rest of society. To achieve these ends the solidarity sought to give the fact of the death of a member wide publicity, rather than concealing it.

In rural Normandy in the late sixteenth century the practice was to ring church bells in a pattern which revealed the age, sex and social status of the deceased. Urban practices were more elaborate. For instance, in 1575 the confrères of the Holy Sacrament at Troyes gave orders that on the death of a member the clerk should robe himself in his official gown and red hat. Holding his staff of office in one hand and a handbell in the other, he was to go to all the principal crossroads of the city announcing who had died, and the place and hour of his or her burial.

The funeral itself was a mixture of Christian rites and pre-Christian pomp and ceremonial dressed up in Renaissance or Baroque forms of a sort which seventeenth-century Puritans in England as well as the Catholic precisionists in France, the Jansenists, found highly distasteful. At the centre of the display was a great procession in which the spiritual forces of the poor (the beggars of Christ or Woden), the young, the old, secular and religious clerics and the confraternity were marshalled. Headed by the confrères bearing the banners and crosses of the solidarity, the procession accompanied the bier to the church where the priests had their say, to the grave where more clerical rites were performed, and stood by while coins and foodstuffs were distributed to the poor. Then the procession accompanied the bereaved family back to their house (in Florence and many other places widows and daughters had to remain at home during the church and graveside services). Once there the confrères symbolically welcomed the family back into the community of the living. Later, at the anniversary of the death of the confrère, or at an annual general meeting, solidarity members accompanied a hired priest in saying prayers for the soul of the departed in purgatory. Some confraternities went further and held that the 'good works' of members (the distribution of charity and participation in the church sacraments allowed to lay people) were enough to allow them to pass directly into paradise without first passing through purgatory; this in any case was the message sent off by letter to St Peter (the apostle who holds the keys to heaven) by one of the brotherhoods of Our Lady in the Netherlands in 1456.

In addition to presiding over funerals, confraternities were agencies of group solidarity among living laymen. According to the teachings of the later medieval Church, as presented both in the written word and by paintings and frescoes (such as Leonardo da Vinci's 'Last Supper' in Milan, painted in 1495–7), a corporate banquet by a religious organization was meant to be a re-enactment of the Last Supper taken by Christ and His twelve Apostles before His betrayal and crucifixion. But for many rural confraternities in the sixteenth and seventeenth centuries, the annual banquet was merely an occasion for happy conviviality. In Languedoc the festivities began with a collective act, the slaughter of a pig. This evoked death in two ways; first, the death of the pig itself, and second the release of the human soul which the beast might be carrying around in its body. After the pig was roasted, shares of the carcass were distributed to all members of the confraternity or parish. By eating this meat they transformed it into nourishment and later into human excrement, which after it had become a fertilizer would give life in future. Thus by feasting, drinking, dancing and joking together, the members of the group reaffirmed their mutual solidarity and their determination to enjoy life to the fullest, while it lasted.

For humble people who did not belong to a confraternity, but who were no less determined not to be overwhelmed by the fact of death, the wake performed a similar function. Tables loaded with food would be laid on in the church itself or in the churchyard from which everyone who shared in the space of the village could eat their fill. Great kegs of homebrewed ale would be drunk. The feast would be followed by story-telling by the old and larking about by the young. Wind instruments and drums would sound and soon everyone would be dancing both inside the church and in the burial ground beside it.

Saints

The cult of saints was the third element in the trinity of tolerated practices through which the medieval Church tried to bring the Christian message to all people. The dangers inherent in saints – that they could readily be assimilated into an animistic world – were clearly recognized by St Augustine (d. 430). Yet in the end the great Bishop of Hippo in north Africa came to accept the fact that pagans would not come forward to be baptized unless they were convinced that some dead Christians would answer prayers and work miracles of healing, drought prevention and the like. Backed by Augustine's tremendous authority – the author of *De Civitate Dei* (*The City of God*) is perhaps the most important of all the early Church fathers – from the fifth century onwards the cult of saints became a standard element in the Church's policy of accommodation and conversion.

The saints whom early modern European kings, peasants and most people in between thought able to intervene miraculously in everyday affairs fall into two categories: those of international and timeless fame such as Mary, the mother of Christ, St Anne (Mary's mother), St Michael and St Sebastian; and those of purely local prominence and repute. In neither category were many canonized peasants to be found. Instead most saints were recruited from the ranks of the élite who, in life, had not had to perform manual labour.

Localized saints were often the dead people who while they lived had first brought the gospel to an area and were later credited by Church and people with mystic properties similar to those of the pagan god they had supplanted. Thus the symbol of St Herbert who worked in those parts of Luxembourg where Diana the huntress was worshipped in the early Middle Ages (a Roman import from Greece) was a full grown stag with a cross attached to its antlers. Also numerous were the saints who took over the specialized healing powers of sacred trees or wells. In the sixteenth century in Champagne the shrine housing the remains of St Bertaud was thought to have the power to cure madmen, and in Brie the shrine of St Fiacre attracted people who were suffering painfully from haemorrhoids. Every parish church, confraternity, craft and mystery had its own particular patron protector saint. For instance, in France the patron of textile workers who transformed raw hemp and wool into cloth was St Blaise, a fourth-century saint and martyr. Through her martyrdom (a transformation) St Blaise was connected with the idea of a rope drawn up to heaven and, by a further analogy, with the rope used to snare the legendary dragon woman Mélusine. In Naples the patron saint was Gennaro. In 1631, when the volcanic mountain Vesuvius was erupting (in Roman times it had completely engulfed the town of Pompeii), churchmen carried St Gennaro's relics about the city to invoke his protection from a similar fate (Naples still stands).

Nowhere was the corporate nature of the culture of saints more in evidence than in sixteenth-century Spain. Here it was often the custom for an entire village population to take a vow to observe the rituals appropriate to their chosen saint protector. Just which dead miracle-working Christian would be invoked depended upon the circumstances surrounding some recent catastrophe; fashions in saints change. For example, according to the exhaustive reports of local religious practices sent to King Philip II in 1575, in the town of Fuente de Pedro-Naharro in the diocese of Cuenca

they observe the Feast of Our Lady Saint Agatha and fast on her eve, and began to do so because when the sun rose on Our Lady Saint Agatha's Day there were thirteen dead from the pestilence, and it was decided from devotion to observe said holy day and fast on her eve...[7]

This vow to fast was done in the expectation that in future St Agatha would take it upon herself to prevent future visitations of the plague.

In Spain, and doubtless in most other parts of Europe as well, the initiative for the worship of a particular saint might come from the common people or it might come from a member of the social élite just as it had in St Augustine's time. Early modern kings who were consciously attempting to win the loyalty of a local population and who in any case fervently believed in wonder-working saints themselves, took special care to visit humble rural shrines and to collect relics. Thus, in April 1528 the Emperor Charles V, Martin Luther's inveterate foe, stayed overnight in mean quarters in the little town of Alabalate de Zorita so that the next morning he could adore the miraculous cross which an inspired dog had unearthed some years before. As a special boon which was expected to work both ways, the Emperor was given the two small chains from which the cross was hung so that he could keep them as a talisman about his person. Some rulers surrounded themselves with vast collections of relics in the expectation that these sacred things would help to convince their subjects that they were the chosen agents of God. In 1517, on the eve of the Reformation, one of the largest collections of old bones, rags and other saintly artefacts in Europe was owned by Martin Luther's later protector, Frederick of Saxony. And among the literate people who could afford to buy books (following the invention of the printing press in or near Mainz *c.* 1450) one of the best sellers was the *Legenda Aurea* (the *Golden Legend*). This was a collection of saints' lives compiled by Jacobus de Voragine in the thirteenth century and printed in many editions after 1483.

According to the teaching of the Church hierarchy, saints were merely intercessors between suppliants and the high God and had no power to work miracles on their own. Yet among the unlettered it was often held that each particular statue of a saint or representation on a stained glass window had animistic properties; the image which was intended only to jog the memory into recalling the virtues of the saint had itself become the message. Thus, in Bazezney in Lorraine in the seventeenth century a woman asked whether it was the statue of Our Lady at Sion, the statue of Our Lady at Fricourt or that of Our Lady of Le Maix which had brought disaster to one of her friends. The idea that saints' images could cause misfortune as well as good was also found in lower Brittany. Around 1610 a missionary priest was shocked to see statues of saints being abused to punish them for failing to perform miracles after the proper rituals had been performed. In the Loire and Somme regions wine-makers were still whipping statues of St George when their wine harvest failed as late as the eighteenth century. Obviously rituals performed before statues of saints were imperfect mechanisms by which to control the weather.

Although some village animists looked at statues of saints as objects which could be punished, far more widespread was the contradictory belief that shrines dedicated to particular saints could be made to work wonders if they were appealed to by the unified moral community. Since most villagers were at enmity with some of their neighbours most of the time (St John's Eve not excepted) the temporary suspension of mutual hatreds in order to go on a pilgrimage marked an occasion of special sacredness. The pilgrimage would be even more effective if several villages usually at odds with each other over pasture and water rights and abducted daughters joined in a common cause. Thus, in the Champagne during the great drought of October 1556 cadres from many villages marched under their banners to the shrine of the virgin St Mathie in the cathedral at Troyes to pray for rain. It was also held that intercessory saints would pay special heed to the pleas of suppliants who had come a long way and endured many hardships in the course of their pilgrimage. In the village of Ivry in the Île de France before 1672 it was the custom to make the hazardous journey to the shrine at Créteil to pray for good harvests. To get there the pilgrims had to cross the treacherous River Seine and then the Marne, all the while realizing that they had to retrace their steps to get home. A similar sense of camaraderie was felt by the bands of pilgrims who met each other for the first time while on the high road to a great international shrine such as that of St James at Compostella in Spain. Whatever their individual social status or village of origin the pilgrims formed a temporary *communitas* which was no longer governed by ordinary rules of behaviour. According to modern anthropological theory, the coming together of disparate people with a common purpose in a pilgrim band gave temporary substance to the millennial dream of peace and brotherhood among all people. Yet early modern reality was sometimes less tidy. Thus in the cold spring of 1579 the people of Courlon-sur-Yonne asked their curé to join them on a pilgrimage to a neighbouring village chapel to pray for better weather. Coming upon a meeting of two roads which both led to the shrine, the curé insisted they go by one route but the lay people demanded that they go by the other. The argument was not settled until the laymen threw the curé into the River Yonne and proceeded on their way.

The Mass

According to the teachings of the Catholic Church (and on this point the Church was *not* prepared to compromise) the condition of peace and brotherhood or sisterhood among communicants was a necessary precondition for receiving the elements of the Mass. The Church also taught that partaking in the sacred elements at least once a year at Easter (the day Christ rose from the dead) was one of the 'good works' which cut down the length of time one's soul would later spend in purgatory. It further held that the gates of paradise would be forever closed to a person who on the point of death did not confess his or her sins and receive extreme unction at the hands of a priest; to die unshriven was the greatest of the catastrophes which could overcome an early modern Christian. In order to avoid this horrid fate each day it was essential to gaze upon a statue of St Christopher – such as the 5 metre high image which still stands in one of the western towers of the cathedral at Amiens – or upon a small portable image of the saint.

The Mass itself was a ritual which, whatever his moral worth, only a fully-ordained priest could perform. Standing before a consecrated altar, the priest recreated Christ's sacrifice upon the Cross for mankind by miraculously transforming the ordinary substances of bread and wine into the body and blood of Christ. This process was technically known as transubstantiation.

Built into the scheme through which the Church intended to monopolize control of the supernatural were two stumbling blocks which prevented its full acceptance by most ordinary early modern Europeans who were not yet on the point of death. The first was people's reluctance to go to confession. Until the introduction of private confessional boxes in the diocese of Milan soon after 1560 and in France and Germany by the late seventeenth century, the act of confession was done in public within the hearing of one's neighbours. At Sennely-en-Sologne, a village perhaps typical of hundreds of others, in the late seventeenth century people refused to use the recently installed confessional boxes fearing that their neighbours would still hear what was going on. According to the distraught curé:

a boy who has abused a girl before marriage waits until death to confess it; thieves, perjurers, incendiaries and generally all those who have committed horrible and punishable crimes, wait until the last hour to confess them to a priest and give as a reason that it is not good to trust their corporal well-being to their malicious neighbours.[8]

What further dissuaded people from preparing themselves to partake in the sacred elements (or at least the bread, the wine was reserved for priests) was the need to put themselves in a condition of peace with their neighbours. This process went beyond the mere need to confess one's sins and perform the acts of penance prescribed by the priest (saying prayers, giving alms, going on a pilgrimage). It also required that one restore the lost honour of the person one had offended. But most people were unwilling to restore their enemies' honour by publicly asking for their forgiveness, especially when they stood to gain by continuing the dispute. In Piedmont in northern Italy a late sixteenth-century report noted that in many parishes people would not come to take Easter communion because they were in litigation against their neighbours or against their priests. This attitude was not confined to remote upland regions where the habits of the feud still held sway as they did in Piedmont or in northern Lancashire. In the lowlands of the Île de France at Clichy it was noted in 1671 that Christophe Nicholas had failed to attend church for a year because 'he could not bear to see another man of the parish with whom he was at enmity, and last Easter he preferred not to make his Easter duties than to be reconciled to him'.[9] In practice then the requirements of the *Pax* served to emphasize that the community was divided into the obedient few (many of whom were on the verge of death) and the passive many. Yet the fact that whole parishes seldom or never fulfilled the conditions necessary to achieve the *Pax* was not imcompatible with the old semi-pagan explanatory systems. Ordinary people saw the condition of peace as a phenomenon far out of the ordinary. Used too often, and once a year at Easter was too often, it would lose its potency as a means of compelling the gods who controlled the world to obey the will of suppliants.

For most ordinary Europeans the ritual of the Mass was a form of magic. Reports from pre-Reformation Germany and many other parts of Europe show people flocking to the churches in vast crowds; to house them a great number of new churches were built. But what many of these people came to see was a priest in the act of compelling God to become visible in the form of sanctified bread and wine. Village cunning people claimed they could control forces but few could automatically make them appear in this way. Moreover, the rituals of the Mass provided ordinary people who went forward to take communion with a useful magical artefact – the consecrated wafer. Kept under their tongue after it had been given them by the priest and taken home and preserved in a jar kept near the hearth (an East Anglian custom according to Keith Thomas), it would later prove useful if someone in the family was struck down with an illness. Consecrated wafers were also a well-known cure for warts; inserted into animal fodder they could also restore the strength of a sick plough ox.

The strange attraction which the elements of the Mass had for ordinary semi-Christians was acknowledged by the Church when it authorized the use of windowed vessels (monstrances) in which the sanctified elements could be publicly displayed. Depending on their point of view, ordinary people were at liberty to think that the longer they contemplated the monstrance the greater the amount of virtue they stored up against the eventualities of purgatory. Alternatively, contemplating a monstrance could give one greater magical potency. In any case a monstrance was a wonder-working relic which most people respected. Thus in 1530 the monks at Lytham in Lancashire persuaded a mob who were about to attack the priory in a property dispute to return quietly to their homes by bringing a monstrance into their midst.

An urban refinement

In the cities of Europe on Corpus Christi Day, a festival created by the Church in the late Middle Ages, the sacred elements formed the centrepiece of an elaborate float which was borne in procession through the streets bringing holiness in its wake. Corpus Christi Day was the high point of popular religious expression and was supposed to be the occasion when strangers and newly married couples were welcomed into the urban neighbourhood and when existing social hierarchies were affirmed as at Coventry and Venice. In time of tension it might also be the day when people who did not share the religious views of most of their neighbours were forced to flee for their lives. In the Catholic cities of France in the 1560s (at a time when they numbered about a fifteenth of the population of the country as a whole) the people most likely to suffer this fate were the Huguenots (Protestants). In the patois used by people around Tours in the Loire valley (the core area of monarchical control during the early Renaissance) the words *le roi Huguet* referred to ghosts of people who had come back to work harm at night. Since most Huguenot meetings were, of necessity, held secretly under cover of darkness a connection between Huguenots and the evil spirits was easily made. Moreover, contrary to the practices of Catholics, the Bible-reading Huguenots wore sombre dress, refused to participate in games or community religious rituals, or even to hang banners on their houses on Corpus Christi Day. All of these things set them apart from their urban neighbours.

In Lyon tensions between Catholics and Huguenots ran particularly high in 1561–2 at a time when the French king, Charles IX, was under pressure to grant the Huguenots the right to worship openly as full citizens. Forsaken by their annointed king and natural protector, Lyon's oligarchs and Youth Abbey members were thus led to think that the only way they could rid themselves of the polluting Huguenots was to do the task themselves. On Corpus Christi Day 1561 the shout went up 'for the flesh of God we must kill all the Huguenots'; badly mauled many Huguenot artisans and craftsmen temporarily left the city. The following year in the province of Maine, villagers who looked for leadership to the Holy League, which had been created by a fanatically Catholic élite to defend Catholic values against all-comers including the Crown, systematically massacred local Huguenots on Corpus Christi Day. Yet these brutal killings paled into insignificance when compared to the more than 3000 Huguenots who were killed on or soon after 24 August 1572 during the St Bartholomew's Day Massacre which was occasioned by the marriage of the Protestant Henry of Navarre to a royal princess, Margaret de Valois. During the era of Reformations religion and politics became hopelessly intermixed.

The Reformations

Between 1517 (when Martin Luther nailed his ninety-five theses to the door of the Castle Church at Wittenberg) and 1563 (when the Council of Trent ended its long deliberations with a firm statement of Catholic principles), the monolithic structure of the Christian Church was shattered. Instead of a single body of authority (the rich diversity of opinions *within* that Church during the late Middle Ages was unknown to ordinary Christians) there were now several groups collected into churches or sects, each of which claimed to have a monopoly of the truths necessary for salvation. The most important of the churches were the reformed Catholic, the Lutheran, the Zwinglian, the Calvinist and the Church of England. No less important were the Anabaptist sects.

Except in three or four of the free cities of the German Empire and in the Dutch Republic (which gained effective independence from Spain in 1609), religion was not allowed to be a private matter between an individual and his or her conscience. In all other polities and nations the decision about which religious denomination would become the sole tolerated church within the polity was made by the ruling princes or, in the case of the German Imperial cities, by the city oligarchy. Once made – after a period of hesitation which might last for weeks or years – this decision was backed up by church or lay courts (i.e. the Inquisition of Spain or Venice, the Consistory Courts of Protestant Geneva) and the full authority of the State. All people who dissented from the State church and were perceived to be in a position to influence others in their choice of faith, were in danger of being fined, imprisoned, banished or executed.

By the 1580s these policies of intolerance – and by later standards, of religious bigotry – had succeeded in preserving Spain, the Italian states, Bavaria and certain other parts of southern Germany for the Roman Catholic Church and in silencing the Protestants of Poland. In France, because of the strength of Calvinism in the urban south, the final full triumph of the Catholic Church was delayed until the revocation in 1685 of the edict of toleration which Henry IV – of St Bartholomew's Day fame – had given at Nantes in

1598. While the issue was still in doubt in France, much of northern Germany as well as all of the Scandinavian countries opted for the Lutheran Protestant alternative. Parts of Switzerland held fast to the Zwinglian beliefs while elsewhere in the mountainous confederation Calvinist forms prevailed, based on Geneva. Calvinism also prevailed in Protestant circles in France (the Huguenots) and in the Palatinate, and, in a modified form, in England.

In deciding which set of religious principles to adopt, rulers were ever mindful of geo-political, commercial and military considerations. In the Holy Roman Empire of the German Nation where the Reformation began these all came into lively play during the religious wars which ended with the Peace of Augsburg in 1555, a treaty which ignored Calvinism and divided the Empire into Catholic and Lutheran regions. Military and other considerations again came into play during the Thirty Years' War (1618–48) which ended with a treaty which finally recognized the Calvinist presence, but again ignored the Anabaptists and other sects.

If lists of printed books are anything to go by (without printing the Reformation would not have developed as it did, and indeed might have been quashed entirely), even in Italy among the better sort there was a widespread longing before 1517 for an evangelical Christ-centred form of religion which would give each individual a sense of being able to control his or her own spiritual destiny without the need to resort to superstitious practices. Before the full implications of the Protestant founders' teachings were worked out by their followers, these perceived needs for a more individualized Christian religion seemed to be met by the teachings of the three great Protestant leaders, Martin Luther (d. 1546), Ulrich Zwingli (d. 1531) and John Calvin (d. 1564).

Though these three leaders differed on many points of doctrine (especially on the meaning of the service of communion, the old Mass) they all agreed that individual men and women could only be saved for eternal life if they had a lively faith in Jesus Christ which was granted to them by God's Grace and by reading, hearing and believing the words of the Old and New Testaments. Theirs was a religion based firmly on a corpus of written scriptures – the Bible – which ostensibly had little use for visual images such as statues of saints or of the crucified Christ. In regions newly given over to Zwinglianism and Calvinism, such as those in the Netherlands between 1544 and 1569, the destruction of images – iconoclasm – was especially widespread; perhaps half of Europe's artistic heritage was lost in this way. Ironically in the Germanies before 1525 it was the visual images presented by printed woodcuts which did as much as any other single agency – including verbose Lutheran preachers – to bring unlettered men and women into the Lutheran fold.

Besides their insistence on the fundamental importance of the written word, Luther, Calvin and Zwingli also agreed that the Catholic system of 'good works' was incapable of controlling God's will. Their intention was that, rather than being protected by corporate solidarities, moral communities, confraternities, pilgrimages and the intercessory power of priests, individual Protestants should be left entirely naked before their God. Thus, according to the new teachings if a layperson were afflicted by an evil spirit (i.e. became mad), the demon could no longer be exorcised by a priest as had been the case in Catholic times.

Built into the three Protestant leaders' schemes were several contradictions. One hinged on the fact that not every person who heard or read the Bible arrived at the same conclusions about what it meant as a guide for daily life. Luther's original intention had been to abolish the social distinction between laypersons and the clerics who interpreted the Scriptures for them; as we saw earlier anti-clericalism had been rife in many parts of pre-Reformation Europe. But as Luther came to recognize during the course of the German Peasants' War (1524–6), if every layperson were allowed to be his or her own priest, the result would be anarchy. As a consequence, in the new Lutheran Church a separate priesthood came to be as much a part of social reality as it had been in the pre-Reformation Catholic Church. Similarly, in John Calvin's conception of a proper *Civitate Dei* as set forth in his *Institutes of the Christian Religion* (1536) a separate priesthood was held to be an essential part of a divinely ordered society. By the mid seventeenth century in all of the Christian Churches priests or ministers – all of them male – wore the distinctive black or dark coloured clothes which set them apart from laymen; in earlier centuries only monks and nuns had worn distinctive costumes.

Another difficulty built into the Protestant schemes of salvation hinged on the meaning of God's Grace. According to Calvin, building on the work of St Augustine of Hippo, God had foreknowledge of who would be saved and who would be damned (the concept of predestination) and there was nothing a poor sinner could do to alter his fate. This made it hard to justify in theological terms the perceived political need to compel every man and woman to belong to a Protestant state church.

The difficulties inherent in the Protestant schemes were taken into account by the Catholic fathers who met at Trent just south of the Alps between 1545 and 1563 to hammer out their new religious position as well as by the new proselytizing order, the Society of Jesus, the Jesuits, which was officially established in 1540. The Council of Trent affirmed that 'good works', belief in purgatory and in the virtues of the recognized saints, were still an essential part of the Christian life. And as the Jesuits in particular made clear, even though God knew who would be saved in the end, each living man and woman had a free choice to assist God in the task of salvation by participating in the sacraments. The fathers at Trent also affirmed that God's continuing word made itself known through the Holy Ghost acting through the mediation of the leader of the Catholic Church as well as in the ancient Holy Scriptures; with papal amendments God's word endureth forever.

Pervading the whole of the Reformation period was a deep-seated feeling among people who were prepared to give credence to at least part of the Christian message, that the end of the world was at hand. This sentiment, which was shared by Luther, gave a sense of urgency to the affairs of men which many earlier periods had lacked. Yet not everyone agreed what the end of the world would mean. People like Luther who were not social radicals or levellers simply thought that the material world and all mortal life would soon disappear and that Christ was about to come back to earth to judge the quick and the dead. In preparation for this final cataclysm it was essential to find a godly prince and godly church leaders – be they elders of the Calvinist sort, or bishops and priests of the Lutheran, Catholic or Anglican varieties – who would reform earthly society according to standard early modern ideals of degree, order and propriety.

At the level of the parish, god-fearing people who were carried away by this eschatological mood often sought to put their house in order before the end of the world came upon them. Left to their own devices by their prince, they usually did not frame their attitudes in specifically Lutheran, Anglican or Catholic terms; instead they simply wanted to apply what they took to be Christian principles to everyday life. A case in point were the changes which occurred in the parish of St Michael in Worms. In 1524 the church wardens and most respectable members of the congregation were highly dissatisfied with their priest, one Johann Leininger, not because he was a Catholic, but because his immoral ways had ruined the reputation of the parish. For some time Leininger had been living with the woman whom he had appointed to the post of church sexton; all the parishes round about spoke mockingly of the priest who slept with his sexton (a post usually reserved for men). Moreover, Leininger had misappropriated parish funds, used cloth which his parishioners had purchased for mass vestments for clothes for his bastard child, and had wrested control of parish records away from the churchwardens. He also demanded fees in advance before he would give the final sacraments to a dying woman. Justly feeling that Leininger had betrayed their trust, the churchwardens deposed him and put in his place a respectable married ex-monk who happened to be a Lutheran. They assumed that the new man would minister to their needs according to the Scriptures and uphold the honour of the parish.

Far more radical than people like the parishioners of St Michael were the millenarians. Basing their chiliastic ideals on obscure prophesies in the biblical books of Daniel and Revelation and on the teachings of Joachim of Fiore in Calabria (d. 1202), millenarians held that the coming cataclysm would be a battle between Christ supported by his millenarian allies and the forces of anti-Christ. Lutheran propagandists identified this latter person as the Roman pope; other candidates included the Great Turk and the Whore of Babylon. In preparation for this final battle between the Titans, the millenarians held that they had a moral duty to strike down all of the ungodly allies of anti-Christ, by which they generally meant all those in positions of authority. If this option were not readily available (heads of state and leaders of aristocratic armies weren't keen on social levellers) millenarians could withdraw from the everyday world and gird up their loins for the coming conflict. In any case they were convinced that the world war would ultimately be won by the forces of the godly and that Christ would come to establish an earthly kingdom which would last for a thousand years. Only after this millennium had come to an end would the material world disappear and Christ come to judge the quick and the dead.

The best known of the millenarians in the early sixteenth century were the Anabaptists. Because they openly questioned many of the core ideas which bound more conventional societies together, every point for which the Anabaptists stood marked a position far beyond that which territorial rulers and most ordinary godly people were prepared to accept. In no sense the cutting edge of the Reformations, their very existence created a barrier before which respectable Christians drew back in horror.

First emerging in Zwingli's Zürich in the mid 1520s (like Zwingli they denied that there was a miraculous transformation of the elements used in the communion), Anabaptists most readily gained converts among men in the traditional trades; blacksmiths, millers, shoemakers and tailors. In the village world these were the sort of people who often served as intermediaries with the world outside. In the regions around Leiden Anabaptists were particularly numerous among the unskilled textile workers who were victims of the putting-out system. Yet initially there were also a sprinkling of minor nobles, merchants and former law students. One such ex-student was Francesco della Sera of Padua – Italy was not immune from heresy – who argued that 'it was better to learn a trade and earn my bread with my own hands in the sweat of my brow than to do it by striving and arguing cases'.[10] Never numbering more than a few thousand souls in the early modern period and located in widely scattered regions, the Anabaptists were too individualistic and too anti-intellectual to agree on a single creed. Yet in general terms they held to a literal interpretation of the Bible which rejected all the Catholic formulations made since Christianity gained acceptance as a tolerated religion in the Roman Empire in AD 313 (the Emperor Constantine's Edict of Milan). For them the twelve hundred years of scholarly endeavour to bring Christianity into line with changing élite needs was meaningless sophistry.

Anabaptists had no use for the concept of the Trinity (Father, Son and Holy Ghost) or for St Augustine's ideas about predestination. Instead, these millenarians held that it was possible in this life fully to imitate Christ and to enter into a condition of sinlessness. And if a condition of sinlessness were possible, it was also possible to do away entirely with any priesthood or ecclesiastical organization. In the eyes of respectable people, no less anti-social than these assertions was the Anabaptist insistence that the only baptism which was valid was that undertaken by a fully mature regenerate adult; thus following Christ's example when He was baptized at the age of 30 by John the Baptist. In a world where more than half the population were under the age of 15, this Anabaptist concept, if it had been generally accepted, would have left most people outside the jurisdiction of any organized Christian grouping.

Anabaptists shunned the ordinary world which they held to be ruled by agents of the Whore of Babylon. In the segregated, egalitarian, male-dominated communities which they sought to create before and after the experience at Münster in 1534–5 (see p 194), three principles served as guides; modified communism, the rule of the saints and polygamy. In practice polygamy usually seems to have meant that no mature woman would be allowed to remain single, but instead was prevailed upon by the elders to marry a worthy already-married man and to put herself under his discipline. Modified communism meant that while individuals continued to control their own lands, tools and equipment, reserves of grain and other necessities were stored in communal barns. Fully committed Anabaptists were workaholics who did not take kindly to providing supplies to idlers. Yet if a fellow believer were ruined because his possessions had been seized by the agents of the anti-Christ (the State) or were overcome by some natural disaster, he could draw his sustenance from the communal store. The third principle, the rule of the saints, meant that the only government which Anabaptists recognized as fully legitimate was that provided by themselves. Within an Anabaptist community, such as those found in Moravia, discipline was upheld by elders who represented the consensus of the community. Backsliders were publicly humiliated in front of the congregation and, if need be, socially ostracized.

Whenever possible Anabaptists ignored ordinary outside secular authority. Believing literally in Christ's admonition that it was wrong to kill a fellow human being, they would not serve in national or territorial armies. Similarly, they refused to take oaths in a court of law, to serve as magistrates or to pay regular taxes. By avoiding payment of taxes and expenditure in war, the Anabaptist communities which escaped harassment tended to grow relatively wealthy. This was yet another reason why they were disliked by outsiders.

Yet it was not so much the comparative material wealth of Anabaptist communities which proved attractive to converts as their unquestioned sense of moral purpose and individual worth. With the decline of the monastic ideal in the northern world in the late Middle Ages, few communities could match the Anabaptists' experience in recreating the sense of endangered community which had bound the first Christians together in the three centuries of persecution after the death and purported resurrection of their Christ. Inner conviction strengthened the more than 2000 Anabaptist martyrs who are known to have been drowned, beheaded, burnt at the stake or otherwise judicially murdered by secular authorities, as well as the thousands of other Anabaptists who were assessed crippling fines.

Several things prevented the Anabaptists from becoming the dominant religious group among ordinary God-fearing Christians in the early modern period. One was their failure to find an influential convert of the stature of the Roman Emperor Constantine (d. 337). Instead of a Constantine equipped and prepared to issue an edict of toleration, the Anabaptists only managed to recruit leaders who, in the eyes of the respectable world outside, played the role of anti-Christ.

More than anything else the Anabaptists were discredited by the horrific events at Münster in north-western Germany in 1534–5. Coming in from Leiden and other Rhineland cities and rural areas, Anabaptists expelled the prince bishop of Münster and seized control of the city by force. Under the charismatic leadership first of Jan Mathys and then of the handsome libertine Jan Brockelson, the Anabaptists established a theocratic despotism which in its cruelty was unrivalled by most conventional Christian secular régimes, at least before the 1520s. Hundreds of non-members who did not escape during the first stages of the occupation were killed and their property confiscated for the use of the richly robed and bejewelled Anabaptist leaders. All books except the Bible were burnt on the pretext that it alone contained all the truths that anyone needed to know. Unattached women were forced to enter into polygamous marriages; Brockelson alone was serviced by fifteen wives. Anabaptist elders who protested at this imposition of polygamy by King Brockelson were killed or imprisoned by their fellow sectarians. This reign of terror only came to an end in June 1535 when, in a rare show of élite solidarity, combined Catholic and Lutheran armies starved the surviving remnant of Anabaptists into submission.

Much chastened by this experience, Anabaptists became increasingly inward looking, girding their loins in quiet preparation for the coming Apocalypse. After 1535 small communities flourished in the Netherlands (where they were known as Mennonites), in the Swiss Tyrol, in upper Austria and Moravia (where they were known as Hutterites). In most of these regions they were subjected to periods of sharp persecution. However, some of the north German princes, such as the Duke of Brandenburg, saw the quietistic Anabaptists as exemplars of the Protestant work ethic and encouraged them to settle in their cities. Thus in northern Europe by the end of the sixteenth century the tendency was for Anabaptist congregations to become increasingly urban-based and to consist largely of upwardly socially mobile artisans and craftsmen. In Moravia and south-central Europe, on the other hand, Anabaptists were largely rural based and in the material sphere followed the traditional peasant way of life.

Two centuries after Münster, in the 1730s, groups of Mennonites and Hutterites made their way to Pennsylvania and other parts of North America to take up new lands. A century or more later, Canadian and American descendants of these people, who still adhered to most of the old Anabaptist principles, once again crossed the Atlantic, this time to serve as missionaries of millenarianism in West Africa. Here they helped to found the churches which, if present trends continue, will survive long after the collapse of all the main-line Christian churches in western Europe.

The task of conversion

The Protestant and Catholic Reformations were the first occasion in the history of Europe when well-meaning urban élites bearing the Great Tradition made a concerted effort (the early medieval effort by monks was far more patchy) to instil ideas which were compatible with their own into the minds of semi-pagan rural people. So that there would be no shortage of qualified clergymen to preach the word of God and to minister to the needs of the people, in both Protestant and Catholic lands training colleges for ministers and priests were established, or existing colleges were put to new uses. By 1700, if not earlier, most rural parishes were staffed by clerics who were better trained and better paid than their late medieval predecessors had ever been.

To supplement the efforts of the parish clergy, in Catholic lands new religious orders such as the Jesuits, the Oratorians and Lazarists were established. Soon highly trained members of these new orders were out in the countryside holding evangelical rallies, preaching repentance from sin and burning pagan trinkets in 'fires of joy'. Since the Catholic missionaries seem to have had a shrewder understanding of the psychology of rural people than their Protestant counterparts (though both were products of the urban-based Great Tradition), in the years before 1730 they had considerable success in bringing to rural people both the word of God and a vision of God offered by the sacraments and dazzling Baroque ceremonial.

Two general principles guided the reforming bishops, elders and synods in their attempts to bring the knowledge of Christ to the people. First, there was to be a clear separation between the profane – the things of this world – and the sacred – the things which pertained to the Christian God. Second, all religious observances were to take place within the organizational framework of the parish so that they could readily be controlled by the parish priests or ministers. Both principles were essentially new and both had revolutionary social implications. In essence the separation of the sacred from the profane meant the secularization and de-mystification of everyday life and the removal of religion into a separate compartment of social existence. For most peasants, this entailed a high degree of inconvenience and the need to alter customary patterns of ritual behaviour, or at least to find new ways in which to act them out. In most parishes people were now forbidden to use church buildings for dancing, feasting and general merriment as had been done in the past. As a bishop of Milan put it, conviviality in church was 'indecent and contrary to Christian discipline'. Similarly cemeteries were fenced off and set apart from the world of the living.

The uses which people made of their time were also compartmentalized and made to fit the patterns of the new urban-organized religion. In Catholic lands the number of saints' days (holidays) on which people were not supposed to work was cut back: in France by 1666 to only ninety-two (this excludes the fifty-two work-free Sundays) and in Spain by 1624 to 150. In Protestant lands work-free saints' days were abolished almost entirely.

In nominally Calvinist Holland where, to the amazement of foreign visitors after around 1610, free-thinkers, atheists, Jews, Moslems and Catholics were openly tolerated, no special sacredness was attached to the Sabbath. In the 1630s Sundays were used by the Dutch:

for the holding of dance schools, beer and brandy-wine parties, lotteries, sales, juggling, fairs, auctions, hiring servants, baking and brewing, digging ditches or for laying in the church yard during the sermon.[11]

In Anglican England the situation was quite different. Here all ordinary people were expected to be at work six days a week (except at Christmas) and to spend Sunday mornings in prayer in church. This expectation was strictly enforced. During the first forty years of the seventeenth century church courts in lowland England tried numerous Sabbath breakers who had gathered in harvests, ploughed, threshed corn, shoed horses, cut people's hair, carried out a constable's duties, put servants to work or any number of other standard rural chores. Until King James I published his Book of Sports in 1618 (much to the consternation of Protestant precisionists – the Puritans) people were also forbidden to walk in the fields or play games on Sunday afternoons; instead they were supposed to spend this time in quiet meditation about their sins and the effects sin would have on their life in the world to come. After the Civil War and Restoration, the Anglican squires who filled Parliament still saw fit to maintain the sanctity of the Sabbath (in legislation in 1677).

Across the Channel in France, church officials also made every effort to close down inns, taverns and other places where people could buy alcohol and amuse themselves while religious services were held in the parish church. Offenders might be excommunicated and in theory cut off from normal intercourse with believing Christians. Yet in the mid eighteenth century, after more than a century of missionary endeavour, drink and Christianity were still incompatible. In Bignon in the diocese of Nantes missionaries found the people to be 'hard, undevout and wine-bibbing'. Similarly in St-Julien-de-Vouvantes the people much preferred to spend their time drinking local cider to attending mission exercises. Here, as elsewhere, by not knowing how to Christianize the profane – perhaps an impossible task – the élite lost contact with the people they were attempting to acculturate.

Though holiness was withdrawn from the everyday social world inhabited by ordinary people the same may not have held true for the world inhabited by men of business. In his *Protestant Ethic and the Spirit of Capitalism* (1905) Max Weber suggested that capitalists of the Calvinist persuasion differed from the traditional Catholic merchants found in say Leonis Baptiste Alberti's Florence in their notion of a 'calling'. Sensing that they were predestined to be saved but aware of the fact that they might possibly be damned, Calvinist businessmen felt that they had a duty to God to follow a path of worldly asceticism in their conduct of everyday affairs. They had to live modestly without ostentation, rationally calculating their use of time and money, so that they could increase their capital accumulation. According to Weber, success in capital accumulation was lively proof of the accumulator's moral and eternal worth. Yet just how closely this thesis fits the realities of bourgeois existence in post-reformation Europe is still a matter of lively scholarly debate.

In the life of ordinary people, of no less potential importance than the segregation of time was the Protestant and Tridentine Catholic insistence that the parish should become the principal focus of religious life. Although parishes had been in existence for centuries, in rural Flanders, in Venice and doubtless in many other parts of Europe, Christian religious observances had not been closely tied to parochial organizations. By making certain that they would be in future, the reformers hoped to snuff out all semi-pagan forms of religion and to ensure that no Christian could engage in religious practices that were not approved by the State.

To further these ends all rival organizations and informal groups which in the past had enabled believers to ignore their parochial obligations were either abolished outright or brought firmly under clerical control. In Protestant lands, the lay-dominated confraternities and religious guilds were abolished and their properties confiscated. In France, Italy, Spain and other Catholic lands the confraternities were reorganized and given new functions. Thus in

Milan during the administration of Archbishop Carlo Borromeo (1564–84) – later the patron saint of Portugal – every parish was required to create a new confraternity which was to indoctrinate the youth of the parish. Here too, all existing confraternities given over to the adoration of the Eucharist on Corpus Christi Day and on other days of the year were placed under centralized priestly controls. Similarly in Mâcon in France, Bishop Colbert made it clear that people were 'parishioners first and *confrères* afterwards'.[12]

One both sides of the credal divide Youth Abbeys and Realms were either dissolved or converted into training organizations for the young. Wherever the influence of reformers prevailed – and this was by no means everywhere – popular semi-pagan festivals such as St John's Eve, May Day, Twelfth Night and Carnival were gradually superseded by Christ-centred festivals. Thus in Montpellier in the late 1550s, Huguenot authorities banned public dancing and all the traditional festivals, and in Châlon-sur-Saône the rituals of St John's Eve were officially suppressed in 1648. The catalogue of these acts of suppression is almost endless.

Ordinary people did not always accept these well-intentioned élite prohibitions willingly. In 1663 Bishop Caulet of Pamiers, a prelate who had banned dancing in his diocese, was serenaded by rowdy youths during the night of St John's Eve and on the two succeeding nights. Similarly, many parishioners who considered themselves to be devout Catholics did not take kindly to the many bishops and lesser clergy who insisted on taking down statues of unauthorized saints or saints whose nakedness was too clearly revealed or who were too closely associated with the animal kingdom. In 1682 at Sennely-en-Sologne, women prevented the removal of an offending statue of St Anthony which the bishop had requested, saying that the bishop did not love the saint because he was a secret Huguenot.

Christian education

Whether Protestant or Catholic, the new urban-oriented religion laid great stress on the need for laypeople to know the word of God as a matter of personal experience. It was not enough merely to attend church. Instead, what was required was a lively knowledge of the fundamentals of the faith as interpreted by authorized ministers of religion; almost everywhere conventicles and informal meetings of laymen and women to discuss scriptures and sermons were discouraged. Rather than allowing Christians to come to a knowledge of God by themselves, all the mainline churches established training programmes for children, many of which centred on forcing them to learn catechisms by heart. In many parishes priests or lay school-teachers set Sunday afternoons and holidays aside for this purpose.

In some parts of Europe programmes of this sort paid handsome dividends, if dividends can be measured in the number of people who regularly took communion. In Spain by the mid seventeenth century most of the adults, other than vagrants, who were questioned by the clergy about the mysteries of the faith knew the essential facts about the life of Christ and His redeeming love, and could distinguish the three persons of the Trinity. At least 90 per cent of the people regularly took Mass, perhaps because they knew that if they did not the priest would post their names on the noticeboard and bring disgrace upon them. In all these matters the priests of Spain were greatly assisted by people's eagerness to denounce religious deviants to the agents of the Inquisition.

In some parts of Lutheran Germany as well, for example around Strasbourg, a comparison of visitation reports from the 1520s and 1550s suggests that people remembered what they had learned in catechism classes in their youth and tempered their behaviour accordingly. According to a report made in 1555 by Johann Marbach, the president of the company of pastors, the people in the villages were regularly coming to church on Sundays and were 'more peaceable and civilized than before'. Similarly, in Catholic Bavaria, where Lutherans were a persecuted minority, most adults who thought of themselves as Lutherans knew the Creed, the Lord's Prayer and other fundamentals of their faith.

Yet probably more typical of Lutheran lands overall was the situation in the county of Nassau-Wiesbaden where, as we saw earlier (p. 165), in 1594 most rural people were still unregenerate semi-pagans. Here and elsewhere children much preferred to go fishing, skating or dancing to going to catechism classes. During their years of adulthood they continued in ignorance of basic Christian truths. Typical of the reports coming in from visitations is this account of the Duchy of Wolfenbüttel in the 1570s:

It is the greatest and most widespread complaint of all pastors hereabouts that people do not go to church on Sundays .... Nothing helps; they will not come. And the same obstinacy exists on weekdays when the catechism is preached. Only a small part of the population attends these sermons so that the pastors face near empty churches .... No wonder then that the people respond miserably in catechism examinations. Even if one finds a man or woman who remembers the words, ask him who Christ is, or what sin is, and he won't be able to give you an answer.[13]

The failure of the State-supported Reformation to take full hold of the minds and hearts of rural people in the Germanies was paralleled by the experiences of many rural clerics in Catholic France and in Anglican England. However hard a priest such as Christophe Sauvageon, curé of Sennely-en-Sologne between 1676 and 1710, or a vicar such as Richard Greenham of Dry

Drayton in Cambridgeshire tried to win people for Christ they simply refused to listen. According to Greenham's own account he

spared no pains amongst his people .... His constant course was to preach twice on the Lord's day, and before the evening sermon to Catechize the young people of the Parish. His manner also went to preach on Mundayes, Tuesdayes and Wenesdayes and on Thursdayes to catechize the youth and again on Fridayes to preach to his people ... besides his publick preaching and catechizing, his manner was to walk out into the fields and to conferr with his Neighbours as they were at plow.

Greenham left the parish in 1591 largely because of the 'intractablenesse and unteachablenesse of that people'.[14] Similarly in Earls Colne during the ministry of Ralph Josselin, only a small proportion of the people who should have participated actively in the services of the church did so. At Easter 1669 only twenty people of the 500 qualified parishioners took communion and in 1670 only twelve. Ten years later the situation improved slightly when thirteen women and four men did their Easter duties. Here the abstainers were supported by the community consensus. In Catholic France where attendance levels at Easter were much higher – often 90 per cent or more – the people who refused to expose themselves to the 'Word' had to make more of an effort to justify their behaviour; here they were the deviants.

The Reformations in perspective

In lands which were not haunted by a popularly supported Inquisition the Reformations in religion furthered changes at the village and neighbourhood levels. In earlier times semi-pagan festivals and ritual observances had bound rich and poor together in a set of common assumptions about how to control Nature. These assumptions remained in place ready for emergency use even though villagers could seldom bring themselves to form a full perfect moral community. But now under the new dispensation – the Reformations – common assumptions disappeared and local populations were divided into a minority of godly believers and the rest. Often even the godly few were divided; in France between solid conventional Catholics and the precisionist Jansenists; in Germany between solid Lutherans and inward-looking Pietists; in England between solid Anglicans and the Puritan precisionists who were dissatisfied with the religious status quo and later between both parties and Archbishop Laud's Arminians. This last division sharpened the tension which in 1642 led to civil war. Yet even when the consequences of division were less catastrophic than this, the differences among the few who saw themselves as the chosen of God were a new dynamic force in the shaping of people's perceptions of who they were and what their local, regional and national societies stood for.

The great witchhunt

Beginning in the second third of the sixteenth century and ending around 1680 large areas of western Europe were in the throes of a massive hunt for witches. The scale of this hunt entirely eclipsed the small localized scares of the fifteenth century. Although the precise figures may never be known, during this century and a quarter at least a hundred thousand village people were sentenced to death as witches by law courts controlled by the bearers of the Great Tradition. No general explanation has yet been found which will explain this phenomenon in its many varied social settings. However, it is clear that it reflected changes which were taking place both in the mentality of selected village peoples (the *accusers*) and in the mentalities of the élites who controlled the courts of law.

Until 1680 one thing which nearly all western Europeans had in common, whether they were unlettered or learned, Protestants, Catholics or negligent sceptics was the belief that an ill-disposed but not necessarily identifiable person had the ability to work harm by occult or magical means. Since this belief had been no less common in the fifteenth century and earlier centuries than it was during the great witchhunt, it does little to explain this phenomenon. In the realm of ideas at the village level one change which was necessary before the great witchhunt could begin was the replacement of the old idea that the forces which controlled the world were morally ambivalent with the Christian notion that there was a clear distinction between good and evil. Once this idea was firmly planted in accusers' minds – the groundswell of interest in the Christian explanatory scheme was in part a cause and in part a consequence of the Protestant and Catholic Reformations – it was possible for accusers to link evil with one particular person, the active agent, the witch.

In most villages during the great hunt the person who was accused of being a witch was someone who had been born and brought up in the sacred space of the village and who had formerly been accounted a full member of the moral community. In these villages evil was found *within* the village itself. Yet in some of the villages which were afflicted during the great hunt vestiges of the old idea that evil came in from the outside still lingered on. For example in St Claude, Neuchâtel, Forcigny and other villages around Geneva after Calvin had made that Swiss city a bastion of reformed Protestantism, several accused witches were alien immigrants from the Savoy.

Left to their own devices – this is a vital qualification – most village-level accusers of witches between the mid 1500s and 1680 were almost solely concerned with acts of *maleficium*. The ways in which a reputation for being a bad witch was built up over the years is perhaps best shown by quoting George Gifford, an Essex cleric who wrote a reasonably unbiased discourse on the practices of witches in 1587 during the reign of the first Elizabeth. According to Gifford:

Some woman doth fal out bitterly with her neighbour; there followeth some great hurt .... There is a suspicion conceived. Within fewe yeares after shee is in some iarre with an other. Hee is also plagued. This is noted of all. Great fame is spread of the matter. Mother W is a witch. She hath bewitched goodman B. Two hogges died strangely; or else hee is taken lame. Wel, Mother W doeth begin to bee very odious and terrible unto many. Her neighbours, dare say nothing but yet in their heartes they wish shee were hanged. Shortly after an other falleth sicke and doth pine, hee can have no stomacke unto his meate, nor hee can not sleepe. The neighbours come to visit him. Well neighbour, sayth one, do ye not suspect some naughty dealing: did yee never anger mother W? Truly neighbour (sayth he) I have not liked the woman a long tyme. I can not tell how I should displease her, unlesse it were this other day, my wife prayed her, and so did I that shee would keepe her hennes out of my garden. Wee spake her as fayre as wee could for our lives. I think verely shee hath bewitched me. Every body sayth now that Mother W is a witch in deede, and hath bewitched the goodman E. Hee cannot eate his meate. It is out of all doubt; for there were [those] which saw a weasil runne from her housward into his yard even a little before hee fell sicke. The sicke man dieth, and taketh it upon his death that he is bewitched; then is Mother W apprehended, and sent to prison, shee is arraynned and condemned.[15]

The transformation of simple village-level anti-social *maleficium* into something which the Christian élites considered much more grievous – a crime against God – was a process which took place either in a court of law or a prison while an accused witch was awaiting trial, or in the minds of accusers who had been made to accept the new élite stereotype of a witch. Forged by the Christian Church during two centuries or more of bitter conflict with Waldensian and Cathar heretics (these people were Christian fundamentalists deeply influenced by the teachings of the Persian mystic Mani who died in AD 276), this élite stereotype took it for granted that the Devil was no less real than was God. As King James VI of Scotland put it in 1597, playing upon the principle of inversion:

since the Devill is the verie contrarie opposite to God, there can be no better way to know God, than by the contrarie ... by the falshood of the one to considder the trueth of the other ....[16]

The extent of élite interest in the Devil is reflected in the catechism written by the Dutch Jesuit Peter Canisius around 1550 in which the Devil's name was mentioned sixty-seven times and Christ's only sixty-three.

The élitist delusion held that Satan was assisted in his hellish work by a well-organized network of human agents, the witches. These misguided people had renounced their loyalty to the lay rulers who exercised temporal power in Christ's name and to Christ himself; in most realms this was a capital offence. The delusion further held that the witches were periodically borne aloft by monstrous animals or broomsticks and flew long distances to meet with the Devil and their fellow witches at a 'Sabbot'. At this hellish festival they worshipped Satan by parodying the Christian Mass and other rituals; thus according to notions conjured up in the fertile minds of celibate priests and monks, the holy water used by witches at a Sabbot consisted of the Devil's urine or semen.

With the exception of England, where the notion of a Sabbot did not catch hold, and of France, in most other regions the propagators of the élite stereotype held that a witches' Sabbot ended with feasting on human babies, a sexual orgy and other obscenities. The élitist delusion further held that the witches had given their souls to Satan and in return received a Devil's mark on their skin which would not bleed when pricked with a pin. They were also given the power to work all manner of evil on the people of God; blasting their crops, wrecking their farmsteads, killing their cattle, causing newly married men to be impotent and bringing death and disease to the households of the godly.

The effects of the élitist-style witchcraft closely paralleled the effects of the sort of witchcraft known to village people from personal experience or hearsay. This probably explains why they were willing to turn to courts of law for relief. Yet even at the height of the great witchhunt many ordinary people still had only a very confused notion about the identity of the master of the witches. Thus, in the mountainous Ajoie district in the Jura, a district in which a single dialect was spoken, village people could not agree among themselves on the name by which the master of evil was known. Between 1594 and 1617 they variously spoke of him as Noiron, Herpet, Pisaulx, Sautaurain, Frenical, Niquesse, Robin, Greppin and Griffon. Magistrates perhaps erroneously assumed that all of these names referred to their own monolithic concept of evil, the Devil. Yet even among the élite there was some confusion about the identity of the two polar forces which supported the élite witch stereotype. For example, for Jean Bodin of Laon, the author of a guide book for French magistrates intent on identifying witches (the *Démonomanie* published in 1580), the God whom witches had supposedly rejected was not the gentle Christ of the New Testament but instead the cruel monotheistic Jehovah of the Jewish Old Testament whose agents had taught that all other people's tribal gods were devils. It has recently been suggested that Bodin himself was an apostate who had rejected Christ in favour of Jehovah.

Thus far we have not mentioned the gender of most of the people who ended up in a court of law accused of practising witchcraft. Before the mid 1500s and the advent of the great witchhunt many accused witches were men. For example, in fifteenth-century Neuchâtel in Switzerland twenty-nine of the thirty-six people accused of witchcraft were males. Then too nobody could have been more manly than the Knights Templars against whom Philip the Fair of France used the charge of witchcraft with such devastating effect in the years after 1307 (the Order of Templars was utterly destroyed). In courtly circles in the fifteenth century witchcraft accusations were often used as a means of eliminating political dissidents. In uncivil Scotland as late as 1590, King James VI accused his troublesome cousin Francis, Earl of Bothwell, of meddling in witchcraft and causing the storms which nearly shipwrecked the king when he was sailing to Denmark to claim his bride.

In marked contrast to this earlier pattern, during the great witchhunt the overwhelming majority of the people who were accused of witchcraft were women. Thus in Essex 92 per cent and in Luxembourg and the Cambrésis nearly 80 per cent of the accused were women. Just why this sexual bias existed has not yet been fully determined. But in an era of rapid change when old rural values were being questioned and held up for ridicule by outside élites and by the new *coqs de village*, it was natural that people looked around for scapegoats. Among the more obvious candidates were women of mature years who served as midwives and nurses and who were reputed to have special links with the supernatural forces which surrounded the village. In Austria and Schleswig-Holstein in what was then Denmark more than half of the people who were later accused of witchcraft had earlier served their rural communities as healers or diviners. Under the old value system these cunning people had a moral authority which most men lacked and perhaps secretly envied. Then, too, the old widowed women who were likely to find themselves accused of witchcraft were often much poorer than they had been when in the prime of their married life; out of loneliness they often pestered their neighbours for the loan of a cup of milk, an invitation to a marriage feast and the like. And as we saw in Chapter 2, the people who moulded the opinions of the male population in the sixteenth century assumed that women were lustful irrational beings who would willingly engage in the carnal act with the Devil himself. In 1522 a famous but slightly paranoid man who had a keen understanding of popular prejudices could automatically assume that witches were women. According to Martin Luther:

sorcerers or witches are the Devil's whores who steal milk, raise storms, ride on goats or broomsticks, lame or maim people, torture babies in their cradles, change things into different shapes ....[17]

In Luther's Germany, in contrast to, say Florence, few men were whores.

In order for the great witchhunt to come into being it was essential that the laws and court systems set up by the élite co-operated with village accusers in seeing that a suspected witch was put on trial, found guilty and judicially murdered. In Spain, alone of all the large states of western Europe, this co-operation was not forthcoming. Ever since the 1520s the Inquisition had been reticent to accept the claims of village accusers and to put suspects on trial for their lives. This position was itself put to the test in 1609 when Alanso de Salazar Friás and other members of the Inquisition were sent to Lagrōno in the Basque country to investigate 5000 people whom locals accused of witchcraft. After studying thousands of pages of written testimony Salazar came to the conclusion that in no single case was there any empirical proof that the spells and curses the accused had uttered had actually caused misfortune or bodily harm. Building on these findings Salazar recommended to the Inquisitor General and his council that all of the accused be declared innocent. Ignoring pleas to the contrary the Inquisitor General accepted Salazar's recommendation in 1614. After that year no case of village-level *maleficium* which came to the attention of the central Inquisition ended in conviction. Similarly, except in the lands which were under the control of the Venetian Republic, in the Italian city states and kingdoms, where witchcraft trials were also left in the hands of the Inquisition, most hearings ended with the exoneration of the accused.

In England, where the relevant members of the élite, the Members of Parliament, held that witches existed and that they could work bodily harm by magical or occult means, the enabling Acts which made the great hunt possible were passed in 1542, 1563 and 1604. But in contrast to most other parts of Europe where lay courts were used, in England the decision about whether a witch had actually committed the foul deeds of which he or she stood accused rested with grand and petty jurors who came from the county or shire in which the *maleficium* was felt. These ordinary men (no women were jurors) were, in theory, in a position to know something of the witch's earlier reputation in her village and were far less likely to be totally influenced by the élite stereotype than were the great judges of the Common Law Courts. In consequence most English witches were judicially murdered for merely committing *maleficium* rather than for belonging to an anti-Christian sect of devil worshippers.

On the Continent most territorial rulers felt uneasy about letting any judicial decision rest in the hands of ordinary people and modernized their court systems according to the tenets of the Italianate Roman Law. Under this system, the judges and their well-trained court assistants (bearers of the Great Tradition) compiled the evidence accusers laid before them (a procedure known as the *Inquisitio*) and doctored it to fit their preconceptions in the process. Here the accused could say nothing in their own defence. Since it was highly desirable that the accused admit to their guilt before they were sentenced (the judges, too, had consciences) torture was used to extract a confession.

The use of torture (specially designed thumb screws, laced boots, the rack, the wheel and the like) together with the discretionary power allowed to judges under the *Inquisitio* procedures, largely explains why at least 10 per cent of the population of a south-western German town such as Rothenburg might find themselves before a court charged with practising witchcraft. For under torture not only did a faint-hearted person freely admit to an interrogator – who asked the right leading questions – to being a witch of the élite-stereotype sort, she or he also named all of the other persons who had supposedly attended a local witches' Sabbot. Since the judges had the option of seizing and torturing these people as well, everything was set for a chain of accusations.

In the urbanized German south-west where the witchhunt reached an intensity greater than that found in most other parts of so-called civilized Europe (between 1561 and 1670 3229 people, 2527 of them Catholics, were executed) confessions obtained under torture confirmed the worst fears of the judges and led them to track down every last suspect. The suspects thus detected included many sorts of people besides lonely old women; wealthy merchants and their wives, school-teachers, innkeepers and just about anybody who had earlier inadvertently wronged or slighted the tortured accuser. In 1627 the magistrates finally began to recognize not that witches did not exist but that they and their near associates on the bench would all be burnt to death as witches if they accepted the validity of all the accusations made under torture. This realization came much earlier in Calvinist Geneva and as a result magistrates there seldom followed up accusations made under torture.

In rural Cambrésis the chain of reactions set in motion by the use of torture appears to have incriminated only other village people, not the élite. For example, in 1623 a woman named Catherine Salmon who was associated with the villages of Fressier and Hem-Lenglet admitted under torture that she was a devil worshipper and claimed that her son Crespin was as well. Madame Salmon also denounced Colette Jardet who in turn denounced her own son; all four were executed as witches. And because local people and magistrates held that witchcraft ran in families, they also put Madame Salmon's sister Barbara and her daughter Gilliette on trial. Gilliette was later strangled and burnt; her aunt escaped with a sentence of banishment.

Aside from the special case of Spain, the reason why a few regions such as the primitive highlands of Scotland and the rural parts of the Kingdom of Naples managed to survive with their population of cunning women and midwives intact was that no outside élite saw fit to meddle with the moral relationships of local people. But in regions which were of deep concern to outside élites and which were undergoing rapid internal social change, the absence of witchcraft accusations was probably a reflection of the fact that the new *coqs de village* felt themselves to be secure, both with respect to their fellow villagers and to the outside élites. For instance, in the Essex village of Terling, where the processes of social differentiation were as marked as anywhere else in England, no accusations of witchcraft came to the attention of the courts during the great witchhunt.

By way of contrast, in Luxembourg and the Cambrésis, regions in which at least 838 trials were held, the new rural élites were clearly riddled with feelings of insecurity and inadequacy. As we saw earlier in this chapter, during the first part of the sixteenth century the moral behaviour of the people in both regions had been more or less ignored by outside élites. All this changed in 1570 when they were brought under the firm control of the Habsburg ruler, Philip II of Spain, and proselytizing Tridentine bishops such as Pierre Binsfield of Trier. Another Catholic cleric who was much concerned with the moral behaviour of people in these afflicted regions was the Jesuit Martin del Rio who published books on the evils of witchcraft in 1599 and 1601. Together with other missionary priests and pioneer school-teachers, these men encouraged each person of consequence in Luxembourg and the Cambrésis to believe that it was his or her own sins against God which had led Him to punish them with illnesses and misfortunes. Interpreting this message in their own way, village people assumed that this God/Devil caused the misfortunes which had been sent upon them through the mediation of a witch. And just as this new confusing sense of guilt was internalized within the breast of each individual, so too was the reality of the new dividing line between the sacred and the profane. Absolute goodness was now seen to reside *within* the very centre of the village in the person of the priest and the congregation of the godly. Likewise the absolute evil which tried to trap the unwary and bring their souls to hell was now brought fully *within* the village and sometimes within the family.

In the Cambrésis and Luxembourg many of the people who accused others of being witches were adults of some substance who desperately wanted to reject the old notions about the efficacy of corporate pagan rituals and to accept the new urban ideas about personalized sin. Overwhelmed by a sense of guilt about their inability to do so, they cast about for a scapegoat whom they could accuse of *maleficium* or worse. These feelings were picked up by many of their clients and employees. Thus among the people who in 1599 levelled charges of witchcraft against Reyne Percheval, a widow who had lived all her life in Bazuel, was Pierre Wattelier, a 30-year-old thatcher who was frequently employed by the *coqs de village*. Wattelier accused Reyne of causing the death of one of his cows. Another accuser was Reyne's son-in-law who claimed that she had caused the death of his daughter Maria, (the accused's granddaughter). The son-in-law's court room testimony was confirmed by Jean Lenain, an alderman of Bazuel, and Georges Cloquette, a constable. Another widow accused Reyne of bringing sickness into the household of Jean Paretier by occult means. Paretier, a 50-year-old alderman, confirmed this testimony and added that Reyne had caused one of his lambs to be born without a skin.

Reyne Percheval was not among the small minority of accused witches who withstood the pressures to confess or who died of gaol fever before she did so. Arrested and tortured Reyne found herself transformed by her own words from a mere practitioner of *maleficium* into a devil worshipper. She admitted to having sexual intercourse with the Devil who called himself Nicollas Rigaut, to renouncing her baptism, to having attended a Sabbot in the company of Isabeau Dubaille and to have practised her foul craft of evil-doing for seventeen or eighteen years.

In the acculturation of rural Europe the public execution of witches served an important didactic purpose. As far as the judges were concerned, the fiery removal of the witch helped to establish the bounds of morally acceptable behaviour. Before the fires were lit, the pretended witch was made to confess her sins against God and the territorial prince who claimed to rule in His name. She then had to ask to be received back into the fold of humankind. Following this request the attendant priest or minister gave her absolution and assured her that her sins were forgiven. For the hundreds or sometimes thousands of people who had come from near and far to see the spectacle, the lessons were all too clear. Devil-worshipping witches actually existed and the power to combat them now rested not with the village moral community, but with the new order of Church and State.

But at a deeper level of understanding which accepts the modern scientific premise that no person can control forces by occult or magical means (jet planes are built by skilled engineers and mechanics and not by witches) the burnt witch was something different from what early modern judges supposed. Under the old order of moral values she had been a wise woman or healer who was revered for her abilities to control the forces of the supernatural in ways which were as likely to be beneficial as harmful; she had been a vital part of the moral defences of the village. Now under the new early modern order, she was rejected and cast off as a scapegoat just as another healer who was said to work miracles was rejected around AD 30 and put to death on the cross at Calvary.

Tracking down and destroying a witch-scapegoat from within a village was an extremely expensive business which the goods confiscated from the dead victim – usually a person of little wealth – would scarcely begin to defray. In a world where the monopoly of justice was becoming increasingly centralized (see Chapter 6) it was necessary for village officials to send messengers back and forth to the high court judges at every stage in the proceedings as well as to pay for the cost of imprisoning, torturing and executing the sacrificial victim. In the Cambrésis the cost of executing a single witch might amount to the price of twenty or thirty cows. This expense would be met by a special levy from which local men of substance would not be exempt. And after the witch's ashes had been scattered to the four winds, custom demanded that the local and high court judges be lavishly entertained at a costly public banquet. For the local *coqs de village* this feast was of especial significance. It was a public affirmation that for a short time they were at one with the social superiors they so desperately wanted to emulate, and that they had temporarily succeeded in assuaging their sense of guilt.

The sudden rise of the witch craze in the second third of the sixteenth century was matched by the suddenness of its decline. Between 1660 and 1680 judges everywhere began to follow the earlier lead of the Parlement of Paris (an appeal court for the northern third of France) and to apply stricter rules of proof to the evidence which came before them. One by one they came to recognize that no empirical link could be established between any particular suspected witch's ritual activities and the misfortunes which subsequently befell the accusers.

Just why Europe's judicial élite and their princely masters went one step further and began to doubt that the Devil was seeking to overcome the Christian social order by using witches has yet to be ascertained. In the German South-West the new self-confidence of magistrates after about 1650 seems to have been a factor; accusers of witches now found themselves fined or drafted into the army. Perhaps the lessening fear of the Devil was also linked to the precipitous decline of Neoplatonism (which had endowed every material thing in the universe with forces and depended upon correspondences between macrocosm and microcosm) and the rise of a more mechanistic but no less erroneous world view (we now know that the universe is not analogous to an ever-constant functioning machine). By the late seventeenth century, the high-tide of the Age of Reason, the élite came to assume that scientists and philosophers such as Descartes, Newton and Galileo could adequately explain most happenings in the material world. They were convinced that by the use of reason, happenings which were currently inexplicable would in time be explained. As Sir Robert Filmer put it in 1653, 'There be daily many things found out and daily more may be which our fore fathers never knew to be possible.'[18]

The belief that there was no limit to man's potential to understand and control Nature through rational means was incompatible with the belief in witchcraft, magic and perhaps with the concept of a God who participated actively in everyday affairs. Thus around 1670 a sophisticated Parisian lawyer felt able to confess to Father Beuvrier that at the bottom of his heart he felt that the Christian scheme of redemption and punishment was 'all a fairy tale' and that 20,000 other cultured Parisians shared his views.[19] Writing about his contemporaries in Restoration England Dudley, fourth Lord North found that very few 'especially among the vulgar' believed in life after death.[20]

Yet at the level of the village it would be a long time before most people gave up believing in signs and witches. In Spain more than a century after the Inquisition had ceased to regard witches as anything other than victims of malice or as troublemakers, rural people still besieged them with accusations. For instance, in 1680 the Inquisitors at Saragossa were confronted by twenty-eight lay people and a priest who accused a middle-aged woman named Maria Perez of practising *maleficium*; as usual the Inquisition found that she was innocent. But if the central courts found accused witches innocent, the neighbours sometimes took justice into their own hands. According to one French official's claim, in the years between 1593 and 1601 nearly 300 exonerated witches were lynched or stoned to death by their neighbours in the Champagne. In Norway, village witches were still being murdered by their neighbours well into the eighteenth century. And in late seventeenth-century England, according to the brother of Chief Justice Lord North, if a judge did not heed the popular clamour and condemn an accused witch to death, the country people would cry that 'this judge hath no religion, for he doth not believe [in] witches'.[21]

Thus despite the painful efforts of Christian missionaries, teachers and judges to acculturate rural people to their own urban-based views, by 1680 two evolving, but distinct cultures had clearly come into existence; popular culture – in which changes took place relatively slowly – and élite culture in which changes took place more rapidly. In our next and final chapter we will examine the interaction of these two cultures in dealing with the problems posed by poverty, the need to maintain law and order, and other secular concerns.

Notes and references

1   G. Strauss, 'Success and failure in the German Reformation', *Past and Present*, no. 67 (1975), pp. 62–3.
2   Richard Gough, *The history of Myddle* (edited by D. Hey) (London 1981), p. 18.
3   A. Macfarlane, *Witchcraft in Tudor and Stuart England: a regional and comparative study* (New York 1970), p. 311.
4   P. Burke, *Popular Culture in Early Modern Europe* (London 1978), p. 212.
5   J. Rossiaud, 'Prostitution, jeunesse et société dans les villes du sud-est au xve siècle', *Annales E-S-C*, **31** (1975), p. 323.

6   P. Ariés, *The Hour of Our Death* (translated by Helen Weaver) (London 1981), p. 24.

7   W. Christian Jr, *Local Religion in Sixteenth Century Spain* (Princeton, NJ 1981), p. 35.

8   G. Bouchard, *Le Village immobile: Sennely-en-Sologne au XVIIIᵉ siècle* (Paris 1972), p. 291.

9   J. Bossy, 'The Counter-Reformation and the people of Catholic Europe', *Past and Present*, no. 47 (1970), p. 56.

10 G. H. Williams, *The Radical Reformation* (Philadelphia 1962), p. 190.

11 K. Sprunger, 'English and Dutch Sabbatarianism and the development of Puritan social theology (1600–1660)', *Church History*, **51** no. 1 (1982), pp. 28–9.

12 Bossy, 'The Counter-Reformation', p. 60.

13 Strauss, 'Success and failure', p. 53.

14 M. Spufford, *Contrasting Communities: English villagers in the sixteenth and seventeenth centuries* (Cambridge 1974), pp. 327–8.

15 Macfarlane, *Witchcraft in Tudor and Stuart England*, pp. 111–12.

16 S. Clark, 'Inversion, misrule and the meaning of witchcraft', *Past and Present*, no. 87 (1980), p. 117.

17 E. William Monter, *Witchcraft in France and Switzerland: the Borderlands during the Reformation* (Ithaca 1966), p. 31.

18 K. Thomas, *Religion and the Decline of Magic: studies in popular beliefs in sixteenth and seventeenth century England* (London 1971), p. 660.

19 J. Delumeau, *Catholicism between Luther and Voltaire: a new view of the Counter-Reformation* (translated by J. Moiser and introduction by J. Bossy) (London 1977), p. 219.

20 Thomas, *Religion and the Decline of Magic*, p. 172.

21 ibid., p. 460.

6 *The wider circles of sociability*

By the 1550s, a century after the invention of the printing press in or near Mainz in the west of the German Empire, an increasingly sizeable minority of ordinary Europeans were becoming literate. At the very least, people who were able to read their own vernacular language – though not necessarily to write it – were no longer guided in their thinking and behaviour solely by the customary thought patterns of their own localized oral culture. Instead, they could be influenced by printed materials created for a regional or national market. However, whether this influence worked for a change of the sort associated with modernization or for a new kind of continuity has yet to be fully determined.

Although the whole subject of mass literacy is hedged about with uncertainties, it is probably true to say that in early modern Europe far more people had the ability to read – a skill which normally proceeds learning how to write – than to both read and write. Parents who had children who were under the age of 6 or 7 and too young to contribute in any meaningful way to the family economy might well send them across the road to a semi-literate neighbour – who might be a woman – to learn to read. Then before the child had time to acquire the second more liberating skill (writing), he or she might be called home to farm full time or to work in the shop. The demands of mundane existence being what they were, this child might never find time to learn how to write. Thus, because full literacy was economically determined, it was only the better sort of peasant or the more skilled of the artisans who could both read and write.

In itself, the ability to read or at least to pick one's way through a simple printed text does not free the reader from the tyranny of received opinion, whether it be that of the village, that of the urban élite and the reformation of

Detail from 'Justice' by Peter Bruegel the Elder, 1559

manners, or that of the ruler of the state. A person who can merely read but who cannot write is still essentially passive in the same way that illiterate people who are entirely dependent upon what they hear in an oral culture are passive recipients of the opinions of the village elders. Full emancipation from received opinion only comes with organizing one's own thoughts in a coherent fashion and putting them down in writing – perhaps preparatory to sending them off to a printer. All the steps in this process can be done in secret without the need to call in any censorious intermediary.

A comprehensive understanding of the dynamics of early modern society requires that we know just how many people were in fact fully literate; whether this requirement can be met is another matter. Among most historians it is an article of faith that the ability to sign one's name on a marriage register, a *terrier*, or a political document such as the English Protestation Oath of 1642 reflected the person's full literacy. Thus we know from the marks and signatures affixed to the new *terrier* drawn up for the seigneury of Wissous in the Hurpoix in 1600 that twenty-five of the 100 village heads of households were able to sign their name. Among these were nine of the fifteen Wissous *laboureurs*, a baker, a merchant, a stonemason and a quarter of the wine-growers. This Wissous pattern – about a quarter of the males able to sign by 1600, mostly among the better off peasantry, and a far lower proportion of women – closely parallels the pattern in most of the region north of a line stretching from St Malo to Geneva. South of this line in France and probably in most of the rest of the Mediterranean world as well, the proportion of men of non-genteel status who were able to sign by 1600 or even by 1720 or 1820 was far lower. Yet, to assume that true literacy rates can be derived from the evidence of signatures such as those from Wissous may be fallacious. Historians who have personal experience in today's Third World know of people who have mastered the art of signing their name on a pay slip or cheque but who cannot write anything else or read a single word. For all intents and purposes these people are still totally illiterate.

Laying to one side the unanswerable question about the correlation between signatures and rates of full literacy in early modern Europe, it can be said with certainty that in several Protestant lands State authorities positively encouraged their subjects to learn at least how to read. Protestantism was a religion firmly based on the Bible. Thus in post-Reformation Sweden, where the State was especially quick to realize the potential of the printed word, full membership in the church and community after 1648 was limited to people who had the ability to read the Bible, commentaries on the Bible and the printed sermons which best served the purposes of the state authority. In France as well, the rise of Calvinism after 1520 encouraged the Catholic hierarchy and state authority to see to it that schools were established in every market town and large village. Here people could be taught to read to themselves and to others the government-approved printed works which pointed out the weaknesses of Huguenot teachings and the spiritual worth of Catholic belief and practice. Here they could be inculcated with the stereotype image of Huguenots as incestuous sodomites and rapists who violated every cherished Catholic sexual norm. Legislation in 1539 forbade French schoolmasters to expound to students sensitive works that were dear to Huguenots, such as the epistles of St Paul. In Albi in 1547 (Calvinism was particularly strong in the urban French south) a teacher who disregarded this law was arrested. Though the chaos occasioned by the Wars of Religion after 1562 gravely weakened this movement towards mass literacy, it was renewed with even greater force in the seventeenth century. Coupled with this move was even greater state finesse in the use of censorship and thought control. Dissident literate intermediaries such as Jean-Baptiste de Guigues, the priest at Tourettes who in 1709 was caught reading Jansenist literature aloud to illiterate women and boys at a *veille*, were promptly disciplined.

Yet, in addition to state encouragement of education as a means of propagating an ideology of order, degree and obedience (the push factors), there were also pull factors in the move towards mass literacy. Rural families such as the leaseholders in Altopascio in Tuscany who hoped that their sons and perhaps their daughters might be socially mobile upwards either by being better informed about market conditions for products from the family farm, or by being equipped to find better status jobs in the cities, recognized the importance of the gift of full literacy. Among urban parents who were not completely broken by poverty this awareness was particularly acute. By the late seventeenth century, in the seething competitive milieu of a large city full literacy had become almost a prerequisite for success. Though rural areas generally lagged behind the cities, almost everywhere where village people perceived the need to use the market economy, though not necessarily to join it, parents were anxious to have a schoolmaster in their midst. Thus in Boissy-sous-Saint-Yon in 1605, when villagers learned that their schoolmaster had found a more remunerative post elsewhere, they clubbed together to offer him better pay and better lodgings.

For the literate ordinary early modern European, the large elaborately printed books of the sort found in the collections of great universities or in cathedral libraries were prohibitively expensive. Instead, they were dependent on reading materials that were printed on eight, twelve, sixteen or twenty-four sheets of cheap paper which would at most cost 2 or 3 sous or pence, the equivalent of less than half a day's wages. In addition to their cheapness, these chapbooks, as they were called, had to be light enough for a chapman or vender to carry around in packs from one village fair to another and from door to door. By their very nature, these works were not likely to survive very long after they were sold. Once read they made convenient toilet paper (privies were the libraries of the poor) or were used for miscellaneous odd purposes such as stopping up mustard bottles. Thus, in order to know what it was that people actually read, historians are dependent on the inventories of the remaining stocks left on hand by printers, such as the Oudet family of Troyes (who printed chapbooks between 1670 and 1722), or on the collections of bemused members of the élite such as Samuel Pepys, an avid collector between c. 1682 and c. 1687.

Since few of the printing presses found in the capitals and leading provincial cities of Europe were subsidized by the State or by private philanthropists, the printers who catered to the mass market by and large printed only the sort of thing which they knew customers would buy. Some idea of the scale of this market can be seen from the inventory of a London printer such as Charles Tias. In 1664 Tias had on hand 10,000 chapbooks ready for sale and the paper required to print an additional 80,000. A few decades later, in 1722, Jacques Oudet in Troyes, son of one of the first publishers of the famed *Bibliothèque Bleue*, had on hand 36,000 little volumes and the paper needed for an additional half a million. In France the number of different titles offered for sale in any given year increased from more than 1000 in the seventeenth century to 4000 in the eighteenth.

In Europe overall, after the first flurry of interest in the Reformations had died down and the proportion of religious books had decreased, nearly a third of the chapbooks offered for sale continued to deal with religious subjects. In Catholic countries ordinary people never seemed to tire of reading about the miraculous lives of saints and of godly martyrs who had put themselves in a position to die for their faith. In late sixteenth- and seventeenth-century Protestant countries, where saints were either abolished or played down by those in authority, the standard theme in the religious chapbooks was that the ghoulish sins, which were so titillating to read about, would be punished by heavenly agents. Most tales ended with the anti-hero or heroine's death bed repentance, an object lesson which no cleric would find unorthodox. Another immensely popular category of chapbooks was those dealing with what readers took to be historical personages; brave knights such as Roland the companion of Charlemagne, or Pierre de Provence who battled with armies of dragons and infidels to free the chaste maiden whom he or his noble superior would later marry. In the twelfth century chivalrous tales such as these had been the common fare of bored winterbound knights and storytellers. But by the late sixteenth century, when the élite culture was drawing apart from the popular culture, few gentlemen aside from demented throwbacks such as Cervantes's Don Quixote thought them worth reading. Their adolescent sons, however, often thought otherwise. Richard Baxter, the Puritan divine whose writings serve as a source book for modern students of the Protestant work ethic, confessed that in his youth (he was the son of a yeoman), 'I was extremely bewitched with a love of romances, fables and old tales which corrupted my affections, and lost my time.'[1]

Not all of the romances and merry books printed by enterprising printers and sold by chapmen were escapist literature pure and simple. In England, in marked contrast to France, a good proportion of the chapbook heroes were apprentices who made good either through the providential intervention of miraculous forces or through their own hard work. A good example of the latter genre is the tale of Jack of Newberie written after 1594 by Thomas Deloney, a former weaver. Set in the time of King Henry VIII, Jack's is the tale of a virtuous apprentice clothier who married his former employer's wife and set himself up in the cloth trade. After her death he married again, but this time for love. By the time that Henry VIII needed troops to fight against the Scots, Jack had several hundred happy men and women in his employ and was able to raise and equip a contingent of men for the king's service. Disdaining the reward of a knighthood as unworthy of a true clothier, this entrepreneur asked only that the king be as benevolent to the poor as Jack of Newberie had proven himself to be.

Ordinary people's aspirations to better their status or at least the quality of the personal letters they wrote were reflected in the pages of another important category of popular literature – the almanacs. Here they would find standard letters on which they could model their proposals of marriage as well as letters to lawyers and associates in business. Almanacs also contained other sorts of practical advice such as when to plant crops and when to go to market. Some of this information was timeless common sense; some of it was tied to the phases of the moon and to the conjunctions of the constellations which made up the signs of the zodiac. Another stock-in-trade of almanac makers was the prediction of the year's coming events. Until the 1670s and 1680s even the élite accepted this as a worthwhile intellectual endeavour. Thus, during the French Wars of Religion no one thought it odd that Catherine de Medici, the Queen Regent of France, patronized one of the most famous of these charlatan prognosticators, Nostradamus. But a century later with the rise of a more mechanistic view of the universe, élite confidence in astrological predictions collapsed. This left this dubious field fully in the possession of hack writers who would write anything they felt would appeal to popular tastes. Yet in England and the Dutch Republic, almanacs published in the late seventeenth century had a place both for the old mystic and for the newer mechanistic view. Readers could find in their almanacs simplified reports of the latest developments in science, information they could obtain nowhere else.

For really topical information, however, ordinary early modern Europeans depended on newspapers or news-sheets. Because of government censorship, these tended to proliferate only during periods when the authority of the central government had nearly broken down; in the German Empire during the debates on the Reformation in the 1520s and during the Thirty Years' War, in France during the Wars of Religion and the Fronde and in England during the Civil War. News-sheets reflected and stimulated a rise in political consciousness among ordinary people who were far outside what the élites liked to consider the proper bounds of the political nation. Thus in urban northern Italy in the early seventeenth century, where at least six weekly newspapers were printed, it was found that 'even the barbers and even more vile artisans were discussing reason of state in their workshops and meeting-places'.[2]

Underlying all the other anxieties which racked the minds of Europe's ruling classes in the two centuries before 1720 (when tensions lessened and the stability of the existing social order seemed assured), was the fear that a populace stirred up by the hostile propaganda found in news-sheets, pamphlets, prints and broadsides would seek to overturn what the élite held to be the proper ordering of society. To understand this we first need to consider the changes which were taking place in the organization of states and in the patterns of sociability of the people who were at the summit of each political nation.

State politics

Well before 1713, the date of the Treaty of Utrecht which ended the war between the France of Louis XIV and England and the Dutch Republic, it was crystal clear that the small independent, oligarchic city states, which in northern Italy, the Low Countries, southern Germany and the Baltic lands had played such an important role in the shaping of late medieval and Renaissance civilization, were now anachronisms and that effective real power lay with the relatively centralized great states of the north. In the Italian peninsula the realities of decay first became openly apparent in 1494 when Charles VIII of France swept through the country, virtually unopposed, on his way south to assert his claims to the Kingdom of Naples. A third of a century later, in 1527, the inability of the alliance system forged by the Italian city states to provide for their mutual defence was demonstrated by the ease with which the troops of the Habsburg Emperor, Charles V, overran and wrecked papal Rome. Most authorities see this event as the effective end of the Italian Renaissance and of Italian political influence elsewhere in Europe. And as for the old semi-independent cities in the Germanies, such as Nuremberg and Frankfurt-am-Main, by the end of the sixteenth century their commercial strength and with it their political influence was already in marked decline. In the next century this decline was accelerated by the disasters of the Thirty Years' War (1618–48). During these years when Christ and his angels slept (to borrow a phrase from an earlier period), the lands of the Empire provided the setting for the battles and bloody frays fought out between the shifty mercenary armies of France, Spain and Sweden. Emerging from the debris of the war fought on German soil by other nations (most of the purely German issues were settled by 1622 when the Protestants of Bohemia were defeated by the forces of the Catholic Emperor) were the three hundred odd old-established duchies, electorates, territories and free cities which continued to pay lip service to the shadowy authority of the Emperor, together with the core of two new aggressive nation states, Austria and Brandenburg-Prussia. But in contrast to Austria and Brandenburg-Prussia, which became leading states in the eighteenth century, the older polities of the Empire became increasingly inward-looking and intent only on building up their territorial rulers' complete control over their subject populations, a process which Marc Raeff has recently identified as the creation of 'the well-ordered police state'. Under these conditions, or at least so the old orthodoxy held, cities could not flourish. However, work in progress by Jonathan Israel suggests that this was the golden age of German-Jewish urban commercial growth. Be this as it may, at any rate to the west of the Empire, in the northern Netherlands, Amsterdam continued to be a vital, exuberant centre of capitalist endeavour. Its leading burgesses (immortalized by the paintings of Rembrandt) controlled the richest of the seven provinces, Holland, and with it the remaining provinces of the Dutch Republic. Yet by 1713, the commercial strength on which the prosperity of Amsterdam rested was rapidly being overtaken by the English. Once again it was a large state, an imperial power, which eclipsed the power of a smaller polity.

In the great polities of north-western Europe – France, Spain and England – by the 1520s and 1530s the old medieval balance between the Crown and the semi-autonomous great landholders in the localities (in which, among the nobles, the king was little more than the first among equals) was being replaced by something new. This was the relatively centralized state headed by a king who had a moral authority and real power which was different in kind from anything which a great provincial noble possessed. Although most kings continued to rely on long-established institutions and privileged corporations of the sort which a completely absolute monarch would have discarded in favour of more efficient mechanisms of government, they, nevertheless, now held the initiative in all the concerns of government that interested them most, which is to say dynastic politics and war.

The principal engine which altered the balance between the Crown and the nobility was the new demands of war. Important innovations in the casting of metal and the use of gunpowder had led to the creation of powerful new cannon which could quickly blast apart even the most elaborate old-style fortifications. Allied to the invention of functioning artillery were innovations in the use of small arms – the primitive harquebus of the 1420s and the later more sophisticated muskets which by the 1550s could kill or maim an opponent at 300 paces. Used in conjunction with phalanxes of mercenary soldiers trained in the use of pikes – an exercise in which the Swiss mercenaries excelled in the early sixteenth century, only to be overtaken by the Spanish by the end of the century – footsoldiers dominated the field of battle in a way which would have been unthinkable during the earlier age of chivalry and mounted heavily-armoured knights. All of these innovations were extremely costly and could only be paid for by kings and princes who by one stratagem or the other could tap the taxable resources of large populations. Thus in France, during the last phases of the Hundred Years' War with England, King Charles VII (d. 1461) forced the Estates General (a late medieval consultative body) to agree that they no longer had the authority to grant or withhold taxation. In future this authority rested solely with the king or, in those provinces that retained their provincial Estates, with these lesser bodies. The king knew that the provincial Estates could if necessary be overawed into compliance by his great officers of state.

Confronted with the threat of armed invasion of their lands, even great nobles who in the past had only paid lip service to their kings' claims of sovereign power now had to find ways of adjusting themselves to the new realities of power politics or face the consequences. In France, the last of the great nobles to learn this harsh lesson was Louis, Prince of Condé, a rebel who placed himself at the head of the Frondeurs in the 1640s and ended his days rowing ladies about the lake in Louis XIV's Versailles. In England the last of the great nobles who tried to assert the near autonomy of their provinces against the Crown were the Earls of Northumberland and Westmorland, leaders of the abortive Rising of the Northern Earls in 1569, and the Earl of Essex, the would-be conqueror of Ireland who ended his days on the scaffold in 1601. In Castile, the principal Spanish kingdom, great nobles recognized as early as 1556, when Philip II came to the throne, that the fount of almost all the honours, pensions and posts necessary to maintain them in the style to which they were accustomed lay with the Crown in the new capital city of Madrid. Some of them had already learned this lesson under his predecessor, Charles V.

The Court

To a far greater extent than in the recent past, by the 1550s at the centre of the new political world lay the Court of the king. Consisting of councils of state, departments of finance and special courts staffed by swarms of bureaucrats who had either purchased their offices (as in France), or been granted them because they seemed competent (as in England), or because they needed tangible rewards to keep them loyal (as in Spain), this was the core grouping of government bodies which, when they wished to, could supervise the lesser privileged groupings and institutions of which the hierarchical social order consisted. In the task of impressing subjects and visiting dignitaries with the God-given near divinity of the sovereign prince (the Divine Right of kings) no less important was the role of the Court as the chief ceremonial centre of the realm. To the courts of monarchs such as Philip II and Philip IV of Spain, Louis XIII and Louis XIV of France or Charles I of England were attached as many of the great Baroque painters, architects, musicians and playwrights from Italy, the Low Countries or the realm itself as the Crown found it within its means to maintain. For all these masters of the art of giving concrete visible or audible form to the mystique which surrounded kings, the role that was assigned was to set the sovereigns above and apart from even the mightiest nobles and churchmen of the realm.

Though it is doubtful whether any early modern king actually aimed at achieving absolute power within his realm, any tentative move in this direction was blocked by certain very real limitations. In a large state such as Spain not the least of these limitations was the physical impossibility of one man knowing precisely what all his subordinates were doing in his name. In order to govern at all it was necessary to delegate responsibility. This was best done by appointing ministers from somewhere other than the top rungs of society, men who were utterly dependent upon the king's will for their power and who could, if necessary, be broken and reduced to nothing. Thus, a clever manipulator of men such as Louis XIV of France made it a policy never to give high office at Court to princes of the blood. Clever kings and queens who did not allow themselves to be ruled by one favourite or one relative, also found it useful to maintain two or more factions within their councils so that they could play one off against the other to their own advantage; for example, in the France of the 1670s, Colbert against Louvois. But if factions were a practical necessity for the maintenance of early modern kingship and with it the complex of interrelated privileged corporations and bodies which constituted the political nation, they were also a source of dissension which might extend well beyond the hothouse atmosphere of the Court itself.

In early modern Europe nobody of consequence who hoped to better his own position or that of his family could do so without 'connections'; clientage and patronage were the very stuff from which politics and élite sociability were made. Based on the town and country houses of great ministers of state, leading magistrates and the greater nobility, these connections fanned out to include all the lesser lay and ecclesiastical offices in the localities over which the Crown had the power of patronage. They also included many of the privileged corporations over which the Crown had no direct control. It was a prudent minor officeholder who knew what his chief patron was up to and was prepared to change horses in midstream if it seemed likely that his benefactor was about to fall from grace. A reasonable amount of success in keeping the disparate factions and groupings in a state of equilibrium such as that which Louis XIV achieved after 1661, demanded that the Crown keep abreast of all these patronage–clientage connections and direct them to its own appointed ends. If a king were too incompetent or lazy to do so (failings which in the end proved fatal to Charles I of England) or in time of a royal minority, too young, the social balance suffered accordingly.

Estates

To rule successfully as an early modern king a sovereign had to be ever mindful of the legitimate demands of the various privileged corporations and bodies found within the realm. As a result of the Reformations, one of the privileged bodies which was most amenable to a reasonable degree of royal control was the state church. Of the non-ecclesiastical privileged bodies, ruling oligarchies of the larger cities were among the most important. Other privileged bodies were located near the Court in the shadows of the king's palace itself; still others lay in the localities or in semi-autonomous provinces or, as in Spain, in the dependent kingdoms. Some were primarily courts of law where justice was done between plaintiffs and defendants. Others were assemblies, courts or Estates which held that they had the power to ratify laws and give consent before new forms of taxation were levied.

In England, the smallest and, even before the events of the Reformation made the sovereign the supreme head of the Church, the most highly centralized of the new emerging nation states, the privileged body which did most to forestall the Crown's moves to unsettle the old accustomed equilibrium of élite power bases was Parliament. Parliament consisted of three groupings – King, Lords and Commons. These, however, were not as distinct as might at first appear. For among the members of both houses were royal councillors who – if they kept abreast of affairs and the state of public opinion in the political nation at large – might persuade Lords and Commons to approve most of the legislation and to grant most of the taxes requested by the Crown.

By no means all legislation in England was initiated by the Crown. Although the Lords, temporal and spiritual, who formed the House of Lords were assumed to represent only their own particular interests, the members of the House of Commons were assumed to represent the interests both of their own constituents in the localities and the best interests of the entire nation. Elected by an electorate which, according to Derek Hirst, by 1641 consisted of between 27 and 40 per cent of the adult male population, most of the

members of the House of Commons were country gentlemen who were or
had recently been respected members of their county's commission of the
peace. As Justices of the Peace they and their colleagues on the commission
were in effect the unpaid administrators and governors of their localities. As
Members of Parliament it was their task to see that local grievances were heard
and set right. Yet their other role was not forgotten. As early as the 1520s
when Cardinal Wolsey and Henry VIII were attempting to ride rough-shod
over the accustomed privileges and liberties of subjects in the matter of
taxation, Parliament helped to stay their hand. Popular risings in East Anglia
and Kent also served to drive the point home.

During the next hundred years, so long as the Crown did not attempt to
push forward with innovations too quickly (and many were made) Crown
and Parliament were generally able to co-operate. MPs were shrewd enough
to recognize that Parliament was by no means a necessary element in the day
to day governance of the realm. Instead, its main functions were to serve as a
forum for national opinion, as an enabling body when changes in the law were
necessary, and as a body which granted taxation (though the Crown had other
sources of finance as well).

Depending upon where one stands in the controversy currently dividing
orthodox and revisionist historians, the House of Commons and their
supporters in the Lords (or was it the other way round?) did not begin to see
themselves as a conservative force in opposition to the innovations of
Divine-Right monarchy until 1604, 1629 or 1640. In any case, so
unacceptable were the innovations Charles I made in his English kingdom
(favouritism towards churchmen who denied the core Calvinist tenet of
predestination, non-parliamentary taxation) and in his subject kingdoms
(Strafford's attempts to create absolutism in Ireland; the decision to impose
the Anglican Prayer Book on Scotland), that in 1641 Parliament refused
further co-operation. With the King's resort to armed force was coupled his
famous warning that the common people might use the squabbles of the élite
as the occasion

[to] set up for themselves, call parity and independence liberty, devour that estate
which had devoured the rest, destroy all rights and proprieties, all distinctions of
families and merit, and by this means this splendid and excellently distinguished form
of government end in a dark, equal chaos of confusion, and the long line of our many
noble ancestors in a Jack Cade or Wat Tyler. [famous rebel leaders in 1381 and 1450][3]

This dire warning together with their fear that there was no acceptable
alternative to the rule of kings led many Members of Parliament (on an
average *younger* than the rebels; schools and universities had done their work
well) to join forces with King Charles. So too did many of the gentry in the

provinces, who in the civil war which followed found themselves fighting against brothers, uncles and nephews. Unable to reach a settlement after the king was defeated in battle, put on trial and beheaded in front of the new Banqueting Hall in Whitehall where masques glorifying the monarch had earlier been performed, the monarchy was restored in 1660 and steps were taken to ensure that the common people at any rate should never 'set up for themselves'.

Although the new king, Charles II, trod carefully, it was clear to many thoughtful observers who were part of the political nation that his aim was to become an absolute monarch of the sort which English patriots took Louis XIII and Louis XIV to be. Charles II's brother and successor, James II, was much less cautious about concealing his true intentions and sacked traditional officeholders in the localities and granted toleration to his Catholic co-religionists. Sensing that everything they held dear was threatened, in 1688 great aristocrats and leading gentry joined forces to depose James II and brought in a Protestant king and queen, William III and Mary II in what is called the Glorious Revolution. The new sovereigns promised to uphold the principles of a monarchy which acknowledged that its powers were limited by Parliament. In all of this the immediate winners were the great aristocracy who through their system of patronage and clientage and a carefully curtailed electorate were able to stand forth in partnership with the Crown as the effective rulers of late seventeenth- and eighteenth-century England.

In the Spanish kingdoms the principal institutions whose members saw them as barriers to the absolutist tendencies of the Crown were *cortes* (estates). Emerging in Spain in the late twelfth and thirteenth centuries (nearly a century earlier than in France), the various *cortes* usually consisted of representatives of the three leading social orders: the clergy, the nobility, and the rich citizens and oligarchs of the cities. The principal perceived function of a *cortes*, such as that found in Castile or in Valencia, Catalonia or Aragon, was to uphold the customary privileges of the kingdom against the Crown by demanding redress of grievances and granting or withholding consent to taxation and to new laws. The underlying ideal which they sought to maintain was the old feudal adage that 'that which concerns all, must have the consent of all'. However, while they were in session, representatives in the various *cortes*, in common with most of the other estates on the Continent were reluctant to accept full responsibility for deciding about levels of taxation, knowing full well that they might be intimidated by the king or by the army he kept outside the hall. Instead, they insisted that they had to refer to their constituencies in the localities for final ratification of an agreement. The delays which all this entailed were one of the reasons why most kings were hostile to Estates and as much as possible tried to do without them. Among the principal realms it was only in England that the representatives to the local equivalent of an Estate – the House of Commons – were equipped from a very early date with full plenary power which enabled them to come to decisions which were immediately binding on their constituents.

In Spain, the most critical of the conflicts which resolved the balance of power between the centralizing authority of the State and a *cortes* came at the beginning of the reign of Charles I (the Habsburg Emperor Charles V). This was very much earlier than the constitutional conflicts in France and England, and centred around the urban dominated Cortes of Castile. Their cherished customs and liberties already eroded by the young king's immediate predecessors and grandparents, Ferdinand and Isabella, and by the Crown's chief officials in the localities, the hated *corrigidors*, in 1520 the Cortes refused to consider the demand that they come equipped with full plenary powers to vote the king the funds he needed to make good his title as Emperor of the Holy Roman Empire of the German Nation. According to Perez Zagorin, among the better sort of rebels the aim of the rebellion once it got underway was to forge some kind of alternative government which would have reduced the king to the position of a limited monarch of the sort which in England only finally came into being after 1688–9. The fatal flaw in this forward-looking scheme, which was intended to preserve the best of the past, was that it did not include the great nobility. Sensing that the cities of Castile represented in the Cortes were divided among themselves and that the Emperor might soon return from Germany backed by an army of mercenary soldiers, the nobility formed themselves into a league and one by one forced the rebellious cities into submission.

With the military defeat and the execution of a hundred or more ringleaders, the Cortes of Castile fell into decline. Although it occasionally stirred restlessly, on the whole during the remainder of the early modern period it obediently approved whatever measures the Crown demanded, and in Castile, at least, there were no further large-scale revolts of any kind. Fully aware that he owed his position to the loyalty of the *grandees*, yet unwilling to fall under their sway, Charles V like his son and successor, Philip II, spared no effort to grant them pensions, honours and offices which would keep them contented. It was under these two exceptionally able kings that the practice further developed of governing Spain – and its empire – through a series of interlocking committees staffed largely by nobles. Once the strong hand of an able king was removed by death and the Crown lapsed into lethargy (broken only during the Count of Olivares's ministry between 1621 and 1643), the result was utter confusion at the centre of government.

In France during these years, effective opposition to the destabilizing policies of the Crown during the reign of Louis XIII, a king who had little interest in government, and during the royal minority which followed his death in 1643, did not rest with the twenty or so Estates in the peripheral provinces, or with the memory of the moribund Estates General which had last met in the abortive session of 1614. Instead it lay with the Parlement of Paris, a court of appeal and of first instance with jurisdiction over the northern third of France, excluding Normandy. Because of its location in the French capital, the Parlement of Paris enjoyed a pre-eminence over the seven other *parlements* found in the provinces. It was this body which in 1648 broke out in revolt in a series of encounters known as the Fronde. In order to establish the context in which these events took place, it is essential to look a bit more closely at the way in which the magistrates of Paris perceived of themselves, and at their corporate relationship with the Crown.

Since the 1560s and the halting reception of the teachings of the Counter-Reformation in France, the Parlement of Paris had become a bastion of religious and moral orthodoxy. Before lower court judges could be appointed to the Parlement they had to secure certification from their parish priests that they were regular churchgoers and active in Catholic-style good works. Given this sort of encouragement they developed an ethic of their own which set them apart from nobles of the sword and lesser bureaucrats. The epitome of moral righteousness, the members of the Parlement of Paris also saw themselves as the guardians of the ancient quasi-feudal constitution. An important aspect of their work was to register any royal edict before it was taken to have passed into law. Without this approval the edict was held to be invalid in the area of Parlement's jurisdiction; the same principle held with respect to the other *parlements* in the provinces. Beginning around 1527, the Crown in the person of Francis I – the Renaissance dandy *par excellence* – instituted a procedure known as the *lit de justice* in order to force the Parlement to register an edict. Held in a great hall which was filled with all the impressive trappings of monarchy, the king in person requested the parlementarians to act in a way befitting loyal subjects. Outmanoeuvred, the parlementarians almost always gave in and obeyed.

This then was the sovereign court which in the late 1630s began to grow restive about the policies of the Crown. Under the guidance of Cardinal Richelieu, after 1635 Louis XIII showed that he was determined to smash the Habsburgs in the Empire and in Spain whatever the cost to ordinary Frenchmen and to the French élites. Taxes doubled and quadrupled, and so did the number of corrupt tax collectors and bureaucrats in the fiscal chambers of government. This coincided with bad harvests, dearth and famine in many parts of the country.

Matters finally came to a head in 1648. By this time both Louis XIII and Richelieu were dead and the Crown was held by a 10-year-old boy, Louis XIV. During his minority he was under the tutelage of Cardinal Mazarin, an Italian much hated by most of the French political nation. In 1648 after a *lit de justice* in which the boy-king demanded the registration of yet more onerous

fiscal measures, the Parlement of Paris became the centre of overt opposition
to the Crown. Going well beyond their usual constitutional role, the
parlementarians took upon themselves the task of judicial review and insisted
that no new taxes or tax offices should be created without their consent. They
also abolished the post of *intendant*, the royal officers in the provinces who
had competence to override lesser bodies in the governance of the localities.
Thanks to the proliferation of news-sheets, this confrontation between
Crown and Parlement soon became public knowledge. Great crowds of
Parisian artisans and workers cheered the leaders of the Parlement and
surrounded the gaols where some of them were imprisoned. Worried lest the
menu peuple no less than the parlementarians might set up for themselves, the
King left Paris and attempted to starve the city into submission. After
considerable manoeuvring on both sides, the Crown eventually reached an
accord which gave the parlementarians much of what they had demanded.
This then ended the first phase of the Fronde.

The second phase followed almost immediately. Although members of
Parlement were suspicious of nobles of the sword, they allowed one of them,
the Prince of Condé, to champion their cause. This marriage of convenience
between old-style aristocratic dissent and the more enlightened dissent of the
parlementarians proved disastrous to both parties. By 1651, besides his own
household retainers and tenants, Condé had at his disposal a troop of 6000
mercenary soldiers furnished by the Duke of Lorraine, a great landholder in
eastern France with pretensions to autonomy. Drawn up against these were
royalist forces which consisted of several thousand mercenary soldiers who
had last seen service in the recently ended Thirty Years' War in the German
Empire. Sparked by disturbances at the centre of government, this second
phase of the Fronde soon spread to Normandy, Guyenne, Provence and
wherever else local estates, *parlements* and coalitions of nobles had serious
grievances against Mazarin's destabilizing policies. Yet with the memory of
recent events in the Germanies fresh in their minds (the wanton killing of
helpless peasants and the sacking of cities by mercenaries in search of thrills)
the French élites decided to forget their differences. By 1652 Louis XIV was
welcomed back in Paris, followed the next year by the return of Mazarin.

After the death of Mazarin in 1661, Louis XIV ruled without any single first
minister. Despite his intellectual limitations, during the next half century he
came as near as any French king ever did to establishing the Crown as the
supreme arbitrator over the affairs of his people. Unwilling to tolerate
religious dissent, the Sun King imprisoned or exiled élitist inward-looking
Jansenists on the one hand and Calvinists on the other. Yet because of the
Crown's unwillingness to abolish all of the late medieval Estates, *parlements*
and other privileged corporations and thus to unhinge the delicate balance
between competing groups and factions, Louis XIV showed that he by no

means intended to establish the form of absolutism that earlier French theoreticians of order such as Jean Bodin, Charles Loyseau, Carden Le Bret and Claude de Seyssel had had in mind. The legacy of overlapping jurisdictions, venal office, incompetence, inefficiency and debt which he left behind him at his death in 1715 was only finally overtaken and overhauled by the befuddled men who came into power at the time of the French Revolution of 1789.

The problem of poverty

However centralized or decentralized an early modern government might be, its primary concern was to maintain the stability of the social order. In the perception of the élites, particularly in the years just after 1500, one of the most obvious threats to that order was the presence of untold thousands of people whose desperate poverty might lead them to riot and to commit acts of wanton plunder and carnage. Thus according to Archbishop Cranmer, the people most responsible for stirring up the troubles in Norfolk in 1549 (Kett's Rebellion), which for a time threatened the stability of the weak régime of the boy-king Edward VI, were impoverished layabouts who had never performed an honest day's work in their lives. In actual fact the ringleaders of this revolt were men whose status was just a shade lower than that of ordinary members of the local ruling élite.

Whether the élite's new consciousness of the problem of poverty after 1500 reflected a real increase in the proportion of poor people in the population as a whole can only be a matter for conjecture. Certainly among the landless, unemployment and underemployment were not problems which suddenly came into being in the sixteenth century. As a highly placed authority much quoted in the Bible put it before Christ was crucified on Calvary around AD 30: 'The poor will be with you always'.

In the broadest sense of the word poverty was (and is) a state of mind no less than an actual physical condition. A person need not be fading away from want of food to be desperately anxious about the perils which the morrow might bring. With few exceptions, early modern Europeans had no extended non-co-resident family upon which they could fall back when they were unemployed and had exhausted their small savings (see Chapter 2). Without these reserves anyone who was struck down by debilitating illness, dismissed from wage employment, dispossessed of a tenement held at the will of a landlord, or overwhelmed by some other misfortune, would either have to subsist on some form of charity or starve to death. At some time in the course of their lives anywhere between a third and a half of Europe's population found themselves in this dire condition. Yet the demands of Europe's charitable resources were never constant. Instead they varied from month to month and from year to year depending upon the state of the harvests, trade patterns in the cities, the availability of land and by-employments, the presence or absence of warring soldiers, and of plague and other epidemic diseases.

Because the rural poor were scattered and largely out of sight, the problem of poverty was seen by those in authority to be most acute in the cities. Certainly the scale of the urban problem was staggering. For example, it was reported of Vicenza near Venice in 1528 that 'You cannot walk down the street or stop in a square or a church without multitudes surrounding you to beg for charity; you see hunger written on their faces, their eyes like gemless rings, the wretchedness of their bodies, with skins shaped only by bones'.[4] Similarly, a survey in 1575 in the north Italian city of Bergomo 'registering only the aged, the sick and children aged fifteen or less' found that nearly 40 per cent of the city's population were paupers; this ignored the untold number of able-bodied paupers whom the authorities chose not to know about.[5] In 1630 probably far more than 40 per cent of the population of the new Spanish capital of Madrid were also paupers. Although the city had no solid economic base and was regarded by foreigners as the most sordid city in Europe, its population in 1630 numbered 170,000 souls compared with only 25,800 in 1561. Here, as in all early modern cities, urban poverty was in fact closely linked with rural poverty. In years of bad harvest or war even a small provincial city such as Provins in Brie in eastern France, might find itself inundated by country people searching for a way to make their living. According to Claude Hutton, a native of Provins, some of the hundreds of strangers who entered the city in 1573 during the Wars of Religion came with the intention of buying bread and grain even though these provisions were pegged at prices three or four times as high as they had been in 1572. Others only demanded to be allowed to work 'without asking any salary other than gruel and bread'.[6] When the authorities failed to meet these demands, the strangers rioted and temporarily seized control of the city.

Before new policies were formulated by the ruling classes in the 1520s two conflicting perceptions governed their attitudes towards the poor. One perception was based on the notion that the poor were created by God in the image of Christ and that all Christians had the moral duty to provide alms to those who were less fortunate than themselves. Because the provision of charity was a form of 'good works' in the Catholic sense, it was held to be a matter of indifference to the Great Bookkeeper in charge of apportioning out time in purgatory whether the recipient was worthy or was patently a work-shy fraud. According to Domingo Soto, a Spanish chaplain to the Emperor Charles V, it might be even more meritorious for the soul of the donor to give alms to unjust men than to give them to the worthy poor. Several other Spanish writers who refused to consider the possibility of abolishing poverty by removing its root causes also stressed the benefits of alms-giving to the donor. Thus, according to Antonio Arbio, whose book *La Familia Regulada* was published in several editions in the early fifteenth century, 'the man who is pious and charitable with the poor of Christ, although he be guilty of many offences, appears as a saint because according to Saint Peter, charity covers a multitude of sins'.[7]

Rural people who had never heard of Christ or St Peter and who had only a vague idea about what Christians meant by sin were also often prepared to be generous in handing out alms to wandering strangers – lest they come back after death to haunt the village. This phenomenon was noted at Sennely-en-Sologne in the late seventeenth century. In England during the same period the provision of free food and lodging to the odd vagrant who was passing through was for somewhat different reasons still seen as an obligation incumbent upon men of gentry or noble status.

Coexisting with these perceptions of the poor as the necessary recipients of random charity which benefited the donor more than it did the poor person were slightly newer (i.e. fourteenth-century) notions. These differentiated between the worthy poor (the elderly, the infirm and orphans) and the unworthy. According to this perception able-bodied beggars – the unworthy – were the Devil's own creatures who of their own volition refused to earn an honest living by the sweat of their brows in accordance with divine command; the need to work was seen as a consequence of the Fall of Man in the Garden of Eden. In Castile legislation governing the punishment of work-shy vagrants first made its appearance in the statute books in 1357, in France in 1350 and in England in 1349. These were the years when European landlords and employers were beginning to come to terms with the demographic collapse occasioned by the first great wave of bubonic plague (1347–9) and the consequent shortage of labourers. In the sixteenth century when it seemed to the more unimaginative of Europe's élite that population had become too plentiful (the reverse of the fourteenth-century situation) these earlier precedents formed the basis of new legislation.

In order to justify this new repressive legislation the élite created a stereotype image of the unworthy poor as being anti-social monsters. The poor man as monster stereotype found its base in a literature of roguery which began to flow from the pens of social critics in the last third of the fifteenth century. Early contributors included Sebastian Brant, author of *The Ship of Fools* published in Basel in 1494, Tesseo Pini of Urbino and Erasmus of Rotterdam. According to the stereotype, beggars were members of a great brotherhood. They had their own special *lingua franca* and distinctive signs and symbols together with their own chosen rulers and sub-rulers; Pini held that there were thirty-nine distinct sub-categories of beggars. Eschewing honest work even when it was offered them by employers, the stereotype vagrant spent his time in taverns playing at dice and taroc (a card game), in brothels gulling other customers or in prison. When vagrants were not in one of these three great schools for scoundrels they were at work robbing travellers, picking pockets at market fairs or public executions or posing as maimed cripples outside churches or other public places. According to the image conjured up by the publicists, a common beggar's trick was to blind or maim a child and then send this human wreck out to beg on behalf of the villainous master. Writing soon after 1597, a year of European-wide scarcity, the Puritan William Perkins claimed that

rogues, beggars, vagabonds...commonly are of no civill societie or corporation nor of any particular Church.... To wander up and down from yeare to yeare to this end to seeke and procure bodily maintenance, is no calling, but the life of a beast.

For Perkins, beggars were 'for the most part a cursed generation'.[8]

What connection was there between the beggar-as-monster stereotype and social reality? In dealing with a somewhat similar phenomenon, the great witchhunt (see Chapter 5), it has been relatively easy for historians to conclude that the achievements credited to suspected witches bore no relationship to what the suspects actually did. But the beggar stereotype can not be so readily explained away. A great brotherhood of the sort described by the publicists *did* exist, not among ordinary Europeans, but among the gypsies. These Indo-European peoples of uncertain origin (perhaps from India) had passed through Egypt (hence the name gypsy), the Balkans and Bohemia on their way into western Europe where they arrived in the fourteenth and fifteenth centuries. Gypsies had their own language (Romany), their own rulers and occasionally stole in the course of their wanderings. Despite the efforts of several governments – they were chased out of Spain in the 1590s – they continued to survive as a group of people who refused to be assimilated into the settled ways of western society. Because fifteenth- and sixteenth-century intellectuals habitually thought in terms of analogies, it is easy enough to see why they might think of vagrants of solid western European stock as similar to gypsies.

Another sort of anti-social brotherhood found in many parts of Continental Europe consisted of demobbed mercenary soldiers; like gypsies such people also had their own *lingua franca*. Accustomed to amusing themselves in time of war by torturing peasant men and raping their wives and daughters, ex-mercenaries found it hard to settle down as honest wage-labourers or farmers after hostilities between the princes had ceased. Those that could not make the transition back to civilian life frequently took to living in bands of brigands. Gangs of desperadoes who saw no reason why they should work for a living while idle priests and rentier landlords flourished all around them were especially common in Spanish cities, in and around Rome (where they were denounced by Pope Sixtus V in 1587) and in eighteenth-century Languedoc and the Beauce.

With its ill-defined frontiers, mountainous terrain, wealthy cities and rich farms, Burgundy was another happy hunting ground for ex-mercenary soldiers. In the late 1450s, just after the end of the Hundred Years' War, a particularly notorious gang of former soldiers who posed as beggars made their headquarters in a public house in Dijon. Using the services of a publican – who got his cut – and information provided by a corrupt police official, the Scottish, Spanish, Gascon and Italian soldiers who made up the band had little difficulty in selling their stolen horses, clothes and treasures to unsuspecting travellers. The authorities first got wind of the gang's membership through a prostitute who lived in the public house and through her were able to apprehend a gang member to whom they promised immunity if he provided information on the rest of the gang. He did, and in the end nineteen of the brigands were hanged.

The activities of the Dijon gang and others of their sort fall well short, however, of the stereotype image of a great graded brotherhood of beggar-thieves. Although in some Continental cities thievish networks of beggars reaching out into the countryside from a central Court of Miracles located in some dank alley *may* have existed in the years after 1450, the case has not yet been convincingly proved. It is even less likely that solid evidence will be forthcoming that such a great brotherhood had ever existed in London.

Who then were the real beggars of early modern Europe? One category consisted of those people whom Christians had almost always assumed deserved to be supported by charity. They were impoverished local residents who were aged, insane, physically handicapped or were children under the age of 15. Among the adults in the first categories who either had to be housed or provided with food in their lodgings, women predominated. Typically, in Rouen in 1586, 1881 women were receiving assistance compared with only 905 men.

A second category of indigents consisted largely of young men from rural areas who were on the move searching for work and social betterment. In Tudor England well over half of these temporary vagrants had professional qualifications and travelled less than 60 kilometres from their point of origin. Far from being social outcasts, they were simply engaged in a prolonged rite of passage which, while it lasted, compelled them to live by doing odd jobs, begging and occasional petty thievery.

A third category of indigents were craftsmen and artisans – often married men – who had been thrown out of work during an economic slump and used up all their small savings. A survey of such people made in Louvain in Brabant in 1546 showed that 70 per cent of the men in this category were trained artisans, 9 per cent were in transport as carters or bargemen, 5 per cent were day-labourers, with 16 per cent falling into other trade groupings. Most such men had had to move about earlier in life during their years of apprenticeship and were now firmly committed to a settled life. Because this expectation was now imperilled by developments over which they had no control, such men were potentially the most dangerous poor people of all. Given half a chance they would seek riotous revenge against hard-nosed entrepreneurial employers, troublesome landlords or whichever social deviants were currently seen as scapegoats; in a Catholic state the Protestants, in a Protestant state the Catholics, and in all Continental states the urban concentrations of Jews.

This leaves us with the fourth category of beggars, the generally isolated individualists who found that they could earn more by begging than they could by taking up a socially acceptable trade. In Norwich there was the case of Mother Arden who by 1562 had managed to accumulate by begging a hoard worth £44 3s. 5d, a sum in excess of what an average yeoman could hope to earn by honest labour in two years. In the perception of Protestants, the mendicant friars who in Catholic countries continued to make their living by begging fell into much the same category as Mother Arden.

Until the decade 1521–30, provisiòn for the indigent was made in a random fashion which better reflected the spiritual needs of living and dead donors than the material and bodily needs of the poor. Though this form of charity was clearly well intentioned, when the need was greatest – during periods of widespread unemployment, dearth or famine – it allowed tens of thousands of people to slip into utter destitution or worse. Under the old charitable régime – which in Spain continued until after the end of the early modern period – people of substance customarily hurled coins among the crowd on festive occasions or after a funeral. Slightly more orderly was the distribution of charity through charitable trusts, such as the almshouses for the elderly set up by pious benefactors, the hostels set aside for categories of travellers such as pilgrims or mendicant friars, or the dowries paid over to poor orphan girls so that they could marry. By the fifteenth century, another form of charity was the aid which some of the craft guilds and confraternities provided for the widows and orphans of their members. And in those few parishes which in the years before the Reformation served as effective centres of neighbourhood life, part of the money collected from non-appropriated tithes (i.e. those not pocketed by lay owners of this form of property) and, more regularly, the small coins dropped into the church poor box were used to help the deserving poor of the parish.

Yet in a period of rapid population growth the funds collected in this unsystematic way were totally inadequate to cope with the problem of poverty. An example was the town of Draguibnon in Provence where the population increased from 2816 in 1471 to 8620 in 1540. Realizing that the parish funds at their disposal were a mere drop in the ocean of want, in 1540 the town elders decided to use them to pay for an annual banquet for themselves, arguing that they no less than the poor were created in the image of Christ. By 1644, in at least a sixth of the villages of France, no provision was made for the poor on the communal level at all.

When it suddenly did break upon the European scene, welfare reform – except in England – was essentially an urban phenomenon. Of the sixty odd Continental cities which participated in the movement which first came to fruition in the 1520s and 1530s, more than twenty were found in the Holy Roman Empire, including Augsburg (1522) and Nuremberg (1522). Fourteen, including Ypres (1525), were in the Low Countries, eight, including Lyon (1531–4), were in France, six, including Geneva (1535), were in Switzerland, and two were in northern Italy. In all of these cities a cornerstone of the new policies was the rigorous prohibition of begging in public places except by indigents who carried valid licences. Except in Venice, the other cornerstone of policy was the creation of a central body staffed by laymen which for greater efficiency administered all the scattered trusts amalgamated into a single central fund.

Now, for the first time, the distribution of charity was seen to be a civil rather than a clerical responsibility. Typically, in Lyon the central administrative body, the *Aumône Générale*, was run by professional men and traders who used the latest, most rational business techniques. As they saw it their first task was to obtain accurate information about the number and categories of the locally resident poor. Next they set out to determine the minimum amount of food and clothing needed to keep people alive. Equipped with this information they siphoned off the sick to receive free medical attention in hospitals, provided mobile indigents with food tickets and distinctive arm badges, and established work projects on town walls and ditches which provided employment for the able-bodied poor. The only people excluded from the benefits of schemes of this sort were vagrants who could not prove that they had residence rights in the city. Though such folk might receive charity during years of economic prosperity, during ill years they were often unceremonially banished. For example, in the round-up of non-resident indigents which took place at Amiens in Picardy during the scarcity of 1644, the city guard deposited an 82-year-old veteran outside the town gates and warned him that he would be whipped or worse if he dared to return.

In Venice much of the impetus for reforming welfare services was provided not by businessmen but by medical doctors who were convinced that crowds of impoverished people coming in from the terra firma in time of dearth or war were a threat to public health. By banning begging in churches, public squares and private palaces, by providing charity through the Scuola Grandi (confraternities), by isolating the sick on the island of Lazzaretto, and by providing able-bodied indigents with low-paid work in the state-owned Arsenal (naval shipyard) or on the galleys which plied the Mediterranean, the Venetian authorities at least gave the appearance of making some impact on the most intransigent of the problems confronting any early modern city.

Here and in several other north Italian cities efforts were made to do more than ameliorate the symptoms of poverty and remove some of its underlying causes. Beginning in the 1520s centralized employment bureaux were established to make it easier for the able-bodied to hear of jobs and to meet potential employers. Elsewhere in Europe such information was still largely passed by word of mouth or publicized at the annual or bi-annual hiring fairs. The Italian genius for organization was also shown in the creation of the Monte di Pietà. Recognizing that for thousands of people a root cause of poverty was indebtedness to crooked money-lenders, in the fifteenth century the Franciscan Observants set up agencies – the Monte di Pietà – which served as honest pawnshops and provided loans at low rates of interest.

North of the Alps in the Holy Roman Empire thoughtful laymen, such as Eberlin von Gunzburg writing in 1521, were slowly coming to the conclusion that if provision were made for the needs of the destitute they would have no reason to commit crimes against the common good. Eberlin's insight was reflected in the new welfare institutions established in Wittenberg and Nuremberg in 1522 and in 1523 in two of the German cities with towering cathedral churches, Regensburg and Strasbourg. The perceived need to demonstrate concern for the plight of the poor in practical material ways also lay behind the establishment of new welfare institutions in Lyon in 1531. Two years earlier in the Rebeine riots hungry poor people who 'had scarcely anything to gain and yet less to lose' had nearly succeeded in seizing control of the city. By establishing the *Aumône Générale* Lyon authorities gave the poor a stake in the continued survival of the existing social order.

Yet in both Catholic and Protestant cities where new welfare institutions were established another less calculating ideology was also at work. Much of it was created by humanist scholars such as Juan Luis Vives, the Spanish author of *De Subventione Pauperum*, the most influential of all the sixteenth-century works on poverty. In common with other humanists, such as Erasmus, Vives considered that man was the measure of all things and that any condition such as poverty which degraded man and made it impossible for him to fulfil his (or her) full potential should be rectified. It is ironic that so little was done to resolve the problem of material poverty in Vives's own homeland, Spain. By the early and mid seventeenth century the intellectual heirs of these early humanists, men such as Sir Francis Bacon, Henry Sherfield and Samuel Hartlib, had come to the conclusion that it might be possible to reorder society so that poverty could be abolished entirely. To 'cloth the naked, feed the hungry, instruct the ignorant and employ the idle' was Hartlib's programme for a just society.

Before this idealistic programme could be achieved, means had to be devised to pay for it. Even when all earlier charitable institutions had been placed under centralized control and administered in business-like fashion, the annual yield was seldom enough to pay for basic services for the poor. In the end most municipalities had to resort to a compulsory poor rate (tax) assessed on all householders who had an income above a set minimum. Yet only in an exceptionally rich and well-ordered city such as Nuremberg could regular taxation be consistently maintained. More typical was the situation in the cloth town of Amiens. During an economic downturn which reached a new low in March 1652, a time when the poor were most in want, substantial bourgeoisie refused to contribute more in taxes to support the poor.

In Amsterdam and several other Dutch cities a partial solution to the finance problem used after 1589 was to compel the able-bodied poor to live in workhouses where they paid for their keep by chopping and rasping Brazil wood for the production of dyes. This was a disgustingly filthy and unhealthy job which few free men would willingly undertake and workhouse inmates who refused to do it were deprived of food. Experiments were also made in using workhouse inmates in other nascent industries. However, privately employed workers and capitalist employers who were worried lest work-house products compete unfairly with their own, successfully prevented these experiments from proceeding beyond a preliminary stage.

In urban France after 1630, Dutch ideas about teaching the discipline of labour to the indigent joined with the ideals of the Counter-Reformation to produce a truly repressive régime for the poor. According to French logic people were always poor by choice; they had consciously rejected the new moral order of absolutism and of Tridentine Catholicism. Seen in this light, the poor were an abomination which if they could not be entirely rooted out by being sent to the West Indies to die of tropical diseases or to Canada to die of the cold (temperatures of $-40°C$ were common in Quebec winters), they could at least be locked away out of sight and hearing of respectable people.

The Great Confinement (the name given by French historians to the élite's new policies towards the poor) began under Richelieu in 1630 and was enacted into general law in 1662 when the memory of popular agitation during the recent Fronde was still fresh in the minds of councillors of state. Under the new order the poor were to be incarcerated in institutions known as *Hôpitaux Généraux*. In Paris, as in Amiens and other provincial cities, only one branch of the 'hospital' was a place where sick indigents received medical treatment. Other wings included prisons for work-shy idlers, and a workhouse for able-bodied vagrants who agreed to work under godly supervision. The workhouse régime was intentionally modelled on that of a monastery. As Nicolas Asseline of Soissons put it in 1622, the poor 'become rich spiritually and since they are assured of the needs of the body, they have all things necessary for the life of the soul'.[9] In Paris by the 1650s, at any one time an average of 10,000 human beings were to be found in these places of confinement.

Yet the Parisian poor were far more numerous than this, augmented as they were by thousands of ruined rural people coming to search for hand-outs or jobs. To deal with the perceived needs of the indigents who were allowed to remain in private lodgings because the *hôpitaux* were too full, godly guardians of the poor turned up unexpectedly at odd hours to check that the poor were morally worthy to be in receipt of charity. In 1708, one of the worst of the many bad years Louis XIV's wars inflicted on France, in the parish of Saint-Sulpice alone, 13,000 people were said to be enduring supervision in exchange for basic charity.

Though historians are usually reluctant to give credence to theories of conspiracy, it would appear that much of the responsibility for the Great Confinement rested with a small group of committed ideologues, the patricians who formed the Company of the Holy Sacrament. Founded in 1629 by the Duc de Ventadour and numbering among its members magistrates in the Parlement of Paris and in provincial *parlements* as well as Chancellor Pierre Séguier, a trusted adviser of Louis XIII, the Company had branches in at least fifty cities. Little else is known about this secret society. Fearful that its members would be lynched by crowds of *menu peuple* or denounced in a court by their many rivals among the faction-torn élite, the Company was careful never to publish lists of its members or to allow them to appear openly in their capacity as members at the centre of the political stage. The Company owed its success to the strategic positions occupied by its leaders and to their undoubted skill in managing client men and women who were less clever than themselves.

At the parish level the Company's sympathizers included thousands of godly women found in the guilds of charity, the *charités*. It was these vindictive ladies who never went hungry themselves who patrolled the streets, and broke into poor people's lodgings to make certain that nobody who was in receipt of charity smoked tobacco, gambled, swore, or cohabited with a person of the opposite sex, all activities in which people of aristocratic birth delighted. Allied with these ladies, 'the witches of the aristocratic white terror', were the celibate parish priests who in urban France retained immediate control of charitable resources under the general supervision of laymen. Before an indigent could receive alms, he or she had to produce a certificate proving that he or she had attended confession, performed Easter duties and accepted the authority of the Counter-Reformation concept of Christ. Yet not all parish priests willingly collaborated with this disciplined compulsory conformity which as one historically-minded observer put it smacked 'of the time of the Goths'.

The most justly famous of the dissident priests was Vincent de Paul of Paris, the founder of the well-born Dames of Charity and the peasant Daughters of Charity, organizations which are not to be confused with the parish based *charités*. When the *Hôpital Général* of Paris first opened to receive its quota of 5000 involuntary inmates who had been rounded up by the police in 1657, Vincent de Paul thought that the general idea of confinement under a modified monastic rule was sound. However, as soon as he became fully aware of the repressive implications of this policy, he withdrew his support and refused to allow his priests to minister to inmates. In such matters, St Vincent was in tune with the popular attitude which held the *Hôpitaux Généraux* and the godly ladies of the *charités* in foul scorn. In Lyon in 1675 attitudes were translated into action when four burly guards of the *Hôpital Général* were beaten up by a stonemason and armed women.

Such incidents did little to stem the tide of repression. In 1724 a decree went out from the French caesar of the day, Louis XV, that all mendicants and vagabonds in the kingdom were to be arrested by the newly reorganized *maréchaussée* (mounted police). Those who would not work were to be sent to the galleys or worse. No mention was made of ways to try to prevent poverty from occurring in the first place. Indeed, in most of the more economically advanced parts of rural France where the new *coqs de village* had come to control their local societies, no regular communal provision for the poor existed. Lumbered with rulers and social superiors who acted towards them in this way, the poor of France were truly a 'cursed generation', though for reasons quite different from those which William Perkins had in mind when speaking of England a century earlier.

In England alone of all the western European states a nation-wide system of poor relief was created in the sixteenth century. As set forth in its final form in the legislation of 1597–8 and 1601, responsibility for the poor of each parish rested with the parish overseers of the poor. Working under the supervision of the local Justices of the Peace and at this one step removed, the central Privy Council, the parish overseers had authority to assess rates on householders for the upkeep of the poor and to decide which of their number should be provided with housing as well as food, and which should be given outdoor relief and possibly supplemental benefits. In contrast to the centralized Continental schemes, in England most of the charitable trusts established earlier were permitted to carry on much as they had before in the provision of selective, casual charity (some still exist in 1984). Moreover, nothing was done to dissuade potential donors from establishing new trusts, founding schools and other training centres. Yet important as this private philanthropy continued to be in the years after 1601, the safety net which prevented all but a very small minority of English people from falling below minimum daily requirements of food, clothing and shelter was provided by the local agents of the national poor law of 1601.

These local agents bore little resemblance to the righteous hags found in French cities in the guilds of charity (the *charités*). In an English city such as London, the parish overseers of the poor were merchants, traders and artisans of middling status and just below who were governed by the ethic of ordinary people rather than by an ideology foisted on them by the élite. Assisting them in their work – not only in their capacity as ratepayers – were a sizeable proportion of all the heads of households in the parish. Thus in 1640 nearly one household head in twenty in the parishes of the city were serving without pay as elected poor law officials. With the rotation of office, this meant that over the course of a decade or two every household head whom neighbours regarded as at least marginally trustworthy did service as a poor law official. Within the context of each parish, the need to administer the charitable funds raised by the rates thus served as a catalyst which brought nearly all household heads together in a functioning *communitas*. These then were the people who in 1641 King Charles I warned might: 'set up for themselves, call parity and independence liberty...[and] devour all distinction of family and merit....'

Admittedly for two small categories of people the poor law policies of late Tudor and Stuart England *were* repressive. Troublesome vagrants and pregnant women who could not prove that they had residence rights in the parish – a term of time set at the discretion of the overseers and JPs – could either be imprisoned (London's Bridewell was established in 1552) or whipped and sent back to their parish of origin where they might expect to find poor relief. Movement between the parishes was controlled by a system of licences granted at the borders of each parish where petty harassment might have to be endured. Alternatively during the years of colonization in America, local authorities might decide that young unemployed potential troublemakers, or pregnant women like Rebecca Moreton of the parish of Dunstan in the West in London, should be forced to serve as indentured servants for periods of from three to seven years in Barbados, Virginia, Maryland or Carolina. Other potential or known impoverished trouble-makers from northern England and Calvinist Scotland were sent out to populate the English plantations in Catholic Northern Ireland. In the late twentieth century the legacy of this seventeenth-century policy still remains a festering sore in British life.

Yet, aside from the treatment meted out to vagrants and unwed mothers, the response of England's amateur poor law officials towards the destitute was, by the standards of the time, surprisingly humane. For example, in the London parish of Wood Street Compter in the 1630s a widow who was chronically in debt took to illegally selling apples in the public thoroughfare. After reviewing her case, parish officials bought up her supply of apples and agreed to pay the rent for her lodgings in the future. In St Bartholomew Exchange parish officials granted impotent old Peter Harley an annual pension of £2 3s. 4d and paid £2 towards his rent. When Harley fell sick they paid out £2 10s. on doctors' and nurses' fees and provided him with a shirt and two pairs of shoes; a total expenditure of £7 2s. 6d in a year for one man. Orphaned children received similar consideration. Those who were still nursing infants were often committed to the charge of a wet-nurse in the healthier climate of the countryside. Those who were old enough to live in an institution were given at least two hours of training each day in writing, reading and the casting of accounts to prepare them for an apprenticeship. In the parish of Dunstan in the West in 1658–9 £5 4s. 9d was paid out 'for a Suite of Clothese...for Stockings Shirts hose shoes and a Hatt' for John Dunstan, an orphan who had been brought up in the parish (hence his surname) and was being put out as an apprentice.[10] The cost of all this was met by the rates, private philanthropy and by the income which parish officials derived from buying houses and letting them out to rent-paying tenants. By way of contrast, in a small town such as Allendorf in Hesse in the German Empire where financial resources were much more limited, people in receipt of household relief through the parish chest could only expect to receive an equivalent of a fifth of their daily food needs. If such people seemed likely to become permanent burdens on the parish, even this token support was choked off.

In London at least, the disruptions occasioned by the Civil War stimulated poor law officials to redouble their efforts. In 1649, soon after King Charles I was executed for, among other things, meddling too much in local affairs, the Corporation of the Poor was created. In its functioning there was little of the bogus piety which marked the work of the nearly contemporary *Hôpital Général* in Paris. In London co-operating parishes pooled their funds to establish inter-parish poor institutions, among others, workhouses. These latter institutions served primarily as training centres for young men and women under the guidance of locally recruited artisans. Workhouse students were permitted to live in their own lodgings and to report in for training each day. In contrast to Dutch or French workhouses, no whips, irons or other persuasive devices appear to have been used. For the founders of the Corporation of the Poor the guiding premise was to educate young people in skills which would enable them to become self-sufficient. To their minds the mark of a just society was not the amount of gold stored in a national treasury but rather the full employment of all hands so that they could begin to achieve their full human potential.

Although not all local poor law officials thought in these exalted terms, especially after the restoration of the monarchy in 1660, for the mass of the people the old poor laws were still regarded as part of the natural birth-right of all true-born Englishmen. Just as in the case of the reified *Law*, the identification of state policies with popular expectations cemented a fundamental bond between the social orders in England which was perhaps unparalleled elsewhere in Europe.

The law

As G. R. Elton, the regius professor of history at the University of Cambridge and a scholar with a deep understanding of conditions in the German Empire as well as in England, has recently pointed out, during the early modern period the law and its courts were 'the real essence and the activating mechanism of all social relationships…all the social structures we can discern lived on and by the law'.[11] Thus it is entirely fitting that we should conclude our foray into the social history of ordinary early modern Europeans with a brief look at this important topic. Our principal theme is that between 1450 and the end of our period there was a gradual change in many ordinary Europeans' perceptions of the criminal justice systems provided by their state and state church. Rather than taking justice into their own hands with resultant high rates of murder, manslaughter and inter-personal violence (the usual result of mob rule) there was a new willingness to settle disputes in either civil or ecclesiastical courts.

Early in our period, when resort to a court of law presided over by gentlemen outsiders was seen as more disruptive to the moral unity of the community than the dispute itself, most village people preferred to settle matters among themselves. Typically at Prescot in Lancashire, a village of around 500 souls, local people more often resorted to their own leet court where they could enforce their own sense of neighbourliness rather than to the Justices of the Peace at Quarter Sessions. Thus between 1615 and 1660 (admittedly rather a late date for a leet court still to be functioning even in the backward North of England) some 1252 assault cases were heard in the leet court compared with only twenty-three assault cases involving Prescot people heard at Quarter Sessions.

In the many thousands of European and English villages which were not fortunate enough to have been able to preserve popular village-controlled courts like the leets (in the Bishop of Worcester's manor at Hartlebury as early as the 1440s cases were apportioned out among the appropriate regular élite-controlled civil and ecclesiastical courts), a common way of proceeding after an arm had been broken in a brawl or strayed cattle had destroyed a peasant's standing crops was to call in a village elder or priest to serve as an arbitrator. In addition to avoiding the need to bring in an outsider, who had little sympathy with local people's ancient sense of natural justice, to the village moral community the point of the exercise was to re-establish harmony between the troublemaker and his victim by exacting due compensation for the harm committed while not disparaging the honour of the perpetrator. This then was quite different from the mechanistic principles used, for example, in the Consistory Court in Calvinist Geneva in the 1570s which meted out predetermined punishments to people in each category of crime committed regardless of individual circumstances. It was different too from the Catholic Church's old insistence that before people could receive communion they must first restore the lost honour of those they had wronged whatever the cost to their own sense of honour.

In uncorrupted backward societies such as highland Scotland before 1600 or Poland before it fell under the sway of Jesuit teachers in the 1650s, when disputes between members of rival kinship/dependency groups arose the leaders of each clan served to arbitrate disputes between their members. As a price of failure was a blood-feud between the clans, the chiefs had a strong incentive to prevent a misunderstanding or hurt born of the anger of the moment from getting out of hand. Thus in 1576 Colin, Earl of Argyll in Scotland entered into bond with William, Earl of Glencairn that if any of their dependants or kinsfolk slaughtered or harmed a member of the other's clan, the wrong would be amended and compensation paid through the chiefs' arbitration. By standing forth as arbitrators, the clan chiefs reinforced their authority over their own people while at the same time enhancing their standing in the eyes of the king in Edinburgh as the upholders of customary justice and authority. In the very different context of a mid sixteenth-century Norman seigneury such as that presided over by the Sieur de Gouberville, the same general principles held. The seigneur was considered to be responsible for the good behaviour of 'his people' and took it upon himself to mete out punishments in a spirit which was entirely in accord with local people's sense of natural justice. Similarly in sixteenth-century Castile where, aside from the king in his capacity as a divinely-appointed sovereign, few great landholders were considered to be an organic part of local society, the Cortes took account of the strains which resort to a formal court placed on people's social relationships, their time and resources. Accordingly it ordered each village to appoint two regular arbitrators to settle minor disputes.

An unintentional consequence of forms of arbitration of this sort was that they left no written records which would enable later historians to determine which forms of crime predominated in one period compared with another and why they did so. However, this caveat does not apply when an accord drawn up by arbitrators was registered by a notary. In most early modern Italian and French cities, but not in England where notaries did not exist, such an accord was recognized as a legitimate alternative to legal action before the courts. Thus, in retrospect Jacques Pié of Paris who in 1609 found himself before a court of law charged with assault would have done better at an earlier stage in the affair to have used a notary's service to make a formal agreement with his opponent. As it was, all he had done was to take Easter Communion with his former victim and then 'sealed their friendship with a drink' not realizing that the wretch would later bring him into court.[12] Surviving notarial records from Paris for the period around 1630 suggest that each year one out of every 150 to 200 inhabitants was involved in a conflict which in the eyes of a court of law would have been a criminal offence. Yet this level of reported conflict was low compared with the situation in rural Prescot in Lancashire where annually during these same years one in twenty of the village population found themselves hauled before either a leet or a JPs court.

In England during the late sixteenth and early seventeenth centuries, a wide variety of cases which touched upon the reputation of the plaintiff (or defendant) were heard in church courts at the level of the archdeaconry. Cases involved accusations of slander, blasphemy, witchcraft, usury, gambling, drunkenness, sexual irregularity and other matters which if left unattended might provoke violent retaliation. At one time or another in their lives perhaps one person in five or six was involved in a case of this sort.

Because of the archaic nature of the procedure used in the church courts they can be seen as a legitimate continuation of earlier Teutonic notions of community justice and natural right. People who, on pain of excommunication if they did not, saw fit to appear before the court to answer charges laid against them by other villagers, churchwardens or bishops during their visitation had the option of pleading not guilty. In this case they were often required to produce four to six compurgators, people of good moral standing, to swear that the defendants were of good repute. Thus in Malden, Essex, in 1575 Thomas Ball, a gentleman who stood accused of fornicating with Eleanor Francis, produced four compurgators, two gentlemen and two esquires, who swore to his innocence. People who could not prove their innocence were required publicly to confess their sin and do penance by standing barefoot dressed only in a sheet in the parish church during time of service and perhaps in the market-place on market day as well. As far as the public was concerned the point of the exercise was that the accused should confess that they had wronged the community by their sin rather than to punish them for their crime. Alternatively, the church courts provided people – often women – with an avenue to clear their name. Thus the reason why Alison Emerson who was accused of being a whore pressed charges against members of the Phillipson family in a Durham church court in October 1592 was to be 'cleared to be an honest woman amongst her neighbours against these words...that hir neighbors afterwards might not charge her with them'.[13]

The willingness or unwillingness of people to use church courts is a useful barometer of community opinion. The courts might be seen as agencies of community-style justice and enforce generally accepted norms. Alternatively they might be seen as agencies of élitist domination, in which case their decisions would be ignored and as far as ordinary local people were concerned the honour of a defendant was left unimpaired. Take the case of John Ayle of Felix Hall in Essex. In the eighteen years before 1631 godly churchwardens and village élites repeatedly brought him before the archdeacon's court for not coming to church on the Sabbath, for keeping a disorderly alehouse on the Sabbath, being drunk in church, cohabiting with a servant and then when she was pregnant, marrying her off to an innocent youth who could bear the cost of maintaining the child. Yet in 1631 the people of Felix Hall chose Ayle to be their constable, the lynchpin of local justice. Here in the minds of village people, natural justice and the Church's justice were obviously not the same.

In Spain it was almost unthinkable that a person who had come before the church courts would be honoured by fellow villagers as was John Ayle in 1631. Here where moral orthodoxy was guarded by the Inquisition established in 1478 (nearly half a century before a similar institution was set up in the world capital of Catholicism, Rome) the church courts were regarded with a degree of respect which was the envy of rulers everywhere. In part this respect was due to the connection which had sprung up in the popular mind between moral deviance and impure Morisco or Converso blood (Moriscos were Christian converts from Islam; Conversos were converts from Judaism). Until the western frontiers of Islam were stabilized in the Balkans in the late 1600s (the lifting of the seige of Vienna in 1683 and the Turkish retreat from Hungary in 1699), Spanish Christians might legitimately think that their few remaining Moriscos were agents of an aggressive foreign power: the Ottoman Empire. Similarly, though the Jews had no state of their own (Israel was not established until 1947) people who had Jewish ancestors were held to be more loyal to international Jewry centred on the cities of Germany than to Spain. Both minority groups were associated in the popular mind with behaviour which Christians held to be immoral; the Jews with usury (lending out money at a rate of interest in excess of 5 per cent) and the Moslems with polygamy and homosexuality. It was also thought that both sorts of people would readily utter blasphemies and criticize Spanish ways and institutions.

All offences associated with impure blood came within the purview of the Inquisition. Since it seemed to aim at establishing a perfect moral order of the sort most people desired, if not for themselves then for everybody else, the Inquisition was well supported at the village level. Indeed it serves to yet further buttress G. R. Elton's thesis that legal institutions closely reflected early modern Europeans' social relationships. Typically, at Lerin in Northern Spain in 1680 a card player who accidentally scratched himself with the blade of his sword while he was at play jokingly uttered the blasphemous phrase, 'it would be a shame to lose such noble blood, which is good enough to redeem the entire human race'.[14] Reported to the Inquisition by his fellow players, he was later let off with a simple reprimand and a light fine. Popular knowledge that most of those who were reported to the Holy Office would be treated to justice tempered with mercy was probably one reason why most people were so free in their denunciations to this court. Yet not all defendants were so leniently treated.

To make good their claim to be the enforcing agency of the will of God in Spain, the Inquisition blanketed the whole of the peninsula with a network of professional troubleshooters, known as familiars, all of whom were tightly controlled by the central court of the Inquisition in the capital. Once or twice every ten or fifteen years the Inquisitors personally visited every village within their jurisdiction in order to hold the sessions which might end in a fiery *auto de fe*. In Saragossa in 1609 at the height of the anti-Morisco campaign, the tribunal sent 150 suspects to the oblivion of death through fire. Yet harsh punishments might also be dealt out by secular courts.

In Western Europe as a whole two quite different types of secular courts were found. The first sort used the inquisitorial forms known to the Roman Law and the second the accusatorial procedures derived from the old Germanic law. Of the two, the system most preferred by Continental monarchs who were aiming at establishing a new equilibrium between themselves and their subjects was that derived from the old Roman Law.

The adoption of this form of law, first in Italy and southern France (where it had never been entirely lost) and then in northern France and by 1532, with the publication of the *Constitutio Criminalis Carolina*, by Charles V in many parts of the Holy Roman Empire, brought with it the rise of a university-trained professional lawyer class. Even on the eve of the reception of the Roman Law peasants in German states such as Württemberg protested against 'the plague of learned lawyers that has been infesting legal business in every court in the land'.[15] In a larger polity such as France the number of lawyers whose stock in trade was to sort out (or cause) flaws in the mechanisms of social relationships nearly came to outnumber priests.

Here in France, beginning in the sixteenth century, legal experts came to the conclusion that unadulterated old-style Roman Law – the compilation made under the Emperor Justinian (died AD 565) – could not be applied to contemporary cases without serious modifications which took account of distinctive French customs and traditions. This realization was one of the influences which led French magistrates and lawyers to feel that they were a special social grouping set apart from the rest of society, including the nobility of the sword. Of course, using patronage and connections, the more successful of their numbers in time came to be appointed to the bench of a sovereign court such as the Parlement of Paris, and with their new post they acquired the status of a noble of the robe. Deeply read in the works of the

Renaissance humanists who stressed the importance of virtue rather than the old noble attributes of blood and inheritance, as well as in the works of the ideologues of the Counter-Reformation, French magistrates saw themselves as the aloof arbitrators of justice and the true civilizing agents of uncouth peasants and artisans alike.

These perceptions were not entirely unknown in Castile. Here students seeking a career in law flocked to the Universities of Salamanca and Valladolid especially in the years before 1640 when the supply of trained lawyers finally came to exceed demand. Yet in that unhappy kingdom most lawyers who did manage to become magistrates put their own interests first, or used their position to arrange things for their friends. In Castile even when an accuser decided to withdraw charges against an accused, the judges usually went ahead and convicted the latter of some lesser offence so that they could assess a fine which they then pocketed.

Dependent as magistrates and lawyers became – after the invention of the printing press – upon a written set of laws on which to base their proceedings, an early task was to codify all of the different customary laws found in a particular jurisdiction. By 1600 some 700 different codes were found in France alone, some general, some particular and many overlapping in ways which only skilled lawyers could sort out. By committing to writing and to printed guides what before had been a flexible set of oral precepts and usages, the lawyers fossilized the law and made it even less accessible to the common understanding of ordinary people. Once codified, the law was subject to interpretation by skilled jurists and modified as first one precedent (a legal decision affecting the interpretation of the law) and then another was added to the corpus of the law. Another source of new law was the edicts of the king, subject to ratification, in those regions where they existed, by a local *parlement* or Estate. Either way the initiative for *making* the law, though not for initiating proceedings that led to its use, rested with those at or near the summit of society rather than with the ordinary people.

In all of the written codes of early modern Europe, the punitive element was uppermost. Offences which threatened the hierarchical social order or the religious status quo were punishable by death. Capital crimes included sedition and treason (which might consist only of drunken mumblings which questioned the legitimacy of the rule of the prince), counterfeiting coins, sodomy and incest, infanticide, heresy and witchcraft, murder, armed assault, burglary and so on. Once accused of any of these felonies by a hostile neighbour, under a system derived from the Roman Law a defendant was almost entirely at the mercy of professional lawyers, magistrates and procurators (public prosecutors). It was they who dragged up the necessary witnesses without whom a verdict of guilty was impossible unless the accused openly confessed his or her crime, first under torture and later of his or her own free will. All of these processes and depositions of witnesses were written down on dockets and, as in France after 1670 might be subjected to judicial review by a higher court such as the Parlement of Paris or, in its much smaller area of jurisdiction, the Parlement of Toulouse or a similar provincial court.

Yet whether subjected to review or not, the lesson for the ordinary person who was contemplating a crime against the social order was clear. Once apprehended, and testified against by witnesses or made to confess under torture, the punishment for heinous crime was death. Thus, in the city and territory of Milan between the years 1625–9, thirty-two people were executed for murder, nineteen for theft, two for rioting, two each for sodomy and infanticide and one for counterfeiting. During these same four years in that Spanish dependency nine people who had committed a number of lesser offences over the years were accounted anti-social beings by their accusing neighbours and by magistrates and were sentenced to death. In Spain itself, or at least in the Montes de Toledo, nearly 90 per cent of all indictments for criminal offences between 1580 and 1690 ended in conviction. Yet here as elsewhere in Europe, as an alternative to the death penalty, judges might impose lesser sentences ranging from mutilation and whipping to involuntary servitude upon a galley of war or, in those states which possessed them, to transportation to the colonies.

Except in a few of the small well-ordered German states after 1648, a basic problem which no early modern government entirely overcame was the near absence of a reliable state-supported police force. Although a small force of this sort existed in France after 1670 (the *maréchaussée* with less than 4000 men) and in Spain (the Brotherhood of Santa Hermandad), both were far too small to begin to police these vast countries properly. And since almost by definition mounted policemen were outsiders to the moral community of the village, they were as popular with villagers as were state tax collectors or the members of anti-smuggling brigades. Not only did the mounted police often ignore local customary usages about how to contain disorder, they were usually nowhere to be found when the friends of executed bandits returned to the village to seek revenge for their partner's death. In the absence of a state police force most communities were entirely dependent upon the service of their own constables and bailiffs. Often characterized by élite satirists as buffoons, in England, at least, many of these local officers in fact performed adequately enough in the context of a face to face mutual surveillance society.

In part because of the absence of a sizeable police force and in part because it fitted in with the perceptions of the élite, the criminal justice systems of all the states of Europe except England officially distinguished three or more classes of suspected criminals. People who were at least marginally respectable were tried by one law and nobles by another. Vagrants and rootless poor men who lived by theft and violence fitted into the third category and could if caught expect to receive only summary justice. Thus in Scotland, just north of the border with England, in August 1607, special police officer William Cranston 'made no bones to kill such fugitives or felons who made resistance'.[16] In Spain the large stone vaults filled with the skeletons of men whom the Brotherhood of the Santa Hermandad took to be bandits were mute testimony to the sort of roadside justice the Brotherhood meted out.

Writing in 1692, the Marquis of Castelnovo noted that 'the soil of Valencia throws up criminals in the way that it sprouts wheat or barley, for their seed is virtually impossible to root out of that whole area'.[17] Much the same thing might have been said of Catalonia or of the southern half of the peninsula, or indeed wherever mountains provided cover for bandits and where competing court jurisdictions made it difficult to determine which authority was responsible for law enforcement. The cupidity of Spanish bandits knew few bounds. In 1616, for example, a gang headed by Pedro Guerre assaulted a caravan under contract to the Duke of Osuna in the Sierra Morena and made off with gold and silver worth 14,000 ducats. In 1643 Pedro Andrews and thirty well-armed henchmen assaulted and robbed travellers on the roads just outside Madrid. And within the capital itself other bandit bands recruited from the countryside had virtual control of many of the main thoroughfares at night.

The bandits who made life a misery for so many people in late sixteenth- and seventeenth-century Spain fell roughly into two categories. The first consisted of genuinely poor men who were unable or unwilling to find honest work – many Spaniards had an aversion to the work ethic – and who had a grudge against the *senyors* from the towns (holders of jurisdictional rights) who were usurping control over common lands (see Chapter 4). Because of their usual choice of victims, men in this category were often seen as friends of the people, an image which bandits such as Francisco Sánchez, a Franciscan friar who was active around 1693, did much to cultivate. Yet in actual fact such bandits were not above preying on poor villagers who refused to pay them protection money or to provide them with shelter. The second category of bandits were hit-men in the employ of a *senyor*, lay judge or other person in authority who wanted to settle scores with rival families or officials by extra-judicial means. In the absence of a neo-feudal or more developed form of paternalism, hit-men were also a useful way of keeping the tenantry in order. Their use was a far cry from the tenants' own well-developed sense of natural justice.

In England alone of all the major European states, the principles of community justice were never swamped either by over-mighty subjects or by the Roman Law. Except in exceptionally troubled regions (the Welsh border, the marches towards Scotland) and during times of disorder when special commissions of oyer and terminer were called into being in Chancery, all criminal cases which might result in the execution of the defendant were heard by one or more of the twelve common law judges. This might either be done in the central law courts in Westminster Hall (the hall still stands) or by a judge on his circuit through the regions during an assize. In either case the defendant always had to be tried before two sets of jurors. These were nearly always men with at least a modicum of property (often yeomen) who hailed from the county with which the defendant was associated.

The first of the juries, the grand jury or indicting jury, was concerned not only with the facts of the alleged crime itself but also with the reputation of the suspects and the accusers within their respective communities and within the context of community norms. If without strong supporting evidence a normally law-abiding person was suddenly accused of, say, highway robbery, the grand jury would usually refuse to indict him. On the other hand, even though the evidence was weak, if the defendant had a long reputation as a troublemaker, the grand jury might decide to hand him over to the county, i.e. the petit or trial jury. This smaller twelve-man jury – from which men the defendant regarded as his enemies would be excluded at his request – would examine the defendant (who might be represented by an attorney), question witnesses and further sift the evidence. Except for certain categories of causes established by Parliament in Statute Law, men charged with capital offences who were literate (formerly a monopoly of clerics) or at least claimed to be literate, might be able to plead benefit of clergy. If this plea were accepted this meant that the crime with which the defendant was charged would be altered to a lesser, non-capital offence (here being able to read or memorize the right phrase was literally a matter of life or death). If found guilty of this lesser crime the defendant might only have to endure a term of years in Virginia or another penal colony; alternatively he might be maimed or branded.

In capital cases in England, once the jury gave its verdict of guilty, the presiding judge or the Crown still had the option of using their prerogatives of mercy. By the eighteenth century and probably earlier, of most concern to the judge in passing sentence was the reputation of the defendant in his or her community, his or her age (youthful offenders might live out their lives usefully) and his or her social status – by executing a high-class person the law demonstrated its impartiality. This lesson was soon common knowledge for in time of assize hundreds of people came into the county town to see what was going on – the judges' grand procession at the beginning which symbolized the majesty of the law and the hangings at the end which demonstrated that justice had been done. The lessons taught on these occasions and by the printed news-sheets which publicized them seem to have sunk home in the minds of people at all social levels. By the end of our period it was not unusual at the conclusion of an assize for only one or two people to be hanged in comparison to the earlier period when twenty or more gibbets might have been called into service.

At the highest and most visible level the Common Law could thus be seen as the embodiment of a unified national culture which did not favour the rich and well-born at the expense of ordinary people. After all it was ordinary people who made up the juries without which criminal justice could not proceed. Yet at the lower jurisdictional levels, in the quarter and petty sessions kept by Justices of the Peace, things may have been different. It was here that most offenders had their first brush with the law after they had been arrested by the local constable or sheriff. If a JP had no cause to extend his paternalism to a poor suspect, the poor man might find himself deprived of everything except his life and his means of livelihood.

The shared expectations of rulers – the JPs and the central government – and those who were ruled most visibly came into play during a time of dearth and widespread unemployment among the artisan groupings. During a crisis of this sort the industrious and the unemployed expected that food exports from the region would cease and that local needs would take precedence over all others. If little food were grown locally, as was, for example, the case in the Forest of Dean where there were many iron foundries and other forest-related crafts in the 1630s, the industrious people expected the JPs to see to it that ample supplies of grain were brought in and sold at prices the unemployed who were living on poor relief or charity could afford to pay. The funds necessary for all this were expected to come from levies assessed on ratepayers.

Among the industrious sort, it was commonly held that the human agents most responsible for the dearth were the middlemen – wholesalers and badgers – who bought up grain when and where it was cheap and later sold it when it was dear, following what are now known as the principles of a free market economy. The industrious sort expected that in the interest of the common good their JPs would call a halt to this sort of entrepreneurial activity. All of these popular expectations closely paralleled those of the rulers and were incorporated into countless royal proclamations and in 1630 summed up in Charles I's Book of Orders. Yet JPs and central authorities whose primary concern was to maintain public order thought it necessary to take further remedial action as well. Seeing alehouses and distillers of beer as consumers of vast quantities of grain, as well as maintainers of inns and taverns where disorderly people might meet preparatory to a riot, in time of dearth a standard procedure was for justices to tighten up licensing controls. Such measures did not always meet with the approval of the unemployed who had nothing better to do with their time than to congregate in taverns.

In the century after 1550 England suffered hundreds of local grain shortages, yet only about sixty of these led to riots which were serious enough to come to the attention of central authority. Those that did occur were not intended by the industrious people as avenues of unlawful behaviour but rather as reminders to those in authority that they should take appropriate action to counter the causes and effects of dearth and that, if they refused to do so, the crowd would do the task for them by staying the export of grain by force, harassing middlemen, and distributing grain to the poor at a just price. Such were the principles of what E. P. Thompson has called the 'moral economy of the crowd'.

In openly defying authority the behaviour of the crowd was anything but random. Instead, it took careful account of the ambiguities and grey areas of the law. Thus in Kent in 1596, the potential rioters who contemplated using force to prevent grain from leaving local ports first took the precaution of consulting an attorney's clerk in Canterbury. Told that it was illegal to use firearms or other weapons in the course of a demonstration, the later rioters were all unarmed. Those in charge of planning riots also recognized that magistrates were less prone to deal harshly with women than with men. Accordingly, a high proportion of the participants in most grain riots were women. Knowledge of what sort of behaviour a particular set of magistrates would permit to go unpunished would be known to anyone in a position to keep themselves informed of the course of events in a previous riot (for example in Malden, Essex, in 1629 the husband of one of the principal rioters had served as a juror the year before).

In sixteenth- and seventeenth-century France where grain riots, to say nothing of tax riots, were endemic, and where there was little common understanding between royal magistrates and ordinary people, the response of authority to a riot was almost always the same; an invasion of troops, summary trials and gibbets groaning under the weight of corpses. But in England the response of authority was more ambiguous. Very often local JPs took to heart the lessons taught to them by the crowd and set about controlling grain supplies, punishing unlicensed alehouse keepers and vagrants, and putting the full machinery of the poor laws into effect. If the former rioters were sufficiently contrite and deferential, JPs often were prepared to let them go with a warning, perhaps requiring them to post bonds to keep the peace. With a conclusion of this sort, a properly conducted riot which enforced the moral economy of the crowd could be seen as a way of strengthening the social order and the rule of law. Not only did a consensus in such matters exist between the rulers and the ruled, it had been openly and visibly reaffirmed.

In England even before the Civil War of the 1640s and the Revolution of 1688–9, the law and the courts proved to be flexible and like willows bent to the winds of change. By the end of the century the reified law and all it stood for, including the moral economy of the crowd, had become the one ideology that bound men and women of all sorts and conditions into a coherent society.

It may well be that far more than any other worldly religion it was the ideology of the law which later enabled England to enter into the era of full industrialization (when machines at long last began to replace the labour of men) without undergoing violent social revolution.

In less organically unified societies such as those found in France, Spain, the larger states of the German Empire and in the Italian peninsula, at the very least the deterrence created by the law and its courts contributed to a marked lessening in the number of violent crimes committed against the person between the beginning and the end of the early modern period. Everywhere the business which cluttered up the calendars of the courts increasingly came to be related to offences against property. Even poor men such as those in the Montes de Toledo between 1605 and 1630 came to realize that justice could best be seen to be done if the victim of a thief took his case to a regular court of law. Here and wherever the Roman Law was used, accusers knew that if at some point in the proceedings they wished to withdraw the charges they could do so and thus demonstrate their magnanimity and moral superiority, both solid traditional social virtues. Yet these priorities were seldom uppermost in the mind of a substantial landholder in the 1690s and later who used the courts to enforce his new-found sense of private property against the customary rights of poor men to collect gleanings after the harvest, gather in wood from the wastes or take fish from the streams. In cases such as this it was not only people of differing status gradations who were in conflict, it was also two opposing world views. One was based on a still lively sense of community and natural justice, the timeless world of the village, and the other on self-righteous individualism – this was the world of the market-place. Whether for good or for ill, it was this latter world-view which would prevail in the years after the early modern period had come to an end.

Notes and references

1 M. Spufford, *Small Books and Pleasant Histories: popular fiction and its readership in seventeenth century England* (London 1981), p. 74.

2 P. Burke, *Popular Culture in Early Modern Europe* (London 1978), p. 262.

3 Quoted by J. P. Kenyon, *The Stuart Constitution 1603–1688* (Cambridge 1966), p. 23.

4 Quoted by P. Burke, *Culture and Society in Renaissance Italy 1420–1540* (London 1972), p. 240.

5 B. Pullan, *Rich and Poor in Renaissance Venice: the social institutions of a Catholic State to 1620* (Oxford 1971), p. 312.

6 J.-P. Gutton, *La société et les pauvres en Europe (xvie–xviiie siècles)* (Paris 1974), p. 39.

7   W. Callahan, 'Corporate charity in Spain: the Hermandad del Refugio of Madrid, 1618–1814', *Historie Sociale/Social History*, **9** no. 17 (1976), p. 116.

8   C. Hill, *Puritanism and Revolution* (New York 1964), p. 227.

9   R. Chartier, 'Pauvreté et assistance dans la France Moderne', *Annales E-S-C*, **28** (1973), p. 574.

10 R. Herlan, 'Poor relief in the London parish of Dunstan in the West during the English Revolution', *Guildhall Studies in London History*, **3** no. 1 (1977).

11 G. R. Elton, 'Ruling, regulating and ravaging', *The Times Literary Supplement* (1 July 1983), p. 694.

12 A. Soman, 'Deviance and criminal justice in western Europe, 1300–1800: an essay on structure', *Criminal Justice History: an International Annual*, **1** (1980), p. 17.

13 P. Rushton, 'Women, witch-craft and slander in early modern England: cases from the church court of Durham, 1560–1675', *Northern History*, **18** (1982), p. 131.

14 H. Kamen, *Spain in the Later Seventeenth Century, 1665–1700* (London 1980), p. 295.

15 V. A. C. Gatrell, B. Lenman and G. Parker (eds.), *Crime and Law: the social history of crime in Western Europe since 1500* (London 1980), p. 33.

16 S. J. Watts, *From Border to Middle Shire, Northumberland 1586–1625* (Leicester 1975), p. 142.

17 J. Casey, *The Kingdom of Valencia in the Seventeenth Century* (Cambridge 1979), p. 218.

Selected
further reading

The following listing, arranged by chapters, is intended to give some indication of the principal books and articles consulted in the preparation of this book, though it is by no means comprehensive. In its present shortened form it is also intended to give students who wish to follow up some of the themes found in the *Social History* some idea of where to begin to look for further information.

Chapter 1 An overview

Abrams, Philip and Wrigley, E. A. (eds.) (1978), *Towns in societies: essays in economic history and historical sociology*, Cambridge

Chaunu, Pierre (1975), 'Les éléments de longue durée dans la société et la civilisation du xviiᵉ siècle; la démographie', *Dix Septième Siècle* nos. 106–7

Cipolla, Carlo (1976), *Public health and the medical profession in the Renaissance*, Cambridge

Clark, Peter and Slack, Paul (eds.) (1976), *English towns in transition 1500–1700*, Oxford

Clarkson, Leslie (1975), *Death, disease and famine in pre-industrial England*, Dublin

Easlea, Brian (1980), *Witch hunting, magic and the new philosophy: an introduction to the debates of the scientific revolution, 1450–1750*, London

Flinn, Michael, (1981), *The European demographic system, 1500–1820*, London

Friedrichs, Christopher (1979), *Urban society in an age of war; Nördlingen 1580–1720*, Princeton

Giddens, Anthony (1979), *Central problems in social theory; action, structure and contradictions in social analysis*, London

Goulemot, Jêan-Marie (1980), 'Démons, merveilles, et philosophie à l'âge classique', *Annales E. S. C.*, **35**

Hildesheimer, Françoise (1981), 'Prévention de la peste et attitudes mentales en France au xviiie siècle', *Revue Historique*, no. 537

McNeill, William (1977), *Plagues and People*, Oxford

Myer, Jean (1975), 'Le xviie siècle et sa place dans l'évolution à long-terme', *Dix Septième Siècle*, nos. 106–7

Slack, Paul (1981), 'The disappearance of plague; an alternative view', *Economic History Review*, **34** no. 3

Wrigley, E. A. (1966), *Population and History*, London

Wrigley, E. A. and Schofield, R. S. (1981), *The population history of England 1540–1871; a reconstruction*, London

Chapter 2   The family, the passions and social controls

Anderson, Michael (1980), *Approaches to the history of the western family 1500–1914*, London

Ariès, Philippe (1962), *Centuries of Childhood; a social history of family life* (trans. by R. Baldick), New York

Belmont, Nicole (1978), 'La fonction symbolique du cortège dans les rituels populaires du mariage', *Annales E. S. C.*, **33**

Berkner, Lutz (1972), 'The stem family and the developmental cycle of the peasant household: an eighteenth century Austrian example', *American Historical Review*, **LXXVII**

Berkner, Lutz and Shaffer, J. (1978), 'The joint family in the Nivernais', *Journal of Family History*, **3**, no. 1

Bideau, Alain (1980), 'A demographic and social analysis of widowhood and remarriage', *Journal of Family History*, **5** no. 1

Bray, Alan (1982), *Homosexuality in Renaissance England*, London

Burguière, André (1972), 'De Malthus à Max Weber: le mariage tardif et l'esprit d'entreprise', *Annales E.S.C.*, **27**

Caspard, P. (1974), 'Conceptions prénuptiales et développement du capitalisme dans la Principauté de Neuchâtel, 1678–1820', *Annales E.S.C.*, **29**

Castan, Yves (1974), 'Pères et fils en Languedoc à l'époque classique' *Dix Septième Siècle*, nos. 102–3

Collomp, Alain (1981), 'Conflits familiaux et groupes de résidence en Haute-Provence', *Annales E.S.C.*, **36**

Flandrin, J. (1979), *Families in former times: kinship, household and sexuality*, Cambridge

Goody, Jack, Thirsk, Joan and Thompson, E. P. (eds.) (1976), *Family and inheritance; rural society in western Europe 1200–1800*, Cambridge

Gouesse, Jean-Marie (1974), 'La formation du couple en Basse Normandie' *Dix Septième Siècle*, nos. 102–3

Hajnal, J. (1965), 'European marriage patterns in perspective', in D. Glass and D. Eversley (eds.), *Population in History*, London

Herlihy, David and Klapische-Zuber, Christiane (1978), *Les Toscans et leurs familles; une étude du catasto florentin de 1427*, Paris

Hunt, David (1972), *Parents and children in history; the psychology of family life in early modern France*, New York

Karant-Nunn, S. (1982), 'Continuity and change; some effects of the reformation of the women of Zwickau', *The Sixteenth Century Journal*, 13 no. 2

Kent, F. (1977), *Household and lineage in Renaissance Florence*, Princeton

Kussmaul, A. S. (1981), *Servants in husbandry in early modern England*, Cambridge

Lamaison, P. (1979), 'Les stratégies matrimoniales dans un système complexe de parenté: Ribennes en Gévaudan, 1650–1830, *Annales E.S.C.*, 34

Laslett, Peter (1977), *Family life and illicit love in earlier generations*, Cambridge

Laslett, Peter (1983), *The World we have lost* (rev. ed), London

Lottin, Alain (1974), 'Vie et mort du couple; difficultés conjugales et divorces: dans le Nord de la France aux xviie et xviiie siècles, *Dix Septième Siècle*, nos. 102–3

Macfarlane, Alan (1970), *The family life of Ralph Josselin; an essay in historical anthropology*, Cambridge

Menefee, Samuel (1981), *Wives for sale; an ethnographic study of British popular divorce*, Oxford

Plumb, J. H. (1975), 'The new world of children in eighteenth-century England', *Past and Present*, no. 67

Quaife, C. R. (1979), *Wanton wenches and wayward wives: peasants and illicit sex in early seventeenth century England*, London

Ronzeaud, Pierre (1975), 'La femme au pouvoir ou le monde à l'envers', *Dix Septième Siècle*, no. 108

Rossiaud, Jacques (1976), 'Prostitution, jeunesse et société dans les villes du sud-est au xve siècle', *Annales E.S.C.*, 31

Shammas, Carole (1980), 'The domestic environment in early modern England and America', *Journal of Social History*, 14 no. 1

Sharpe, J. A. (1981), 'Domestic homicide in early modern England', *Historical Journal*, 24 no. 1

Smith, Richard (1981), 'The people of Tuscany and their families in the fifteenth century; medieval or Mediterranean?', *Journal of Family history*, 6 no. 1

Stone, Lawrence (1977), *The family, sex and marriage in England 1500–1800*, London

Thomas, K. (1959), 'The double standard', *Journal of the History of Ideas*, no. 20

Thomas, K. (1976), 'Age and authority in early modern England', *Proceedings of the British Academy*, **62**

Trexler, Richard (1981), 'La prostitution florentine au xve siècle', *Annales E.S.C.*, **36**

Chapter 3   The structures of rural society

Abel, Wilhelm (1980), *Agricultural fluctuations in Europe from the thirteenth to the twentieth centuries* (trans. by O. Ordish), London

Benecke, G. (1978), *Society and politics in Germany 1500–1750*, London

Bidart, Pierre (1976), 'Pouvoir et propriété collective dans une communauté basque au xviiie siècle', *Études Rurales*, nos. 63–4

Blum, Jerome (1971), 'The European village as community; origins and functions', *Agricultural History*, no. 45 (3)

Bouchard, G. (1972), *Le village immobile: Sennely-en-Sologne au xviiie siècle*, Paris

Braudel, F. (1981), *The structures of everyday life: civilization and capitalism, fifteenth to eighteenth centuries*, London

Burke, Peter (1978), *Popular culture in early modern Europe*, London

Cabourdin, Guy (1977), *Terre et hommes au Lorraine, 1550–1635*, 2 vols., Nancy

Casey, James (1979), *The kingdom of Valencia in the seventeenth century*, Cambridge

Clark, Peter (1983), *The English alehouse: a social history 1200–1800*, London

Davis, Natalie (1978), *Society and culture in early modern France*, Stanford, Calif.

De Vries, Jan (1976), *The economy of Europe in an age of crisis 1600–1750*, Cambridge

Duby, G. and Wallon, A. (eds.) (1975), *Histoire de la France rurale*, vol. 2, *L'âge classique des paysans 1340 à 1789*, Paris

Goubert, Pierre (1960), *Beauvais et le Beauvaisis de 1600 à 1730; contribution à l'histoire sociale de la France du xviie siècle*, Paris

Gutton, Jean-Pierre (1979), *La sociabilité villageoise dans l'ancienne France*, Paris

Hey, D. G. (1974), *An English rural community; Myddle under Tudors and Stuarts*, Leicester

Hilton, R. H. (1975), *The English peasantry in the later middle ages*, Oxford

Hoskins, W. G. (1965), *The Midland peasant; the economic and social history of a Leicestershire village*, London

Jacquart, Jean (1974), *La crise rurale en Île-de-France 1550–1670*, Paris

Le Roy Ladurie, E. (1974), 'L'histoire immobile', *Annales E.S.C.*, **29**

Le Roy Ladurie, E. (1974), *The peasants of Languedoc* (trans. by John Day), Urbana, Ill.

Le Roy Ladurie, E. (1975), *Montaillou: Cathars and Catholics in a French village 1294–1324* (trans. by B. Bray), London

Le Roy Ladurie, E. and Morineau, M. (1977), *Histoire économique et sociale de la France*, vol. 1, *De 1450 à 1660*, vol. 2, *Paysannerie et croissance*, Paris

McArdle, Frank (1978), *Altopascio: a study in Tuscan rural society 1597–1784*, Cambridge

Maddalena, Aldo de (1974), 'Rural Europe 1500–1750', in C. Cipolla (ed.), *The Fontana Economic History of Europe*, vol. 2, London

Muchembled, R. (1978), *Culture populaire et culture des élites dans la France moderne, xve–xvııı^e siècles*, Paris

Munsche, P. B. (1981), *Gentlemen and poachers: the English Game Laws 1671–1831*, Cambridge

Rossiaud, Jacques, (1976), 'Fraternités de jeunesse et niveaux de culture dans les villes du Sud-Est à la fin du Moyen Age', *Cahiers d'histoire*, no. 21

Spufford, M. (1974), *Contrasting communities: English villagers in the sixteenth and seventeenth centuries*, Cambridge

Thirsk, Joan (ed.) (1967), *The Agrarian History of England and Wales*, vol. 4, *1500–1640*, Cambridge

Vassberg, David (1980), 'Peasant communalism and anti-communal tendencies in early modern Castile', *Journal of Peasant Studies*, 7 no. 4

Watts, S. J. (1975), *From Border to Middle Shire: Northumberland 1586–1625*, Leicester

Weisser, M. R. (1977), *The peasants of the Montas*, Chicago

Wrightson, K. (1982), *English Society 1580–1680*, London

Wrightson, K. and Levine, D. (1979), *Poverty and piety in an English village: Terling, 1525–1700*, London

Chapter 4   Contrasts in rural Europe

Bercé, Yves-Marie (1974), *Histoire des Croquants; étude des soulèvements populaires au xvıı^e siècle dans le sud-ouest de la France*, 2 vols., Paris

Bercé, Yves-Marie (1976), *Fête et révolte: des mentalités populaires du xvı^e au xvııı^e siècle*, Paris

Blickle, Peter (1982), *The Revolution of 1525: the German Peasants' War from a new perspective* (trans. Eric Midelfort), Baltimore

Blum, J. (1978), *The end of the old order in rural Europe*, Princeton

Campbell, Mildred (1942), *The English yeomen under Elizabeth and the early Stuarts*, New Haven, Conn.

Clark, Peter (1979), 'Migration in England during the late seventeenth and early eighteenth centuries', *Past and Present*, no. 83

Cohn, Henry (1979), 'Anti-clericalism in the German Peasants' War, 1525', *Past and Present*, no. 83

Cooper, J. P. (1978), 'In search of agrarian capitalism', *Past and Present*, no. 80

De Vries, Jan (1974), *The Dutch rural economy in the Golden Age, 1500–1700*, New Haven, Conn.

Elliott, J. H. (1963), *The revolt of the Catalans: a study in the decline of Spain, 1598–1640*, Cambridge

Fletcher, Anthony (1973), *Tudor Rebellions*, London

Holderness, B. A. (1976), 'Credit in English rural society before the nineteenth century with special reference to the period 1650–1720', *Agricultural History Review*, **24**

Jones, E. L. (ed.) (1967), *Agriculture and economic growth in England, 1650–1815*, London

Kellenbenz, Hermann (1974), 'Rural industries in the west from the end of the middle ages to the eighteenth century', in P. Earle (ed.), *Essays in European economic history, 1500–1800*, Oxford

Kerridge, Eric (1967), *The agricultural revolution*, London

Klima, A. (1979), 'Agrarian class structure and economic development in pre-industrial Europe', *Past and Present*, no. 85

Kriedte, Peter, Medick, Hans, and Schlumbohm, Jürgen (1981), *Industrialization before industrialization* (trans. Beate Scheupp), Cambridge

Landsberger, H. (ed.) (1978), *Rural protests; peasant movements and social change*, London

Le Roy Ladurie, E. (1980), *Carnival; the people's uprising in Romans, 1579–80*, London

Mousnier, R. (1971), *Peasant uprisings in seventeenth century France, Russia and China*, London

Parker, G. (1977), *The Dutch Revolt*, London

Parker, W. and Jones, E. (eds.) (1975), *European peasants and their markets: essays in agrarian economic history*, Princeton

Salmon, J. H. (1979), 'Peasant revolt in Vivarais, 1575–1580', *French Historical Studies*, **11** no. 1

Scribner, R. and Benecke, G. (eds.) (1979), *The German Peasants' War 1525; New viewpoints*, London

Thirsk, Joan (1970), 'Seventeenth century agriculture and social change', in *Land, Church and People, Agricultural History Review*, **18**, Supplement

Thirsk, Joan (1978), *Economic policy and projects; the development of a consumer society in early modern England*, Oxford

Tits-Dieuaide, Marie-Jeanne (1981), 'L'évolution des techniques agricoles en Flandre et en Brabant xive–xvie siècles' *Annales E.S.C.*, **36**

Vivens, V. (1969), *An economic history of Spain*, Princeton

Wunder, Heide (1978), 'Peasant organization and class conflict in East and West Germany', *Past and Present*, no. 78

Chapter 5 The supernatural and the rural world

Anglo, S. (ed.) (1978), *The damned art; essays in the literature of witchcraft*, London

Beé, Michel (1975), 'La société traditionnelle et la mort', *Dix Septième Siècle*, nos. 106–7

Bossy, John (1970), 'The Counter-Reformation and the people of Catholic Europe', *Past and Present*, no. 47

Bossy, John (1975), 'Social history of confession in the age of the Reformation', *Trans. Royal Hist. Soc.*, 5th series, **25**

Bossy, John (1977), 'Holiness and society', *Past and Present*, no. 75

Bossy, John (1981), 'Essai de sociographie de la Messe, 1200–1700', *Annales E.S.C.*, **36**

Brooks, Peter (ed.) (1980), *Reformation principles and practices: Essays in honour of Arthur Geoffrey Dickens*, London

Brown, Peter (1981), *The cult of the saints; its rise and formation in Latin Christendom*, London

Christian, W. (1981), *Local religion in sixteenth century Spain*, Princeton

Clasen, Claus-Peter (1972), *Anabaptism, a social history 1525–1618*, Ithaca, N.Y.

Cohn, Norman (1970), *The pursuit of the millennium*, London

Cohn, Norman (1975), *Europe's inner demons*, London

Collinson, P. (1982), *The religion of Protestants: the Church in English society 1559–1625*, Oxford

Delumeau, J. (1977), *Catholicism between Luther and Voltaire; a new view of the Counter-Reformation* (trans. J. Moiser), London

Dickens, A. G. (1964), *The English Reformation*, London

Dupont-Bouchat, Marie-Sylvie, Frijhoff, W. and Muchembled, R. (1978), *Prophètes et sorciers dans les Pays-Bas xvie au xviiie siecles*, Paris

Ferté, J. (1962), *La vie religieuse dans les campagnes parisiennes 1622–95*, Paris

Galpern, A. N. (1976), *The religions of the people in sixteenth century Champagne*, Cambridge, Mass.

Goff, J. Le (1982), *La naissance du purgatoire*, Paris

Greaves, R. (1981), *Society and religion in Elizabethan England*, Minneapolis

Haigh, C. (1975), *Reformation and resistance in Tudor Lancashire*, Cambridge

Heal, F. and Day, R. (eds.) (1977), *Church and society in England, Henry VIII–James I*, London

Henningsen, G. (1980), *The witches' advocate: Basque witchcraft and the Spanish Inquisition, 1609–1614*, Reno, Nevada

Hill, Christopher (1967), *Society and Puritanism in pre-revolutionary England*, New York

Hill, Christopher (1971), *Antichrist in seventeenth century England*, Oxford

Larner, Christina (1981), *Enemies of God; the witchhunt in Scotland*, London

Macfarlane, Alan (1970), *Witchraft in Tudor and Stuart England; a regional and comparative study*, New York

Midelfort, H. Eric (1972), *Witchhunting in South-west Germany 1562–1684; the social and intellectual foundations*, Berkeley, Calif.

Moeller, B. (1971), 'Piety in Germany around 1500', in S. Ozment (ed.), *The Reformation in medieval perspective*, Chicago

Monter, E. W. (1976), *Witchcraft in France and Switzerland; the borderlands during the Reformation*, Ithaca, NY

Parker, G. (ed.) 'The European witch-craze revisited', *History Today*, **30** (1980) and **31** (1981)

Pennington, D. H. and Thomas, K. (eds.) (1978), *Puritans and Revolutionaries: essays in seventeenth century history presented to Christopher Hill*, Oxford

Reardon, B. (1981), *Religious thought in the Reformation*, London

Sprunger, K. L. (1982), 'English and Dutch Sabbatarianism and the development of Puritan social theology, 1600–1660', *Church History* **51** no. 1

Strauss, Gerald (1975), 'Success and failure in the German Reformation', *Past and Present*, no. 67

Strauss, Gerald (1979), *Luther's house of learning; indoctrination of the young in the German Reformation*, Baltimore

Thomas, Keith (1971), *Religion and the decline of magic; studies in popular beliefs in sixteenth and seventeenth century England*, London

Trinkaus, C., with Oberman, H. (eds.) (1974), *The pursuit of holiness in late medieval and renaissance religion; Papers from the University of Michigan conference*, Leiden

Turner, V. and E. (1979), *Image and pilgrimage in Christian culture; anthropological perspectives*, Oxford

Chapter 6   The wider circles of sociability

Beattie, J. (1974), 'The pattern of crime in England 1660–1800', *Past and Present* no. 62

Berger, P. (1978), 'Rural charity in late seventeenth century France; the Pontchartrain case', *French Historical Studies*, 10 no. 3

Boulet-Sautel, M. (1980), 'Crimes, délits et répression dans la société classique', *Dix Septième Siècle*, no. 126

Brewer, J. and Styles, J. (eds.) (1980), *An Ungovernable People: the English and their law in the seventeenth and eighteenth centuries*, London

Burke, Peter (1974), *Tradition and innovation in Renaissance Italy; a sociological approach*, London

Capp, Bernard (1979), *Astrology and the popular press; English almanacs 1500–1800*, London

Chill, E. (1962), 'Religion and mendicancy in seventeenth century France', *International Review of Social History*, 7

Cipolla, C. (1969), *Literacy and development in the West*, Harmondsworth

Clark, Peter, Smith, A. and Tyacke, N. (1979), *The English Commonwealth: Essays in politics and society presented to Joel Hurstfield*, Leicester

Cockburn, J. S. (ed.) (1977), *Crime in England 1500–1800*, London

Collinson, Patrick, (1981) 'The significance of signature', *The Times Literary Supplement*

Coward, Barry (1980), *The Stuart age: a history of England 1603–1714*, London

Cressy, David (1980), *Literacy and the social order; reading and writing in Tudor and Stuart England*, Cambridge

Elias, Norbert (1983), *The court society* (trans. E. Jephcott), Oxford

Febvre, L. and Martin, H. (1976), *The coming of the book: the impact of printing 1450–1800* (trans. D. Gerard), London

Furet, F. (1977), *Lire et écrire; l'alphabetisation des Français de Calvin à Jules Ferry*, Paris

Gatrell, V. A. C., Lenman, B. and Parker, G. (eds.) (1980), *Crime and the law; the social history of crime in western Europe since 1500*, London

Geremek, Bronislaw (ed.) (1980), *Truands et misérables dans l'Europe moderne, 1350–1600*, Paris

Goody, Jack (ed.) (1968), *Literacy in traditional societies*, Cambridge

Goubert, P. (1973), *The Ancien Régime: French Society 1600–1750* (trans. S. Cox), London

Gutton, J. (1971), *La société et les pauvres; l'exemple de la généralité de Lyon 1534–1789*, Paris

Hill, Christopher (1981), 'Parliament and people in seventeenth century England', *Past and Present*, no. 92

Kamen, H. (1980), *Spain in the later seventeenth century 1665–1700*, London

Langbein, John (1974), *Prosecuting crime in the Renaissance: England, Germany, France*, Cambridge, Mass.

Mandrou, R. (1964), *De la culture populaire aux xviie et xviiie siècles; la bibliothèque bleue de Troyes*, Paris

Myers, A. R. (1975), *Parliaments and Estates in Europe to 1789*, London

Parker, David (1983), *The making of French absolutism*, London

Parry, G. (1980), *The golden age restored: the cult of the Stuart Court, 1603–42*, Manchester

Pound, John (1971), *Poverty and vagrancy in Tudor England*, London

Pullan, B. (1971), *Rich and poor in Renaissance Venice; the social institutions of a Catholic state*, Oxford

Rabb, T. (1981), 'Revisionism revisited; early Stuart parliamentary history', *Past and Present*, no. 92

Samaha, J. (1974), *Law and order in historical perspective; the case of Elizabethan Essex*, London

Scribner, R. (1981),. *For the sake of simple folk; popular propaganda for the German Reformation*, Cambridge

Sharpe, J. A. (1982), 'The history of crime in late medieval and early modern England', *Social History 7* no. 2

Shennan, J. (1974), *The origins of the modern European state, 1450–1725*, London

Somen, A. (1980), 'Deviance and criminal justice in western Europe 1300–1800; an essay on structure', *Criminal Justice history; an international annual*

Spufford, M. (1981), *Small books and pleasant histories: popular fiction and its readership in seventeenth century England*, London

Stone, Lawrence, (1964), 'The educational revolution in England 1560–1640', *Past and Present*, no. 28

Stone, Lawrence, (1965), *The crisis of the aristocracy 1558–1641*, Oxford

Thompson, E. P. (1971), 'The moral economy of the English crowd in the eighteenth century', *Past and Present* no. 50

Walter, J. and Wrightson, Keith (1976), 'Dearth and the social order in early modern England', *Past and Present* no. 71

Weisser, M. (1979), *Crime and punishment in early modern Europe*, Brighton

Zagorin, P. (1982), *Rebels and Rulers 1500–1660*, 2 vols., Cambridge

Index

Villages not mentioned more than once in passing in the text are subsumed under the name of their province or county.